EVALUATION FOR CIVIL COMMITMENT

BEST PRACTICES IN FORENSIC MENTAL HEALTH ASSESSMENT

Series Editors
Thomas Grisso, Alan M. Goldstein, and Kirk Heilbrun

Series Advisory Board
Paul Appelbaum, Richard Bonnie, and John Monahan

Titles in the Series
Foundations of Forensic Mental Health Assessment, *Kirk Heilbrun, Thomas Grisso, and Alan M. Goldstein*

Criminal Titles
Evaluation of Competence to Stand Trial, *Patricia A. Zapf and Ronald Roesch*

Evaluation of Criminal Responsibility, *Ira K. Packer*

Evaluating Capacity to Waive Miranda Rights, *Alan M. Goldstein and Naomi E. Sevin Goldstein*

Evaluation of Sexually Violent Predators, *Philip H. Witt and Mary Alice Conroy*

Evaluation for Risk of Violence in Adults, *Kirk Heilbrun*

Jury Selection, *Margaret Bull Kovera and Brian L. Cutler*

Evaluation for Capital Sentencing, *Mark D. Cunningham*

Eyewitness Identification, *Brian L. Cutler and Margaret Bull Kovera*

Civil Titles
Evaluation of Capacity to Consent to Treatment and Research, *Scott Y. H. Kim*

Evaluation for Guardianship, *Eric Y. Drogin and Curtis L. Barrett*

Evaluation for Personal Injury Claims, *Andrew W. Kane and Joel A. Dvoskin*

Evaluation for Civil Commitment, *Debra A. Pinals and Douglas Mossman*

Evaluation for Workplace Discrimination and Harassment, *William Foote and Jane Goodman-Delahunty*

Evaluation of Workplace Disability, *Lisa D. Piechowski*

Juvenile and Family Titles
Evaluation for Child Custody, *Geri S.W. Fuhrmann and Robert A. Zibbell*

Evaluation of Juveniles' Competence to Stand Trial, *Ivan Kruh and Thomas Grisso*

Evaluation for Risk of Violence in Juveniles, *Robert Hoge and D.A. Andrews*

Evaluation of Parenting Capacity in Child Protection, *Karen S. Budd, Mary A. Connell, and Jennifer R. Clark*

Evaluation for Disposition and Transfer of Juvenile Offenders, *Randall T. Salekin*

EVALUATION FOR CIVIL COMMITMENT

DEBRA A. PINALS

DOUGLAS MOSSMAN

OXFORD
UNIVERSITY PRESS

OXFORD
UNIVERSITY PRESS

Oxford University Press, Inc., publishes works that further
Oxford University's objective of excellence
in research, scholarship, and education.

Oxford   New York

Auckland   Cape Town   Dar es Salaam   Hong Kong   Karachi
Kuala Lumpur   Madrid   Melbourne   Mexico City   Nairobi
New Delhi   Shanghai   Taipei   Toronto

With offices in
Argentina   Austria   Brazil   Chile   Czech Republic   France   Greece
Guatemala   Hungary   Italy   Japan   Poland   Portugal   Singapore
South Korea   Switzerland   Thailand   Turkey   Ukraine   Vietnam

Copyright © 2012 by Oxford University Press, Inc.

Published by Oxford University Press, Inc.
198 Madison Avenue, New York, New York 10016
www.oup.com

Oxford is a registered trademark of Oxford University Press

Library of Congress Cataloging-in-Publication Data

Pinals, Debra A.
Evaluation for civil commitment / Debra A. Pinals, Douglas Mossman.
   p. cm. — (Best practices in forensic mental health assessment)
Includes bibliographical references and index.
ISBN 978-0-19-532914-8
1. Forensic psychiatry. 2. Mentally ill—Commitment and detention.
3. Mental status examination. I. Mossman, Douglas. II. Title.
RA1151.P493 2012
614'.15—dc23   2011026836

The opinions expressed in this book are those of the authors and do not
necessarily reflect the views of the authors' employers.

9 8 7 6 5 4 3 2 1

Printed in the United States of America
on acid-free paper

About Best Practices in Forensic Mental Health Assessment

The recent growth of the fields of forensic psychology and forensic psychiatry has created a need for a book series that describes best practices in forensic mental health assessment (FMHA). Mental health professionals conduct forensic evaluations for a variety of criminal, civil, and juvenile legal determinations. The research foundation that supports these assessments has become broader and deeper in recent decades, and some consensus has emerged among mental health professionals concerning the ethical and professional requirements for such assessments. In the larger context of the current emphasis on "empirically supported" assessment and intervention in psychiatry and psychology, the specialization of FMHA has advanced sufficiently to justify a series devoted to best practices. Although this series focuses mainly on evaluations conducted by psychologists and psychiatrists, the fundamentals and principles offered also apply to evaluations conducted by clinical social workers, psychiatric nurses, and other mental health professionals.

This series describes "best practices" as empirically supported (when the relevant research is available), legally relevant, and consistent with applicable ethical and professional standards. Each book describes the approaches that seem best, while incorporating what is practical and acknowledging that best practice represents a goal to which the forensic clinician should aspire, rather than a standard that can always be met. The American Academy of Forensic Psychology assisted the editors in enlisting the consultation of board-certified forensic psychologists who have special expertise in each topic area. Board-certified forensic psychiatrists were also consultants on many of the volumes. Their comments on the manuscripts helped to ensure that the methods described in these volumes represent a generally accepted view of best practice.

The series' authors were selected for their specific expertise in a particular area. At the broadest level, however, certain general principles apply to all types of forensic evaluations. Rather than repeat those fundamental principles in every volume, the series offers them in the first volume, *Foundations of Forensic Mental Health Assessment*. Reading the first book, followed by a specific topical book, will provide the reader with both those general principles that the specific topic shares with all forensic evaluations and those that are particular to the specific assessment question.

The series editors selected specific topics of the 19 books as the most important and oft-considered areas of forensic assessment conducted by mental health professionals and behavioral scientists.

Each of the 19 topical books is organized according to a common template. The authors address the applicable legal context, forensic mental health concepts, and empirical foundations and limits in the "Foundation" part of the book. They then describe preparation for the evaluation, data collection, data interpretation, and report writing and testimony in the "Application" part of the book. This creates a fairly uniform approach to considering these areas across different topics. All the authors in this series have attempted to concisely address best practice in their area. In addition, topical volumes feature elements intended to make them user friendly in actual practice. These elements include boxes that highlight especially important information, relevant case law, best-practice guidelines, and cautions against common pitfalls. Each volume also contains a glossary of key terms.

We hope the series will be useful for different groups of individuals. Practicing forensic clinicians will find succinct, current information relevant to their practice. Those who are in training to specialize in forensic mental health assessment (whether in formal training or in the process of respecialization) should find helpful the combination of broadly applicable considerations presented in the first volume together with the more specific aspects of other volumes in the series. Those who teach and supervise trainees can offer these volumes as a guide for practices to which the trainee can aspire. Researchers and scholars interested in FMHA best practice may find researchable ideas, particularly on topics that have received insufficient research attention to date. Judges and attorneys with questions about FMHA best practice will find these books relevant and concise. Clinical and forensic administrators who run agencies, court clinics, and hospitals in which litigants are assessed may also use some of the books in this series to establish expectancies for evaluations performed by professionals in their agencies.

We also anticipate that the 19 specific books in this series will serve as reference works that help courts and attorneys assess the quality of forensic mental health professionals' evaluations. A word of caution is in order, however. These volumes focus on best practice, not what is minimally acceptable legally or ethically. Courts involved in malpractice litigation, or ethics committees or licensure boards considering complaints, should not expect that materials describing best practice easily or necessarily translate into the minimally acceptable professional conduct that is typically at issue in such proceedings.

This volume offers a comprehensive review of laws, policies, and evaluation practices concerning the civil commitment of persons with mental disabilities. Civil commitment aims to benefit severely impaired persons who need psychiatric treatment. Despite its benevolent intent, however, involuntary hospitalization constitutes a significant deprivation of liberty. Consequently, the laws governing civil commitment require more than clinical treatment needs alone to justify involuntary psychiatric confinement. They also require evidence that individuals, if not committed, constitute a danger to others or to their own welfare as a result of their mental illness. To ensure such protections, states require that involuntary civil commitment be authorized by judges who decide whether clear, convincing evidence supports the legal conditions required for involuntary commitment.

To obtain that information, courts rely on psychiatrists and psychologists, who offer evidence about individuals' clinical conditions and risk of harm. Fulfilling this role requires that examiners be aware of the relevant legal criteria for commitment and the types of data that will address these criteria. Not all mental conditions meet the criteria for need for hospitalization, and risk of harm to others or to oneself has special contours in civil commitment proceedings. This book defines the history and current status of these legal and clinical requirements, reviews best practices in gathering relevant information for the civil commitment hearing, and offers ethical, clinical, and practical guidance for clinicians who participate in such proceedings.

Among all the volumes in this series, this one may have the broadest application for psychiatrists and psychologists who do not regard themselves as "forensic" clinicians. Civil commitment evaluations are "forensic" to the extent that they are governed by the legal definitions and procedures that are overseen by courts. Nevertheless, unlike most of the other evaluations in this series, civil commitment evaluations typically are conducted by clinicians whose primary day-to-day activities are clinical diagnosis and treatment, not evaluations for courts. Most clinicians offering information in civil commitment proceedings have little reason to identify themselves as forensic examiners, have limited interest in applying their professions to questions in law, and neither have nor need special training in forensic psychiatry or psychology. Their skills at psychiatric diagnosis and treatment qualify them to identify patients' needs, and their ability to identify their patients' potential danger to others is an everyday necessity for mental health practice in psychiatric hospitals. Yet they must know enough about the civil commitment process, its laws, and best practices in collecting and presenting relevant data to judges to apply those skills in this specific legal context. It is for these clinicians—as well as forensic psychologists and psychiatrists who often train them to play this limited "forensic" role—that this volume is intended as a guide to best practices in civil commitment evaluations.

Thomas Grisso
Kirk Heilbrun
Alan M. Goldstein

Acknowledgments

Early in their training, future psychiatrists and psychologists learn that civil commitment proceedings are frequent events in the clinical care of individuals with serious mental illnesses. Being the "keeper of the keys" is an awesome power. We hope that this book will remind novice and experienced mental health professionals that initiating civil commitment can have a tremendous impact on the liberties, health, and daily lives of patients.

This book reflects a broad array of professional contacts across many years of psychiatric practice. We want to acknowledge first the individuals we have treated or evaluated and about whom we have testified in civil commitment proceedings. Facing these individuals in court was sometimes uncomfortable, but nowhere near as difficult as it must have been for the individuals whose lives and problems we were exposing to those present in court. We hope our book will help our professional colleagues to humbly take stock of how it feels to be a respondent and enhance their practice in ways that convey unyielding respect for persons undergoing commitment proceedings.

Debra Pinals would like to acknowledge the editors—Thomas Grisso, Alan Goldstein, and Kirk Heilbrun—for their invitation to contribute to a series of volumes authored by such an outstanding line-up of psychologists. Tremendous colleagues, mentors, teachers and friends have helped shape her clinical and forensic thinking over years. Thomas Gutheil, M.D., Phil Resnick, M.D., and Paul Appelbaum, M.D., all inspired and guided her. Special thanks goes to Ira Packer, Ph.D. for many hours of conversation, intellectual debate, and shared clinical insights. Dr. Pinals is grateful for everything she has learned from students and trainees, as their questions helped her to shape a deeper understanding of the issues surrounding civil commitment. She also acknowledges the support she has consistently received from her family, whose love and nurturing has been boundless and has helped foster personal and professional growth every step of the way.

Douglas Mossman thanks the Glenn M. Weaver Institute of Law and Psychiatry and Dean Louis Bilionis of the University of Cincinnati College of Law for their support for this and several other recent scholarly endeavors. He gratefully acknowledges the advice and encouragement he has received from Professor Michael L. Perlin at crucial points in his academic career. Dr. Mossman also thanks the many psychiatry residents and forensic psychiatry fellows he has helped to train over the last quarter century, whose experiences preparing for and providing testimony during civil commitment hearings have enriched this book.

Contents

FOUNDATION

The Legal Context | 1

*C*ivil commitment is the legal mechanism through which
the government deprives persons of their liberty because of
mental illness. Civil commitment serves two purposes: (1) preventing harm and (2) providing care to persons with mental illness
who need treatment but cannot or will not seek treatment themselves. But under what circumstances should someone be civilly
committed? And what events or conditions are sufficient to justify
disrupting the lives of and detaining persons who have committed
no criminal offense?

Over the past two centuries, U.S. law has answered these questions in ways that reflect a complex, ever-evolving interplay of social
movements, scientific understandings of mental illness, political
trends, and the perceived and sometimes real associations between
dangerousness and mental illness. Most recently, several states'
legislatures have responded to public fears of sex offenders by creat-
ing a specific kind of commitment for "sexually violent predators."
Sexually Violent Predator (SVP) laws typically allow courts to order
long-term postconviction confinement of persons who have committed sexually oriented crimes if those persons have "mental abnormalities" that make them "likely" to engage in additional acts of
sexual violence (see, e.g., Rev. Code Wash. § 71.09.030). Although
the U.S. Supreme Court has held that SVP laws have the same
constitutional basis and legitimacy as other forms of civil commitment (*Kansas v. Hendricks*, 1997), most mental health professionals (and most states' legal codes) distinguish sharply between SVP
laws and the laws and practices governing involuntary hospitalization of persons traditionally regarded as having severe psychiatric disorders. This volume focuses on "traditional" mental health

commitments; *Evaluation of Sexually Violent Predators* (Witt and Conroy, 2008), another volume in this series, discusses SVP laws and related mental health practices.

Sociolegal Purpose and History

Historical Roots: Connections between Mental Illness and Violence

Throughout the Western world, the public has long believed that violence and mental illness are linked. Combined with this belief is a pervasive perception of persons with mental illness as bizarre, pathetic, and undesirable. For centuries, authors and artists have reinforced this perception by depicting persons with mental illness as grotesque, disturbing, and violent. In our era, movies and news media focus on mental disorders as causes of violence far out of proportion to their actual contribution to violence as a whole.

Until relatively recently, treatment and understanding of mental illness were limited, and deciding where to put persons with serious mental illness posed a real social conundrum. During the Renaissance, "ships of fools" sailed from port to port, collecting madmen—a group that often included persons with mental illness who had engaged in criminal behavior—from Europe's growing urban centers (Foucault, 1973). When families were available, they provided care for relatives with mental illness that often involved confinement at home. Some persons with mental illness went to hospitals; others were imprisoned. Containment was the *raison d'être* of early institutions for mental disease, with little consideration given to treatment.

Care of Persons with Mental Illness: Early U.S. History

In the absence of specific sites or special institutions, colonial Americans utilized other sorts of facilities to confine persons with mental illness, including poorhouses, jails, or private cages (Deutch, 1945). Toward the end of the colonial era, Americans responded more compassionately to persons with mental illness and separated their management from that of criminals by establishing hospital wings or institutions specifically for mental health care.

Early laws related to commitment were broad in scope, and admissions to psychiatric hospitals were governed by rather informal procedures (Appelbaum & Kemp, 1982; Appelbaum, 1990). Physicians, family members, or friends had the authority to petition for admission. A guarantee of payment for the hospitalization was sometimes required with the petition, along with a physician's certification that the person to be committed was "insane" (Appelbaum & Kemp, 1982).

As a system of public mental hospitals developed in the United States in the mid-nineteenth century, public advocacy drew national attention to the plight of persons confined in these institutions. In 1843, Dorothea Dix, known for her tireless efforts in advocating for reform within mental asylums, wrote of "suffering humanity" to the Massachusetts legislature: "I proceed, Gentleman, briefly to call your attention to the present state of Insane Persons confined within this Commonwealth, in cages, closets, cellars, stalls, pens! Chained, naked, beaten with rods, and lashed into obedience" (Dix, 1843, ref. no. 973–044). Her pleas led to an appropriation of funds to establish Worcester State Hospital in Massachusetts, and she continued her efforts across the United States.

As states across the country erected more mental institutions, more and more people were confined in them. Psychiatric hospitalization was available only on an involuntary basis until 1881, when Massachusetts enacted the first state law that allowed persons to admit themselves voluntarily (Appelbaum, 1985). Lax standards for confining individuals involuntarily

INFO

The Pennsylvania Hospital, designed to care for patients with physical and mental illnesses, admitted its first patient in 1752. The first institution (an "asylum") specifically designed to care for persons with mental illness was established in 1773 in Virginia.

● An early case
considering justifications
for civil commitment.

began to receive greater scrutiny. Two particularly notorious cases spotlighted problems with early commitment laws.

In the first case, Josiah Oakes, who had been confined in the McLean Asylum in the 1840s in Massachusetts, brought a *habeas corpus petition* forward for his release, saying he was confined illegally. Disapproving family members had committed Mr. Oakes, alleging that he was engaged to a woman of "unsavory character" while his wife was dying (Failer, 2002). In response to Oakes's petition, the Supreme Court of Massachusetts declared that the "right to restrain an insane person of his liberty is found in that great law of humanity, which makes it necessary to confine those whose going at large would be dangerous to themselves or others . . . and the necessity which creates the law, creates the limitation of the law" (*Matter of Oakes*, 1845).

The *Oakes* opinion endorses that commitment had two traditional justifications: exercise of a government's police powers and *parens patriae* powers (see Table 1.1). The *police power rationale* centers on the state's obligation to prevent persons with mental illness from endangering others or themselves. The *parens patriae doctrine* recognizes that some persons needed institutional care for

Table 1.1 | Justifications for Civil Commitment

1. *Parens patriae*
Originally, the power of the Sovereign to act as the caretaker for those individuals who could not care for themselves
2. Police Powers
The State may utilize its powers on behalf of the community and deprive an individual of liberty to protect the safety of that individual or others

their health and well-being, and that in these situations, the state must act to protect its citizens much as parents protect their children. The *parens patriae* rationale as applied to mental health matters grew out of the English monarchy's obligation to protect those who, left to their own devices, would squander their assets (Appelbaum, 1990; Appelbaum & Gutheil, 2007).

In another celebrated case, Elizabeth Packard was committed in 1860 to an institution for the insane based on an Illinois statute that allowed husbands to commit their wives. Her husband, a Calvinist minister who strictly interpreted his faith, had placed Mrs. Packard in an Illinois institution, stating that her unwillingness to concur with his religious views implied her insanity. Mrs. Packard thought she had been "railroaded into the institution" [Group for the Advancement of Psychiatry (GAP), 1948], and her experiences led her to advocate vigorously for commitment law reform. As one historical account of her case activities notes:

> An attractive person and a double-springed tongue gave force and persuasion to the direful romance of this fascinating woman, and she was successful enough, by her feminine arts, to bewitch a whole legislature into the appointment of joint committee to investigate the affairs of the unfortunate asylum. (Illinois Legislation Regarding Hospitals for the Insane, 1869, p. 207)

Mrs. Packard's complaints about mistreatment of persons at the institution in which she had been held contributed to the resignation of then Superintendent McFarland. Mrs. Packard's case became a *cause célèbre*, and she spent her life campaigning to reform commitment criteria and to improve the living conditions in insane asylums. Her efforts resulted in reforming civil commitment laws, including requirements in some jurisdictions for a trial by jury. (See *Lessard v. Schmidt*, 1972, and *Packard v. Packard* at http://law.jrank.org/pages/2582/Packard-v-Packard-1864. html, accessed 7/16/11.) Though Mrs. Packard believed that the jury-trial requirement would have prevented her own commitment, others have argued that it led to greater numbers of commitment by lay juries who were more likely to find people "insane" than were physicians or medical personnel (Deutsch, 1945).

Late-Nineteenth-Century Reform

The Pennsylvania Hospital, designed to care for patients with physical and mental illnesses, admitted its first patient in 1752. In its early days, hospitalizations for mental illness were at the discretion of family and physicians, just as for physical illnesses (Appelbaum & Gutheil, 2007, p. 40). Thus, the belief that an individual needed treatment guided decisions to impose involuntary commitment. As more hospitals were built, however, allegations of abuse, *habeus corpus* petitions, and other legal challenges eventually led to legislative modifications in commitment procedures. Lawmakers sought to address the possibility (highlighted by the *Packard* case) that persons with no mental illness could be deprived of their liberty if ill-intentioned family members could enlist the aid of a physician (Deutch, 1945).

Despite the desire in some quarters to tighten commitment proceedings and limit the authority of physicians and families, commitment processes tended to preserve the determinative role of medical judgment (Appelbaum & Kemp, 1982). In the mid-1800s, Isaac Ray, a leading psychiatrist and superintendent of various mental institutions, chaired a committee of the Association of Medical Superintendents of American Institutions for the Insane (an early version of the American Psychiatric Association) that pushed for clarification of civil commitment laws. The committee recommended informal procedures to commit someone who had families and friends who could remain involved and oversee their best interests. Rather than involving courts, Ray's committee considered having physicians certify an individual as committable and "insane" (at the time, a general term for someone with a mental illness that had no connotation of criminal responsibility) as an informal step in a treatment process (Ray, 1864; Appelbaum & Kemp, 1982). Still, the committee noted that other individuals (such as paupers and persons without family or friends who present a risk of harm to themselves or others) might require procedures that were more formalized through a judicial process. Pennsylvania ultimately adopted a statute largely based on Ray's committee recommendations. It permitted informal commitment processes for persons with family or friends who could help oversee their care and judicial commitment for individuals alleged to be insane and in need of hospitalization and for whom a judge found that treatment was needed (Pennsylvania Laws, 1869).

Developments in the Mid-Twentieth Century
The decades following the Civil War witnessed a gradual return to more relaxed procedural standards that made it easier for persons to be hospitalized (Appelbaum & Gutheil 2007). One form of deference to physician decision making was short-term emergency commitment based on a certification by a physician (Appelbaum & Gutheil, 2007).

By the late 1940s, however, the Group for the Advancement of Psychiatry (GAP; 1948) noted several problems with then-existing commitment laws, including a still-legalized approach that involved public hearings and use of juries whose judgments reflected nonprofessional views. At the time, six states (Alabama, Florida, Mississippi, North Dakota, Georgia, and Missouri) had no mechanism for voluntary admission, and in other states, voluntary admission procedures were a relatively recent phenomenon. The GAP committee also identified problems with antiquated or inappropriate terminology. In response, the GAP committee proposed eliminating terms such as "feeble-minded" or "weak-minded" from statutes and replacing "commitment" with "certification," "insanity" and "lunacy" with "mental illness," and "parole" with "convalescent status" or "convalescent leave." Other problems noted by the GAP committee appear in Table 1.2.

The GAP committee was also troubled by the frequent legal presumption that individuals who underwent civil commitment were incompetent to manage their personal affairs. The committee's sentiment foreshadowed debates and legal cases in the 1970s and 1980s that addressed the question of whether committed patients retained a right to refuse treatment.

Table 1.2 | Most Problematic Features of Commitment Identified by the Group for the Advancement of Psychiatry in 1948*

---

a. Legal service and notice to the patient

b. Insistence of personal appearance in court

c. Exposure of the patient as public spectacle and the public record of such

d. Emphasis on lay judgment as in trial by jury. Utilization of similar procedures to identify mental illness and criminality

e. Acceptance of certification of mental illness as tantamount to legal incompetence, rather than separating these issues

f. Use of anachronistic terminology

g. Inquiry into the patient's financial status at the time of commitment

---

*From the Group for the Advancement of Psychiatry, Report 4, April 1948, p. 2.

In 1952 the U.S. government's Draft Act Governing Hospitalization of the Mentally Ill was published (U.S. Public Health Service, 1952; Appelbaum, 2000). In an era when individuals brought for hospitalization often were routed via law enforcement and jails, this document articulated several ideas for reforming the process of psychiatric hospitalization (including an emphasis on using voluntary hospitalization). The Draft Act also proposed two criteria for involuntary commitment: (1) a risk of harm to self or others, and (2) the need for care or treatment when mental illness rendered someone lacking in insight or capacity and therefore unable to seek voluntary hospitalization. According to Appelbaum (2000), the Draft Act simultaneously promoted

INFO

In the 1940s, the GAP committee was troubled by the legal presumption that persons undergoing civil commitment are incompetent to manage their personal affairs—a view that foreshadowed later debates about whether committed patients retain a right to refuse treatment.

paternalistic views of hospitalization keeping commitment under medical control, but also reflected significant progressive views about patients' rights, including affording patients the opportunity for legal representation and judicial review of their confinement. Several states adopted the principles of the Draft Act in their commitment laws (Appelbaum, 2000).

A flurry of activity related to commitment laws followed publication of the Draft Act, but a subsequent report by the GAP (1966) offered further suggestions for reform. The 1966 GAP report noted that procedures and laws for admission to mental hospitals remained heavily influenced by criminal law. The report recommended that involuntary hospitalization should follow a certification process in which two physicians would carefully describe why a particular individual posed a danger (either to self or others) or needed treatment—thus identifying which of three proposed commitment criteria justified the person's involuntary hospitalization. Patients would also have access to legal counsel at any time, but court involvement would occur only if a patient petitioned for relief via a writ of *habeas corpus*. As a further mechanism to protect patients, a proposed independent review board would conduct periodic reviews of patients' commitments.

The Draft Act, the 1966 GAP report, and subsequent commentary advocating more medicalization of commitment laws ran counter to a broad wave of liberal reform that swept American society in the late 1960s and 1970s. Americans had always espoused beliefs in equal rights, the right to be free from government intrusions, and the right to procedural protections if the government attempts to intrude on an individual's liberty. But beginning with the Civil Rights Act of 1964 and the National Voting Rights Act of 1965, these ideals acquired new meaning in statutes and legal cases that protected previously marginalized groups from discriminatory treatment or undue government intrusion. Examples include legal decisions involving persons undergoing criminal interrogation (*Miranda v. Arizona*, 1966), women seeking abortions (*Roe v. Wade*, 1973), and minors facing sanctions in juvenile court (*In re Gault*, 1967), as well as legislative protections against discrimination in housing or certain public venues (Fair Housing Act of 1968; Rehabilitation Act of 1973).

The same social trends included advocacy for the rights of persons with mental disabilities. Sequestration of the mentally ill and discrimination based on mental infirmity had in former times received official government sanction (*Buck v. Bell*, 1927; Burt, 2001), but by the late 1960s, such practices seemed unenlightened and condemnable. The quality of care delivered in institutions had long troubled advocates for persons with mental illness (Deutsch, 1945). In the 1960s and 1970s, psychiatric diagnoses themselves were unsystematic and unreliable (Appelbaum, 1990), and some theorists questioned the nature and very existence of mental illness (Szasz, 1961, 1974; Torrey, 1972). Suspicions about the legitimacy of psychiatric treatment played out in state and federal courts as right to treatment and right to refuse treatment claims, which also reflected the sad—and even cruel—state of institutional care. In some cases (e.g., *Wyatt v. Stickney*, 1971), right to treatment claims resulted in orders to improve state institutional conditions, with judges refusing to accept excuses related to funding limitations (Bonnie, 2001).

Perhaps the most significant and lasting impact of the liberal reforms related to persons with mental illness were changes to states' civil commitment laws. Articulating a "preference for liberty" in responding to mental illness, California initiated what became a nationwide trend (Karasch, 2003) when it enacted the *Lanterman–Petris–Short Act (LPS Act)* in 1969. The LPS Act endorsed and encouraged voluntary treatment and repealed indefinite commitment, though it included provisions for involuntary interventions with numerous procedural protections. The LPS Act ultimately set a tone of reform that seemed to influence numerous commitment statutes across the United States (Appelbaum, 1994) and gave institutionalized mental patients the benefits of our nation's civil rights protections.

In 1972, a federal court legal decision from Wisconsin (*Lessard v. Schmidt*, 1972) became a watershed event that marked a turn away from *parens patriae* commitments toward basing commitments solely on potential harm to self or others. (Additional discussion of legal cases affecting civil commitment appears later in this chapter.) Over the next decade, every state changed its commitment criteria and procedures to implement most aspects of the *Lessard* holding (Lamb & Mills, 1986). Need for treatment alone would no longer justify civil commitment; instead, only mentally ill persons who met the criteria for dangerousness or could not care for themselves would undergo involuntary hospitalization. Potential durations of commitment were limited, briefer, and predefined. Persons subject to commitment would have access to courts, legal representation, and most of the due

INFO

California's Lanterman–Petris–Short Act repealed indefinite commitment, endorsed voluntary treatment, and set out numerous procedural protections for persons subject to involuntary interventions.

CASE LAW

Lessard v. Schmidt (1972)

Marked a turn away from *parens patriae* justifications for commitment and toward basing commitments solely on dangerousness.

process rights afforded to criminal defendants (Lamb & Mills, 1986).

Commitment reform was one of many forces that contributed to "deinstitutionalization," a drastic reduction in patient censuses at large state mental institutions during the last half of the 20th century. Major advances in psychopharmacology also played a role. In 1952, psychiatrists received the first French reports about the effects of chlorpromazine in ameliorating psychosis (Meyer & Simpson, 1997), which heralded an era in which physicians could give persons with serious mental illness drug treatments that would reliably control symptoms and help them to function better. Chlorpromazine and similar medications developed over the next decade often allowed patients who previously had little hope of recovery to leave hospitals and live in the community (Brill & Patton, 1959).

These psychopharmacological developments coincided with a growing national interest in community-based treatment, exemplified by passage of the Community Mental Health Centers Construction Act of 1963. In addition, attitudes favoring care for persons with mental illness close to home made placement at distant state institutions seem less attractive. Most important, perhaps, were financial incentives and pressures on institutional and community systems of care. Medicaid, Medicare, and the expansion of private health coverage provided funding to pay for treatment in nursing homes and acute-care medical hospitals rather than state mental institutions (Johnson, 1990). At the same time, legal rulings mandated improved conditions in state institutions, which made it more expensive to provide inpatient care (Geller, 2000). As a result, many persons who, in the 1950s, might have received custodial care in state hospitals wound up, in the 1970s, going to other institutional settings, including nursing homes, acute hospitals, jails, and prisons (Talbott, 1979).

Trends Since 1980

By allowing involuntary hospitalization only for dangerousness, legal developments in the 1970s effectively made commitment decisions dependent on whether a person needed confinement rather than on the person's need for care. In the 1980s, court decisions further decoupled involuntary hospitalization from treatment in a series of decisions that restricted when antipsychotic drugs—which mental health professionals had come to regard as a core feature of psychiatric care for most hospitalized patients— might be administered over a committed patient's objection. In one of the most celebrated and contentious medication cases, *Rogers v. Commissioner of Mental Health* (1982), the Supreme Judicial Court of Massachusetts ruled that except in emergency situations, persons hospitalized for psychiatric care could be forcibly medicated only if a court found that they were incompetent to make treatment decisions but would have wanted medications had they been competent. Court holdings in other jurisdictions required an independent psychiatric review of whether the proposed medication was appropriate (e.g., *Rennie v. Klein*, 1983) or a judicial finding of incompetence coupled with a judgment that proposed medications were in the patient's best interests (e.g., *Rivers v. Katz*, 1986).

Another influence on the use of involuntary commitment was the growing number of cases that made mental health practitioners liable for the acts of patients who posed a risk of danger to third parties (*Tarasoff v. Regents*, 1976; *Lipari v. Sears*, 1980; *Jablonski v. U.S.*, 1983; *Naidu v. Laird*, 1988). In several of these decisions, courts made it clear that protecting the public from potential harm was a key responsibility of mental health professionals. In addition, state court decisions in the 1980s further clarified what it meant to receive treatment in the least restrictive alternative setting (Miller, 1992).

CASE LAW

Rogers v. Commissioner of Mental Health (1982)

Ruled that except in emergencies, persons hospitalized for psychiatric care could be forcibly medicated only if a court found that they were incompetent to make treatment decisions but would have wanted medications had they been competent.

CASE LAW
*Tarasoff v.
Regents* (1976)

In a case involving an outpatient who told his therapist of his intent to harm an identified victim, this ruling established a "duty to protect" third parties, even if doing so required breaching confidentiality.

The American Psychiatric Association (APA) responded to these legal developments with its own recommendations (Roth, 1979; Stone, 1975), including a model statute on civil commitment (Stromberg & Stone, 1983). Responding both to the use of dangerousness as the sole justification for commitment and courts' recent right-to-refuse-treatment decisions, the APA proposed that incompetence to make treatment decisions be a necessary condition for involuntary hospitalization. Given his views that the purpose of hospitalization is to provide treatment, Alan Stone, M.D., former President of the APA, believed that to commit persons while allowing them to go without needed treatment was inhumane (Stone, 1985). The APA's proposed commitment statute received a mixed response (Miller, 1992). Civil libertarians argued against the proposition that someone might be deprived of liberty without a finding of dangerousness (Rubenstein, 1985); others defended the APA's proposal while maintaining that commitment statutes should not be vague or overly broad (Appelbaum, 1984).

In December 1986, a *New York Times* article highlighted a trend toward "easing" statutory criteria for committing persons with mental illness (Goleman, 1986). After Washington State broadened its commitment criteria to approximate the APA model statute (Durham, 1985), the state's inpatient census doubled in one year (Pierce, Durham, & Fisher, 1985). In addition to the possibility of increasing hospital censuses, it seemed plausible that if hospital beds were available, patients might not be discharged promptly or given active treatment. Nevertheless, commitment criteria continued to be modestly expanded or "relaxed," often at the urging of advocacy groups such as the National Alliance for the Mentally Ill (now known as the National Alliance on Mental Illness).

Several studies from the 1980s explored psychiatrists' views of existing civil commitment laws and the APA's model statute, as well as the real-life impact of civil commitment procedures. By 1980, 51% of psychiatric admissions to state and county hospitals were involuntary commitments (Rosenstein, Steadman, MacAskill & Manderscheid, 1986), but close examination of commitments revealed great variability in who was committed and why. Segal (1989) argued that different patient populations were the ultimate result of varied criteria for commitment. Roth (1989) believed that limited understanding of commitment law and its application was another significant factor leading to discrepancies in commitments, even if laws involved only dangerousness standards. He suggested that better training of clinicians and clarification of statutes might lead to faster reform than statutory changes themselves. Faulkner and colleagues (Faulkner, McFarland, & Bloom, 1989) showed that features of the system (e.g., locality of the hospital and fiscal and administrative issues) in which one operates have a greater impact on civil commitment than the laws that govern the process. These studies suggested addressing perceived deficiencies of the commitment system would require more than legislative change (Roth, 1989).

Courts' emphasis on placing patients in the least restrictive treatment setting and the ever-climbing costs of hospitalization contributed to the declining use of state hospitals as treatment settings and to increased efforts to provide treatment in community mental health centers. Mental illnesses are chronic conditions, however, and many persons who need ongoing, long-term care—some who have recently left hospitals and others who do not meet commitment criteria—may attend appointments erratically or completely refuse to get outpatient treatment. Without therapy, psychosocial support, and needed medications, these persons are at heightened risk of deterioration. In the last quarter of the twentieth century there was increasing concern about "revolving door" patients, a small but highly visible subset of mentally ill persons who displayed (what was, at least for their caregivers) a highly frustrating cycle of involuntary hospitalization, discharge, stopping treatment, rapid deterioration, and rehospitalization. Mental health professionals and some legal decision makers responded by recommending the use of *outpatient* involuntary civil commitment (Miller & Fiddleman, 1984), in which courts compel persons living in the community to get outpatient treatment with preauthorized involuntary rehospitalization or the imposition of other interventions if they fail to do so.

In the 1980s and 1990s, the American Psychiatric Association prepared two resource documents on involuntary outpatient commitment (APA, 1987, 1999a). The second of these (APA, 1999a) noted that by the summer of 1999, 40 states and the District of Columbia had some legislation that authorized outpatient commitment, though only half of these jurisdictions had some way of implementing it. At the time, available scientific literature had little to say about the effectiveness of existing mandatory outpatient systems and practices. Nevertheless, the APA (1999a) endorsed the idea of mandatory outpatient treatment for a limited group of patients with chronic mental illness who displayed the "revolving door" pattern of decompensation (i.e., worsening symptoms) and rehospitalization due to nonadherence to treatment.

Interest in outpatient commitment has continued to grow during the twenty-first century, as fiscal constraints wrought by managed care and strained state hospital budgets have further limited the overall inpatient bed capacity and length of stay of patients hospitalized with mental illness, and efforts to increase less restrictive community care options have grown. Although outpatient commitment takes on a community-based service framework, it includes an imposition on individual rights and thus requires ongoing assessment of its merits. A well-regarded, careful review of the available scientific literature raises questions about whether the curtailment of liberty that accompanies outpatient commitment produces any effects

INFO

Mental illnesses can be chronic conditions, and individuals needing ongoing, long-term care may have difficulty showing up regularly for appointments or may not adhere to outpatient treatment.

beyond those that would result from making available more intensive, *voluntary* outpatient services (Kisely, Campbell, & Preston, 2011). However, some studies identify merits (both expected and unexpected) of outpatient civil commitment that are not solely attributable to increased services (Swartz, Swanson, Wagner, Burns, Hiday, & Borum, 1999; Hiday, Swartz, Swanson, Borum, & Wagner, 2002; Groff, Burns, Swanson, Swartz, Wagner, & Tompson, 2004), and these support a position that outpatient commitment schemes can be ethically justifiable (Zanni & Stavis, 2007).

Over the past two centuries, revision and reforms of U.S. civil commitment statutes have evidenced an ongoing desire to balance mechanisms for providing safe and effective treatment with procedural protections for persons faced with the loss of their liberty. Statutes and court decisions governing involuntary hospitalization are legal creations, but changes in commitment law reflect fiscal pressures, political trends, and new scientific understandings of treatments for mental illness, rather than mere changes in legal doctrine. In the 1960s and 1970s, the "pendulum" of change swung away from need-for-treatment justifications and toward preventing dangerousness. The pendulum has swung back in recent years, however, and recent laws seem to reflect a combination of both concerns (Anfang & Appelbaum, 2006). We anticipate that in the future, commitment laws will continue to evolve in response to newly emerging treatments, financial constraints on treatment funding, and changes in the larger political climate.

INFO

Interest in outpatient commitment has continued to grow. Although the data are complex, some recent studies have suggested that potential benefits for specific individuals can, in certain cases, follow such interventions.

Civil Commitment Laws and Legal Standards

To those who watch the actual operations of local courts, each jurisdiction seems to have a unique commitment process that reflects local customs and the attitudes of the judge or magistrate who hears cases. Yet in theory at least, civil commitment proceedings implement the rules for decision making embodied in a jurisdiction's statutes. Case law from the past half-century establishes broad limits within which legislatures and courts may design procedures and make decisions. Our review of legal standards thus begins with a survey of how major legal cases have shaped the current landscape of civil commitment law as it relates to clinical practice.

Major Legal Decisions Impacting Practice
LAKE V. CAMERON (1966)

In 1962, Catherine Lake was a 60-year-old "bag lady" (though that phrase was not coined until a decade later) wandering in downtown Washington D.C. A policeman took her to the D.C. General Hospital; from there, she went to St. Elizabeth's (a psychiatric hospital), where she remained for more than 3 years as she sought release via a *habeas corpus* petition. After a district court ruling would have required Mrs. Lake to remain at St. Elizabeth's, an appellate court (*Lake v. Cameron*, 1966) remanded her case for reconsideration under what became known as the "least restrictive alternative" (LRA) doctrine. Writing for the majority, Judge David Bazelon stated that Mrs. Lake did not require the "complete deprivation of liberty that results from commitment to St. Elizabeth's" (p. 661). Before ordering hospitalization, the District Court had to consider whether "alternative courses of treatment" (p. 661)— such as carrying an identification card, or placement in day care, foster care, or a nursing home—might address her needs. In a subsequent decision, Judge Bazelon elaborated a constitutional basis for the LRA doctrine:

CASE LAW
Lake v. Cameron
1966

● Introduced what became known as the "least restrictive alternative" (LRA) doctrine.

[T]he principle of the least restrictive alternative consistent with the legitimate purposes of a commitment inheres in the very nature of civil commitment, which entails an extraordinary deprivation of liberty ... [S]uch a drastic curtailment of the rights of citizens must be narrowly, even grudgingly, construed in order to avoid deprivations of liberty without due process of law. [*Covington v. Harris*, 1969, p. 623 (citations omitted)]

LESSARD V. SCHMIDT (1972)

Mrs. Lake died in 1971 without ever having gained release from a psychiatric hospital (Chambers, 1972). But her case inspired *Lessard v. Schmidt* (1972), a decision from a Wisconsin federal district court that, as we noted above, transformed U.S. civil commitment law.

In October 1971, two police officers picked up Alberta Lessard in front of her home after a reported suicide attempt and took her to a mental health center. At a hearing concerning permanent commitment, the judge found that Miss Lessard was mentally ill and authorized 30 days of confinement. With the help of Milwaukee Legal Services, Miss Lessard brought a federal class action suit on behalf of all adults involuntarily hospitalized in Wisconsin arguing that the state's involuntary commitment statute was unconstitutional. The federal court ruled that because the consequences of commitment were at least comparable to those that followed criminal conviction, a person should not be subject to civil commitment unless the state can prove beyond a reasonable doubt that the person is mentally ill and "that if the person is not confined he will do immediate harm to himself or others." The *Lessard* court also stated that persons facing potential involuntary hospitalization deserved other constitutional protections afforded to individuals who face criminal charges. These included the following:

- effective, prompt notice of the allegations justifying the detention;
- a hearing, within 48 hours, on probable cause;
- a full hearing within 2 weeks on the need for commitment;
- representation by counsel;

- a prohibition against hearsay evidence;

- a privilege against "self-incrimination" (p. 1103), i.e., a warning that statements made to evaluators could be used to support commitment;

- a requirement that those seeking hospitalization consider other, less restrictive alternatives.

Although *Lessard* was binding only in Wisconsin, it became the impetus for several other courts and many state legislatures to revise commitment laws to require an "overt act" as proof of dangerousness.

WYATT V. STICKNEY (1971–1974)

Wyatt v. Stickney dealt not with civil commitment procedures, but with the treatment that individuals ought to receive if they undergo psychiatric hospitalization. In 1970, Alabama cut its cigarette tax, income from which had been earmarked for psychiatric services. In response, Bryce State Hospital laid off 99 employees, including most of its professional staff. Psychologists from Bryce spearheaded an employee suit for job reinstatement. For tactical reasons, they included a patient, Ricky Wyatt (whose aunt was among the laid-off employees) among the plaintiffs and alleged that the layoffs harmed Bryce's patients.

In March 1972, Judge Frank Johnson ruled that conditions at Bryce violated patients' constitutional right to receive individualized treatment that would offer a realistic chance at cure or at least improvement of their mental conditions, and he gave Alabama 6 months to implement the right. When the state failed to do so, Johnson formulated specific, measurable requirements for the hospital, including minimum staff-to-patient ratios and the use of individualized treatment plans. Johnson also wrote detailed requirements for the facilities that even addressed the water temperature for dishwashing and laundry use.

Alabama appealed Johnson's rulings, but the Fifth Circuit Court of Appeals upheld his decision in November 1974, including his notion of institutionalized patients' right to treatment. Although the Supreme Court never endorsed this notion, lawsuits in other states led to court decisions and legislative changes that implemented many of the *Wyatt* requirements outside Alabama (Reisner, Slobogin, & Rai, 2004). Today, *Wyatt*'s impact is evidenced in U.S. statutes and administrative rules governing treatment planning for patients. Evaluators assessing committability often will look at these treatment plans as one source of data to understand the respondent's current situation and goals for ongoing treatment.

CASE LAW

Wyatt v. Stickney
(1971–1974)

- Dealt with the treatment that individuals ought to receive if they undergo psychiatric hospitalization.

- Today, *Wyatt*'s impact is evidenced in statutes and administrative rules governing treatment planning.

JACKSON V. INDIANA (1972)

Jackson v. Indiana (1972) concerned a 27-year-old "mentally defective deaf mute with a mental level of a pre-school child" (p. 717) who was accused of two separate robberies involving goods worth a total of nine dollars. Court-appointed psychiatrists who evaluated Jackson said he could not understand the charges against him or participate in his defense; they also believed that these limitations were unlikely to abate. Nonetheless, the trial court committed him to the Indiana Department of Mental Health until he became "sane" (i.e., fit to stand trial). Jackson's defense counsel argued that Jackson's commitment was cruel and unusual punishment and violated his due process and equal protection rights—it amounted to a life sentence, given the small chance that he had of becoming competent to stand trial.

The trial court and the Indiana Supreme Court disagreed, but the U.S. Supreme Court accepted Jackson's equal protection argument because Jackson had been subject to a more lenient standard for confinement but a more stringent standard for release than persons who underwent ordinary (noncriminal) civil commitments. Moreover, confining Jackson indefinitely solely because of his incompetence to stand trial had violated Jackson's right to due process. In his majority opinion, Justice Blackmun stated, "[D]ue process requires that the nature and duration of commitment bear some reasonable relation to the purpose for which the individual is committed," and that an incompetent criminal defendant should not "be held more than the reasonable period of time necessary to determine whether there is a substantial probability that he will attain that competency in the foreseeable future" (*Jackson v. Indiana*, 1972, p. 738). Once it is determined that treatment has little chance of restoring a defendant's competence, the State must either initiate civil commitment proceedings or release him.

O'CONNOR V. DONALDSON (1975)

Kenneth Donaldson was civilly committed to the Florida State Hospital at Chattahoochee in January 1957 "for care, maintenance, and treatment." For nearly 15 years, he repeatedly demanded his release, claiming that he was neither mentally ill nor dangerous and that the hospital was not giving him any treatment. Moreover, friends and other responsible parties had offered to help care for and support him if that were necessary. In February 1971, Donaldson sued in federal court alleging that the hospital's superintendent

(Dr. J. B. O'Connor) and other staff members had deprived him of his constitutional right to liberty.

Appeals eventually placed matters before the U.S. Supreme Court, which noted that the case raised just "a single, relatively simple, but nonetheless important question concerning every man's constitutional right to liberty" (*O'Connor v. Donaldson*, 1975, p. 573). Though Donaldson denied having a mental illness, a unanimous Supreme Court said that even when individuals suffer from serious mental illness, "there is still no constitutional basis for confining such persons involuntarily if they are dangerous to no one and can live safely in freedom" (p. 575). In a famously ambiguous sentence, the Court set this boundary on civil commitment: "a State cannot constitutionally confine without more [justification] a nondangerous individual who is capable of surviving safely in freedom by himself or with the help of willing and responsible family members or friends" (p. 576). Acting as an agent of the State, O'Connor had done just this and had violated Donaldson's civil rights.

CASE LAW

O'Connor v. Donaldson
(1975)

1
chapter

● Supreme Court set this boundary on civil commitment: "a State cannot constitutionally confine without more [justification] a nondangerous individual who is capable of surviving safely in freedom by himself or with the help of willing and responsible family members or friends."

PARHAM V. J.R. (1979)

Parham v. J.R. asked whether Georgia's statutory scheme for admitting minors to a psychiatric hospital provided sufficient constitutional protections when children objected to hospitalization. As psychiatrist Loren Roth (1980) explained, children generally rely on proxy decision makers—typically their parents—to effectuate medical treatment and other measures that promote their welfare. But what about involuntary psychiatric hospitalization? *Parham* thus addressed the question, "Who shall be given the authority to

CASE LAW

Parham v. J.R.
(1979)

● Held that a
parent's belief that a child
needs hospitalization, coupled
with medical confirmation that
the child satisfies criteria for
admission, satisfies
constitutional due process
requirements.

effectuate the child's rights, and how, procedurally, should the choice of decision-maker for the child be accomplished?" (Roth, 1980, p. 392).

A majority of U.S. Supreme Court justices held that unless parents have abused or neglected their children, they should have a substantial role in making decisions about psychiatric hospitalization. The court reasoned that parents traditionally are responsible for their children's welfare. Therefore, a parent's belief that a child needs hospitalization, coupled with confirmation by a "neutral factfinder" that the child satisfies medical criteria for admission, should provide adequate protection to satisfy constitutional due process requirements. The neutral factfinder need not be a court or judge, said the majority: "an independent medical decision making process, which includes [a] thorough psychiatric investigation . . . followed by additional periodic review of a child's condition, will protect children who should not be admitted" (p. 613). Though the court acknowledged that this process is not error-free and that parents could mislead professionals, "we do not believe the risks of error in that process would be significantly reduced by a more formal, judicial-type hearing" (p. 612).

ADDINGTON V. TEXAS (1979)

Frank O'Neil Addington's mother petitioned for her son's indefinite commitment to a Texas mental hospital after he had been arrested for threatening her. A jury heard evidence that Addington suffered from delusions, had often threatened to hurt his parents and other people, had been assaultive during previous hospitalizations, and had damaged property at his apartment and his parents' home. Addington conceded that he was mentally ill but maintained "that there was no substantial basis for concluding that he was probably dangerous to himself or others" (p. 421). Texas jury instructions allowed for commitment if "clear, unequivocal and convincing evidence" showed that Addington needed psychiatric hospitalization "for his own welfare and protection or the protection of others" (p. 420). Addington objected to these instructions, arguing that the proof requirement should be "beyond a reasonable doubt," as in criminal cases. After the jury found that Addington met Texas commitment criteria, he challenged the decision.

A unanimous U.S. Supreme Court acknowledged that "the particular standard-of-proof catchwords do not always make a great difference in a particular case." The issue deserved careful consideration, however, if only because standards of proof have at-least-symbolic meaning and demonstrate "the value society places on individual liberty" (p. 425).

The court reasoned that an individual's liberty interests are great enough to require the state to prove mental illness and dangerousness by more than a preponderance of the evidence. Yet the court concluded that the "reasonable doubt" standard was too stringent, for two reasons. First, in a civil commitment, the state confines someone not to punish him or to protect the public, but to help the person confined get treatment that he presumably needed. Second, "the lack of certainty and the fallibility of psychiatric diagnosis" made it unclear "whether a state could ever prove beyond a reasonable doubt that an individual is both mentally ill and likely to be dangerous" (p. 429). States should not "be required to employ a standard of proof that may completely undercut its efforts to further the legitimate interests of both the state and the patient that are served by civil commitments" (p. 430). Requiring proof by "clear and convincing" evidence

CASE LAW

Addington v. Texas
(1979)

● Ruled that requiring proof by "clear and convincing" evidence would adequately protect individuals' liberty while still letting a state impose involuntary psychiatric hospitalization when necessary to protect its citizens.

would adequately protect individuals' liberty while still letting a state impose psychiatric treatment when necessary to protect its citizens. Though the Texas statute also included the term "unequivocal," this was not constitutionally required. *Addington* thus establishes that although states may vary as to the standard of proof required to commit an individual, the standard can never be lower than clear and convincing evidence.

VITEK V. JONES (1980)

Convicted robber Larry Jones was moved from his Nebraska prison cell to the penitentiary hospital because of his mental illness. Two days later, he set his mattress on fire and burned himself severely. After receiving treatment at the burn unit of a private hospital, he was sent, without a hearing, to the security unit of the Lincoln Regional Center, a state psychiatric hospital. Jones sued in federal court, alleging that his transfer to a mental institution without a formal commitment hearing had deprived him of liberty without due process of law.

The district court sided with Jones, and following a series of appeals, the U.S. Supreme Court agreed with Jones, too. Although a valid criminal conviction and imposition of a prison sentence permit a state to confine an individual, these actions "do not authorize the State to classify him as mentally ill and to subject him to involuntary psychiatric treatment without affording him additional due process protections" (*Vitek v. Jones*, 1980, p. 494). The court viewed transfer to a psychiatric facility as adding an additional stigma to the individual that could have social consequences. Therefore, the court ruled that

CASE LAW
Vitek v. Jones
(1980)

● Ruled that prison inmates should receive certain procedural protections afforded to other persons who undergo commitment, including notice of allegations, a full hearing before an independent decision maker, and the opportunity to challenge evidence.

prison inmates should receive certain procedural protections afforded to others who underwent commitment, including notice of allegations, a full hearing before an independent decision maker, and the opportunity to challenge evidence.

ZINERMON V. BURCH (1990)

In December 1981, a concerned citizen found Darrell Burch wandering along a Florida roadway and brought him to a community mental health service. There, clinicians thought Burch—who was bloodied and bruised—had fallen or had been attacked. He was also confused and was hallucinating, and he thought he was "in heaven." Yet he signed a form for voluntary admission and another form authorizing treatment at the community center and a subsequent longer-term hospitalization at Florida State Hospital (FSH).

Burch was discharged from FSH after 5 months of treatment, and he began complaining that he had been improperly hospitalized, confined, and treated. Because he had not been competent to sign in voluntarily or to permit treatment, Burch believed he should have had a judicial commitment hearing before being admitted and treated. No such hearing had taken place, however, and Burch sued for damages in federal court, arguing that FSH had deprived him of his liberty without due process of law. The question of whether Burch had legitimate grounds for a civil rights lawsuit ultimately reached the U.S. Supreme Court.

In a 5–4 ruling, the Supreme Court concluded that Burch could pursue his claim, because he and other persons like him were entitled to a hearing that would determine either that he was competent to consent to admission or that he was eligible for involuntary civil commitment.

Zinermon thus implies that a psychiatric facility could face liability for false imprisonment if it allows a patient of questionable competence to sign in voluntarily.

Though the court did not define what constitutes competence to admit oneself for psychiatric care, many patients who come to psychiatric facilities have mental problems that might adversely affect their capacity to admit themselves voluntarily or give consent for treatment. Some hospitals now use forms that require admitting physicians to certify that voluntary patients understand that they are undergoing hospitalization and that there may be limitations on their ability to leave.

In contrast to what some clinicians feared might happen, few cases have been litigated based on alleged violations of *Zinermon.* One reason may be that most patients who enter hospitals voluntarily are competent to do so (Appelbaum, Appelbaum, & Grisso, 1998). Also, foregoing a commitment hearing may cause little practical harm to patients who are so incapacitated as to be incompetent to consent to psychiatric hospitalization and who then receive competence-restoring treatment. This has become even truer as typical stays in psychiatric hospitals have shortened to just a few days. Even in Darrell Burch's case, his injury consisted mainly of losing his liberty without due process; his psychiatric hospitalization had actually helped him. Still, his claims paved the way toward a requirement for greater attention to the more stringent procedures related to voluntary psychiatric hospitalization.

HELLER V. DOE (1993)

This case arose from Kentucky statutes that used a commitment standard for mentally retarded persons (then, the proper designation for persons with developmental disabilities) that differed from the standard applicable to mentally ill individuals. Both laws allowed inpatient commitments of mentally impaired persons who were dangerous to themselves or others and who might benefit from treatment. However, the burden of proof in mental retardation proceedings was clear and convincing evidence, whereas mental illness commitments required proof beyond a reasonable doubt. Also, a respondent's guardians or family members had legal status to participate in Kentucky mental retardation hearings with the same rights as the respondent.

A group of involuntarily committed mentally retarded persons claimed that these differences were violations of the Equal Protection and Due Process clauses of the Fourteenth Amendment. Though lower courts upheld their position, a majority of the U.S. Supreme Court disagreed. Noting that mental retardation is a relatively static condition for which good documentation usually extends back to childhood, the Court held that it was reasonable to require a lower burden of proof than is required for mental illness. Requiring a higher standard for committing mentally ill persons made sense, said the Court, because psychiatric treatment for mental illness is usually much more intrusive than is the treatment that persons with mental retardation receive.

The Court stated that it was reasonable to let family members and guardians participate in commitment proceedings for a mentally retarded person (though not proceedings for mentally ill persons) because close relatives and guardians might have detailed information about the respondent that would prove valuable during a hearing. By contrast, mental illnesses usually arise during adulthood, and proper psychiatric treatment usually depends on matters unrelated to observations made in a respondent's childhood home. Also, previously healthy adults who develop mental illnesses may need private commitment hearings confined to the smallest group possible.

CASE LAW

Heller v. Doe

(1993)

● Held that standards and procedures for hospitalizing persons with developmental disabilities may differ from those required for persons with mental illness.

Table 1.3 summarizes the landmark cases related to civil commitment.

Table 1.3 | Landmark Cases Related to Civil Commitment

Case Name	Relevant Holding
Lake v. Cameron, 1966	Involuntary commitment must take place in the least restrictive alternative
Wyatt v. Stickney, 1971–1974	Consideration of a right to treatment and specific necessary treatment conditions
Lessard v. Schmidt, 1972	Dangerousness and full procedural protections required for civil commitment
O'Connor v. Donaldson, 1975	Without some additional justification, the State may not confine a nondangerous (mentally ill) individual who can survive independently or with the help of available others
Parham v. J.R., 1979	Parents are permitted to authorize their children's confinement to a mental hospital
Addington v. Texas, 1979	Clear and convincing evidence is required to authorize involuntary commitment
Vitek v. Jones, 1980	Prior to involuntary psychiatric hospitalization, a prison inmate is entitled to certain procedural protections
Zinermon v. Burch, 1990	Clinical assessment needed of a patient's capacity to accept voluntary psychiatric hospitalization before allowing the patient to sign in for treatment
Heller v. Doe, 1993	Standards and procedures for hospitalizing persons with mental retardation may differ from those required for persons with mental illness

General Legal Standards of Commitment Criteria
MENTAL DISORDER

As readers of psychology and psychiatry texts and official diagnostic manuals know, no clearly bounded definition of "mental disorder" exists. Not surprisingly, then, civil commitment statutes define mental disorder in many different ways. Some definitions are confusing and circular. For example, § 1.03(20) of New York's Mental Hygiene Laws defines "mental illness" as "an affliction with a mental disease or mental condition which is manifested by a disorder or disturbance in behavior, feeling, thinking, or judgment to such an extent that the person afflicted requires care, treatment and rehabilitation"; § 9.01 explains that needing care and treatment "means that a person has a mental illness for which in-patient care and treatment in a hospital is appropriate."

Michigan law offers one example of what probably is the modal definition found in U.S. civil commitment statutes: a mental illness as "a substantial disorder of thought or mood that significantly impairs judgment, behavior, capacity to recognize reality, or ability to cope with the ordinary demands of life" (Michigan Compiled Laws Annotated 330.1400g). Table 1.4 lists variations on this theme from several states. We discuss the practical implications of definitions of mental illness in Chapter 2.

Table 1.4 | Examples of Statutory Definitions of Mental Illness for Purposes of Civil Commitment

---

Alabama Statutes § 22–52-1.1(1)
Mental illness [means a] psychiatric disorder of thought and/or mood which significantly impairs judgment, behavior, capacity to recognize reality, or ability to cope with the ordinary demands of life.

Arizona Revised Statutes 36–501 (22)
"Mental disorder" means a substantial disorder of the person's emotional processes, thought, cognition or memory . . .

(Continued)

Table 1.4 | Examples of Statutory Definitions of Mental Illness
for Purposes of Civil Commitment (*Continued*)

Idaho Code § 66–317(m)
"Mentally ill" shall mean a person, who as a result of a substantial disorder
of thought, mood, perception, orientation, or memory, which grossly impairs
judgment, behavior, capacity to recognize and adapt to reality, requires care
and treatment at a facility.

104 Code Massachusetts Regs. § 27.05[1]
"Mental illness" means a substantial disorder of thought, mood, perception,
orientation, or memory which grossly impairs judgment, behavior, capacity
to recognize reality, or ability to meet the ordinary demands of life, but shall
not include alcoholism.

Michigan Compiled Laws Annotated 330.1400g
"Mental illness" means a substantial disorder of thought or mood that
significantly impairs judgment, behavior, capacity to recognize reality,
or ability to cope with the ordinary demands of life.

Minnesota 253B. 02, Subd. 13. (a)
A "person who is mentally ill" means any person who has an organic
disorder of the brain or a substantial psychiatric disorder of thought,
mood, perception, orientation, or memory which grossly impairs judgment,
behavior, capacity to recognize reality, or to reason or understand.

New Jersey Statutes Ann. § 30:4–27.2(r)
"Mental illness" means a current, substantial disturbance of thought, mood,
perception or orientation which significantly impairs judgment, capacity to
control behavior, or capacity to recognize reality, but does not include
simple alcohol intoxication, transitory reaction to drug ingestion, . . .

Nevada Revised Statutes § 433.164
"Mental illness" means a clinically significant disorder of thought,
mood, perception, orientation, memory, or behavior which:

1. Is listed in the most recent edition of the clinical manual of the
International Classification of Diseases, ICD-9-CM, . . . or the corresponding
code in the most recent edition of the American Psychiatric Association's
Diagnostic and Statistical Manual of Mental Disorders, DSM-IV, Axis I; and

Table 1.4 | Examples of Statutory Definitions of Mental Illness
for Purposes of Civil Commitment (*Continued*)

2. Seriously limits the capacity of a person to function in the primary aspects of daily living, including, without limitation, personal relations, living arrangements, employment, and recreation.

Ohio Revised Code § 5122.01(A)
"Mental illness" means a substantial disorder of thought, mood, perception, orientation, or memory that grossly impairs judgment, behavior, capacity to recognize reality, or ability to meet the ordinary demands of life.

Oklahoma Stat. Ann. § 43A-1–103
"Mentally illness" means a substantial disorder of thought, mood, perception, psychological orientation, or memory that significantly impairs judgment, behavior, capacity to recognize reality, or ability to meet the ordinary demands of life.

South Dakota Codified Laws § 27A-1–1(18)
"Severe mental illness" [means a] substantial organic or psychiatric disorder of thought, mood, perception, orientation, or memory which significantly impairs judgment, behavior, or ability to cope with the basic demands of life.

Vermont Stat. Ann. 18 § 7101 (14)
"Mental illness" means a substantial disorder of thought, mood, perception, orientation, or memory, any of which grossly impairs judgment, behavior, capacity to recognize reality, or ability to meet the ordinary demands of life, but shall not include mental retardation . . .

Wis. s. 51.001 stats. 13(b)
"Mental illness," for purposes of involuntary commitment, means a substantial disorder of thought, mood, perception, orientation, or memory which grossly impairs judgment, behavior, capacity to recognize reality, or ability to meet the ordinary demands of life, but does not include alcoholism.

"DANGEROUSNESS" IN STATUTES

Commitment laws give effect to the principle that states' police powers and *parens patriae* obligations justify detention of some persons to prevent them from harming themselves or others—that is, to avert "danger." Typically, state statutes specify that commitment is permissible when mentally ill persons exhibit the following sorts of dangerousness:

- Risk that a person might come to harm through self-neglect, "grave disability," or failure to meet basic needs;
- Risk that a person might physically injure or kill himself or herself;
- Risk that a person might physically harm other persons.

In addition, civil commitment statutes in many jurisdictions contain language that allows consideration of a person's need for treatment, the risk of physical deterioration without commitment, dangerousness to property, substance use, and the risk of relapse or mental deterioration. Statutes usually expressly call for the court to order placement in the least restrictive alternative setting available. Chapter 2 explores the meaning of dangerousness and mental disorder in greater depth.

Legal Procedures and Related Concepts

This section, which outlines the types of procedures that initiate and effectuate civil commitment, reflects the particular legal practices in Ohio and Massachusetts, the jurisdictions in which the authors work. Though we have tried to generalize beyond our own experiences to those that practitioners in other locales can expect to encounter, we encourage readers to supplement the following outline with knowledge about the particulars of commitment processes in their own practice locales. For simplicity of exposition, this section (like the majority of this volume) focuses on the legal process that leads to involuntary psychiatric hospitalization rather than involuntary outpatient treatment. We also note that throughout

this volume we generally refer to the subject of the petition as the
"*respondent*" (rather than "patient") and the professional perform-
ing the evaluation as the "evaluator" (rather than "clinician" or
"doctor," terms that connote a treatment relationship).

Initiating the Commitment Process

Jurisdictions in the United States utilize one or more of the following methods to initiate civil commitment proceedings.

FILING AN AFFIDAVIT

Statutes in some states (e.g., Ohio, see O.R.C. § 5122.10; New York,
N.Y. Mental Hygiene Law § 9.27) contain provisions that let ordinary citizens (that is, nonclinicians) initiate certain civil commitment proceedings. In other states, petitions for commitment may
be initiated by professionals who encounter persons with mental
illness in their work, such as police officers, guardians, or superintendents of facilities in which respondents are being detained,
or a prosecuting attorney (e.g., Ind. Code § 12–26-7–2). The
process begins with the execution of a document containing
a declarant's description of the behavior of someone alleged to be
mentally ill. In some jurisdictions, this may involve the declarant's
filing an affidavit, application, petition, or other document with a
court that handles civil commitment proceedings. (An *affidavit*—
Latin for "he has declared upon oath"—is a sworn written statement that the declarant signs before a magistrate or notary, who
affirms the veracity of the declarant's signature.)

The document must be based on the declarant's firsthand
knowledge of recent behavior by the individual alleged to be mentally ill and must support the contention that the person requires
involuntary psychiatric treatment. Some states require that the
document be accompanied by a certificate completed by one or
more examining clinicians, and some states limit declarant eligibility to parties (such as relatives, caregivers, guardians, and room-
mates) reasonably expected to have an interest in the person
alleged to be mentally ill.

In those jurisdictions that require submission of documentation to the court, a judge, referee, or magistrate will review the

information for "probable cause," that is, to determine whether the documentation alleges facts sufficient to justify detention of the individual. The court may then issue a "warrant" or "temporary order of detention," which authorizes law enforcement personnel (and sometimes certain mental health personnel) to apprehend the person alleged to be mentally ill. Following apprehension, the person is either brought before the court (e.g., N. Y. Mental Hygiene Law § 9.43) or transported to a hospital or other suitable facility [e.g., Ohio Rev. Code § 5122.11, Texas Health and Safety Code § 573.012(e)] for assessment. Laws in many jurisdictions specify that such apprehension should take place as inconspicuously as possible. The warrant or temporary order permits confinement only for a short period (typically three to five court days), after which the detained person must have a hearing concerning continued hospitalization.

"PSYCHIATRIC EMERGENCY"

To permit intervention in situations that generate immediate and serious risks of harm, all U.S. jurisdictions permit detention of mentally ill persons whose behavior or condition requires emergency action. Under such circumstances, law enforcement personnel (and, in some locales, health officers or other individuals with statutory authority to detain) may apprehend mentally ill persons and take them to hospital emergency departments or other appropriate facilities for evaluation. Again, statutes often specify that detention should be as inconspicuous as possible.

OTHER OPTIONS

Psychiatric hospitalization is expensive, and in the case of involuntary inpatient care, payment often comes (at least in part) from state coffers. Both to promote treatment in community contexts and to save money, many areas of the country have developed screening processes and "mobile crisis services" (Geller, Fisher, & McDermeit, 1995) staffed by mental health professionals who try to direct persons needing mental health care to the most effective, appropriate, but least restrictive settings. A limited body of empirical data suggests that these teams reduce hospitalization (Guo, Biegel,

Johnson, & Dyches, 2001), yet they often encounter individuals who need treatment but will not accept it voluntarily.

The previous discussion has focused on state actors and public employers as initiators of involuntary hospitalization. Of course, concerned family members and friends may take individuals to hospital emergency rooms, and individuals with mental illness sometimes present themselves to hospitals for evaluation only to find themselves involuntarily detained there. Citizens in many other contexts—for example, school personnel and employers, often acting on the advice of mental health providers—can also take actions that eventuate in involuntary inpatient treatment.

AT THE HOSPITAL

Once an individual has arrived at a health care facility, community responders (often the police) provide information to staff members describing the circumstances that led to the person's detention and the reasons that the person represents a substantial risk of harm to himself or others. Many jurisdictions have created specially colored forms ("pink slips" in Ohio and Massachusetts) to record information about the person that will withstand legal scrutiny if civil commitment is later pursued. Arrival at the facility also "starts the clock" on the time within which clinicians must evaluate and make decisions concerning an allegedly mentally ill person's need for hospitalization.

Time Frames

Within a short time (typically 24 hours) after the allegedly mentally ill person has arrived, a qualified clinician (typically a psychiatrist or other physician) at the detaining facility must examine the patient-detainee. If, in the clinician's judgment, the detainee's condition and recent behavior do not satisfy commitment criteria, the facility must either release the detainee (unless a court has issued a temporary order of

INFO

Within a short time after an allegedly mentally ill person has arrived at a detaining facility, a qualified clinician at the facility must conduct an examination.

detention) or (if hospitalization would be appropriate) allow voluntary admission.

Even if a detainee appears to be committable, the hospital may still be allowed or even be required by law to offer a patient voluntary hospitalization before proceeding with involuntary hospitalization if the detainee is willing to sign in as a patient and can make a competent decision to do so. Otherwise, involuntary detention may continue only if hospital clinicians initiate further legal proceedings that will eventuate in a judicial hearing on commitment. The time within which a commitment hearing must take place varies substantially, from days (e.g., Ohio and Virginia) to weeks (e.g., California and New York), but typically, clinicians have just two or three court days to determine whether involuntary hospitalization is justified and to initiate the appropriate legal filings.

Prehearing Rights of Detainees

All states require hospitals to provide detained patients with written documents that describe their legal rights. State statutes vary considerably as to what these documents must tell detained patients, but the documents often include information about the following:

- the right to make a reasonable number of telephone calls;
- the availability of help in reaching an attorney or, in some states (e.g., New York and Massachusetts), legal advisory organizations created to assist psychiatric inpatients;
- the right to retain counsel (at public expense if the person is indigent);
- the right to examination by an independent clinician (in some states, at public expense if the person is indigent);
- notification (with the patient's consent) about hospitalization to the patient's legal guardian, spouse, relatives, and counsel, if these persons can be found;
- the potential length of detention;

- the right to have a hearing on continued commitment; and
- the possibility that statements made to clinicians may be used in proceedings concerning further detention.

Commitment Hearings

NOTICE BEFORE HEARING

Before the judicial commitment hearing, the patient-detainee—who has now become the "respondent" in a legal case—receives written notice that explains when the hearing will occur, the factual basis for the proposed commitment, and potential witnesses who might testify. The notice must come far enough in advance of the hearing to permit preparation of a defense. In most jurisdictions, the notice also details the respondent's rights at the hearing, including the rights to attend and to have attorney representation (appointed, if necessary, at public expense). In most states, other individuals who would likely be interested in the respondent's case—for example, the respondent's spouse, guardian, attorney, and/or other persons designated by the respondent—must also receive notice.

HEARING LOCATION AND COURT OF JURISDICTION

States vary as to whether commitment hearings are public or private proceedings. Which court holds the hearing also varies among jurisdictions. In Ohio and Texas, for example, hearings are held by the county's probate court, either by a judge or magistrate with statutory power to conduct the hearing. In Massachusetts, district courts hold hearings. Many states' statutes permit commitment hearings to take place in "any suitable location" [Texas Health and Safety Code § 574.031(A)]—for example, the hospital at which the patient is

INFO

States vary as to whether commitment hearings are public or private proceedings. Which court (e.g., probate, district, or other) holds the hearing also varies among jurisdictions.

detained—on the theory that doing so may be less embarrassing and risky for respondents than transporting them to the court-house in shackles.

HEARING PROCEDURE

Presentation of evidence. Though any number of people might initiate proceedings that ultimately lead to civil commitment hearings, the State becomes the legal proponent of any proposed civil commitment. As with a criminal proceeding, the State has the legal burden of production, that is, the responsibility to intro-duce evidence sufficient to support the conclusion that the respon-dent is mentally ill and subject to court-ordered hospitalization. A commitment hearing thus begins with the presentation by the proponent's attorney (sometimes called the "prosecutor") of evidence favoring involuntary hospitalization. The attorney will make the case for commitment by calling witnesses—usually one or more clinicians, and sometimes family, friends, or other nonexpert fact witnesses. Among the facts and conclusions elic-ited from direct examination of the State's witnesses are the following:

- statements and actions by the respondent that led to initiation of the commitment;
- signs and symptoms of mental illness exhibited by the respondent;
- the respondent's psychiatric diagnosis;
- the respondent's clinical prognosis;
- the record of treatment, which may be relevant to justifying hospitalization; and
- the least restrictive treatment setting suitable for the respondent's care.

Following direct examination of each witness, the respon-dent has the right to cross-examine witnesses. Cross-examination questioning (usually done by the respondent's counsel) may include challenging clinicians' credentials, the adequacy of their database, and the soundness of their conclusions. Counsel for the

respondent may also pose alternative explanations for the proponent's behavior, for example:

- "Isn't it possible he was acting in self-defense when he
  hit his mother?"
- "You said my client was hallucinating, but he also
  could have just been talking to himself, correct?"
  or alternative settings for treatment:
- "Is it not true that my client could take the same
  medications as an outpatient?"

Respondent's rights at the hearing. Respondents have several specific procedural rights, including rights to:

- attend the hearing;
- hire or have the court appoint counsel;
- call and cross-examine witnesses;
- testify; and
- hire an independent expert.

States vary on the mechanics of these rights and on whether
a respondent has a right to have the case for civil commitment
heard (or "tried") before a jury. In those states that permit jury
hearings, the default option usually is trial before a judge, with the
option for a jury available if the respondent requests it.

WHO TESTIFIES?

Almost all testimonial evidence at commitment hearings comes
from one of four sources.

- *Lay (fact) witnesses* Courts that hear civil commitment cases
often receive testimony from petitioners—individuals who file
applications for commitment—or from persons who had contact
with respondents shortly before their detention. Such individuals
may include police officers, friends, relatives, spouses, and guardians. These individuals serve the court as fact witnesses. They do
not state opinions, and their testimony should be restricted to
what they have personally observed.

• *Treating clinician* Treating clinicians often initiate civil commitment hearings, and a professional providing care typically has the best information about the respondent's mental condition. In most legal proceedings, a patient could object to testimony by a treating physician or psychologist on the grounds that the communications between them had been "privileged." Civil commitment hearings are different, however, in that many states' rules of evidence include an exception that specifically permits testimony by treating clinicians [see, e.g., Texas Evid. R. 509(e)(6)].

• *Appointed and independent experts* Courts will usually hear testimony by independent experts when they have been appointed or if parties to the proceeding have retained them. Unlike treating clinicians, independent experts do not have doctor–patient relationships with respondents, and their testimony may not be barred by testimonial privilege if asserted by the respondent [see, e.g., Rev. Code Wash. § 71.05.360(9)].

• *Patient-respondent* Finally, almost all jurisdictions give the patient-respondent the right to testify and the right not to do so, analogous to those rights afforded criminal defendants.

COMMITMENT OUTCOMES
• *Commitments for statutorily limited times (e.g., 3–6 months) and required review* In most states, initial and subsequent commitments may be for limited, specific periods—typically 3 to 6 months. Such lengthy hospitalizations are rare these days, but they were common in the 1970s and 1980s, when most current civil commitment laws underwent major revisions. Even today, however, a few persons with severe mental illness do not recover sufficiently

to leave the hospital, even after several months of inpatient treatment. Also, some states are increasingly using outpatient civil commitments in an effort to prevent rehospitalization of patients who would otherwise stop getting treatment after they left an inpatient setting. The time-limited nature of commitment means that courts must periodically review treatment of committed individuals, whether they are inpatients or outpatients. Extensions of involuntary care require new court hearings that apply the same principles, rules, and criteria used in the initial hearings.

- *Appeal rights and procedures* Unless a respondent has "stipulated" to a commitment (essentially, agreed to it), commitment decisions may be appealed via legal procedures analogous to those involved in appealing criminal convictions.

- *If commitment is rejected by the court, how long after, and in what circumstances, may one repetition for commitment?* Most jurisdictions do not state a specific time period after which one may repetition for an individual's commitment. Often, however, courts require new evidence—a new overt act or other new information that justifies a new petition. Committing courts will generally be reluctant to override the decision of a prior court without new facts that would merit opening a new commitment case.

Forensic Mental Health Concepts | 2

In Chapter 1, we explained that trial courts may order civil commitment only upon a finding that an individual

(a) has a "substantial" mental disorder and

(b) poses a "risk" of harm to himself or herself or to others because of that disorder.

Though these concepts may sound familiar to all mental health professionals, their meanings in civil commitment hearings differ in important ways from their meanings in clinical practice. In this chapter, we explore these differences to highlight specific forensic mental health concepts.

Substantial Mental Disorder

As Table 1.4 shows, jurisdictions typically require that an individual subject to commitment have a "substantial" mental disorder affecting "thought, mood, perception, orientation, or memory." Furthermore, the mental disorder must "significantly" or "grossly" impair the individual's "judgment, behavior, capacity to recognize reality, or ability to meet the ordinary demands of life." Thus, a unifying theme in statutory definitions is that to warrant civil commitment, a mental illness must compromise one or more crucial mental faculties so seriously that it creates an obvious impairment in functioning.

Laws in several states use diagnoses to designate disorders that do *not* constitute mental illnesses for purposes of mental illness-based civil commitment. For example, Arizona's civil commitment statute specifically excludes "drug abuse, alcoholism or mental retardation" and "personality disorders characterized by lifelong and deeply ingrained antisocial behavior patterns, including [illegal] sexual behaviors" unless these are also accompanied by "a substantial disorder of the person's emotional processes, thought, cognition or memory" [Arizona Statute 36–501(26)]. Many states' statutes specifically exclude epilepsy and other neurological disorders. Thus, clinicians need to know which clinical conditions are not potential bases for mental illness civil commitment in the jurisdiction in which they work.

In addition to particular exclusions, what "mental illness" means for civil commitment purposes depends on how each jurisdiction construes the phrase in light of the legal contexts, applicable statutes, and regulatory definitions, all of which can vary. In most states, the words and phrases that designate commitment-justifying mental disorders need not fit a formal or official diagnostic scheme. For example, New Jersey's civil commitment statute expressly states, "The term mental illness is not limited to 'psychosis' or 'active psychosis,' but shall include all conditions that result in the severity of impairment described herein."

Often, state case law tells courts to interpret words in civil commitment statutes as ordinary language terms, not professional diagnostic terms. Indeed, case law sometimes expresses skepticism about mental health professionals' diagnostic schemes. For example, in an Ohio decision in which experts did not offer a clear psychiatric diagnosis and therefore testified that the respondent did not have a mental disorder, an appeals court wrote:

> The record . . . presents clear examples of the misconceptions of the experts concerning the statutory definition. . . .
> The experts were apparently using some type of technical professional definition for the ordinary language of the statute.

Instead, the proper test is the meaning that the words convey to the ordinarily prudent person of reasonable understanding and intelligence. . . .

. . . [T]he collective testimony of all the experts describes a substantial disorder of thought, mood and judgment when these terms are considered in light of their ordinary meaning, the manner in which they are used in the statute, rather than in light of some hypertechnical, psychiatric definition . . . [T]he "hangup" of the experts in this case [may be that] they are unwilling to consider anything that they do not professionally recognize as an illness as being a mental illness within the definition of the statute. (*In re McKinney*, 1983, pp. 280–281)

Courts in Illinois and Nebraska have reached a similar conclusion:

[T]oo much emphasis has been placed on the existence or nonexistence of a recognizable psychiatric disease in determining whether a person is "mentally ill" for purposes of civil commitment. Diagnostic classifications in the mental-health field are constantly undergoing revision . . . , and thus it would be unwise to equate the legal term "mentally ill" . . . with the laundry list of diagnoses or psychiatric classifications in vogue at a given moment. . . . [A] finding of "mentally ill" should not be dependent upon diagnostic categories or nomenclature, but on the extent to which a person's functioning is impaired by his mental illness. (*People v. Lang*, 1986, pp. 452–453)
[T]he phrase "mentally ill" is broadly inclusive . . . and . . . the Legislature used these words in their ordinary and popular sense. (*Interest of Pollard*, 1993, p. 17)

In these states and others that treat statutory language similarly, "mental illness" for purposes of civil commitment is a *legal* concept that refers to behavioral evidence of what ordinary citizens would perceive and understand as "disordered" mental functioning, irrespective of whether professionals would regard the behavior as emanating from a diagnosable condition. As one Michigan court stated concerning a mental health expert's attempt to testify about what legal terms mean:

> A psychologist has no special knowledge regarding what the Legislature meant when it defined the relevant terms. Rather, this witness appears to have drawn his opinion of the Legislature's intent by reference to a distinctly non-legislative standard, namely, a manual of the American Psychiatric Association. We do not mean to belittle the integrity of that organization, but it does not enjoy the status of a law-making body. [*People v. Doan*, 141 Mich. App. 209, 214–15 (Mich. Ct. App. 1985)]

For this reason, clinicians who wonder whether a patient might meet criteria for involuntary hospitalization should not assume that only those patients who have severe disorders of thought or mood (e.g., schizophrenia or bipolar disorder) are eligible for civil commitment. For example, in discussing whether a patient with anorexia nervosa might qualify for civil commitment, Appelbaum and Rumpf note:

> The impairments of thought (even in the absence of a formal thought disorder) and of perception that occur in anorexia nervosa, and that clearly impair judgment, behavior, and capacity to meet the ordinary demands of sustaining existence, leave little doubt that it would qualify as a mental disorder for commitment purposes. (Appelbaum & Rumpf, 1998, p. 227)

In a few states, however, statutory criteria use formal or professionally established criteria to identify mental disorders that might justify commitment. In Nevada, for example, the statute requires the assignment of a diagnosis listed in an official diagnostic manual [either the *International Classification of Diseases, 9th Edition* (*ICD-9*) or the *Diagnositc and Statistical Manual of Mental Disorders, 4th Edition* (*DSM-IV*)]. In Utah, a "severe mental disorder" for purposes of civil commitment "means schizophrenia, major depression, bipolar

BEWARE
Do not assume that only patients who have severe disorders of thought or mood (e.g., schizophrenia or bipolar disorder) are eligible for civil commitment.

disorders, delusional disorders, psychotic disorders, and other mental disorders as defined by the" state's Division of Substance Abuse and Mental Health (Utah Code Annotated § 62A-15–102).

Risk or Danger

"Dangerousness" in Statutes

Commitment laws in most states tell courts and mental health professionals to focus primarily on recent and/or severe behavior when evaluating the risk posed by persons with mental illness. For example, Ohio law limits commitment to those persons with mental illness about whom the Court hears clear and convincing evidence of

> threats of, or attempts at, suicide or serious self-inflicted bodily harm; . . . *recent* homicidal or other violent behavior, . . . *recent* threats that place another in reasonable fear of violent behavior and serious physical harm, or other evidence of *present danger-ousness*; . . . not providing for the person's basic physical needs . . .; or . . . behavior that creates a grave and *imminent* risk to substantial rights of others or the person. [Ohio Revised Code § 5122.01(B), emphasis added]

Statutes may require courts to draw additional conclusions about dangerousness beyond ascertaining that behavior or threats occurred, for example, by requiring clear and convincing proof that the danger evidenced by overt behavior persists. Note, however, that *actions* (which may include verbal behavior in the form of threats), not statistically validated risk factors, are generally required for ordering involuntary hospitalization. In some cases, statutes require that the behavior have occurred within a certain time, such as the previous month. Other states balance recentness with severity, so that

INFO

Statutes in most jurisdictions make *actual behavior* (which may include verbal behavior in the form of threats), *not* statistically validated risk factors, a necessary condition for ordering involuntary hospitalization.

past behavior that posed great potential harm might extend the period of relevance for civil commitment.

DANGER TO SELF AND "GRAVE DISABILITY"

All states permit civil commitment of persons whose mental illness has rendered them physically dangerous to themselves (Brooks, 2007; Mossman, Schwartz, & Lucas, in press). In this context, physical danger to oneself includes suicidal behavior (that is, threats of or attempts to take one's own life), non-life-threatening but physically harmful actions (e.g., self-mutilation that would cause permanent injury), and—in almost all states—"*grave disability.*" This last notion refers to the condition of persons who have neither expressed wishes to harm themselves nor made direct attempts to do so, but have so neglected their basic needs that they have put their bodies in peril. Examples of such physical neglect include not eating, not dressing properly or seeking adequate shelter in cold weather, and not attending to one's life-threatening medical conditions.

In four states in which statutes do not explicitly mention grave disability as grounds for commitment, courts have interpreted statutes permitting commitment based on "danger to self" as allowing commitment for being "gravely disabled" (Brooks, 2007). Though Arizona allows for commitment of persons who have displayed "danger to self" by attempting suicide, threatening suicide, or engaging in other behavior that will result in serious physical harm, its civil commitment statute specifically *excludes* involuntary hospitalization based on "behavior that establishes only the condition of [being] gravely disabled" [Arizona Statute 36–501 (26)(b)]. In most states (e.g., Ohio), commitment criteria list suicidal and intentionally self-harming behavior as matters distinct from self-neglect that could quickly cause grave disability. In about 25% of states (e.g., Pennsylvania) commitment statutes subsume suicidal behavior and grave disability under a unitary danger-to-self rubric. In theory,

INFO

Grave disability: a term which, in the civil commitment context, refers to the condition of persons whose neglect of basic physical needs has put their bodies and health in peril.

statutes provide criteria that allow courts to distinguish mentally ill persons whose behavior directly threatens their physical well-being from mentally ill persons whose behavior is merely idiosyncratic, quirky, silly, or foolish—and to commit only the former group.

DANGER TO OTHERS

All states also permit civil commitment of persons for whom clear and convincing evidence indicates that their mental illness has rendered them physically dangerous to others (Mossman et al., in press). As we noted earlier, states usually require that individuals display behavioral evidence of violence toward others in the form of credible threats, attempts to harm others, or actually harmful deeds. Further discussion of this appears later in this chapter.

IN NEED OF TREATMENT

As a consequence of *O'Connor v. Donaldson* (1975), simply needing treatment can no longer be the sole justification for involuntary hospitalization. Wisconsin law, for example, expresses this by stating that even if a person is gravely ill, "no substantial probability of harm" will permit civil commitment "if reasonable provision for the individual's treatment and protection is available in the community" and the person will use such services or can be provided with an appropriate, protective community placement [Wisconsin Statute 51.20(1)(a)2. d].

In some jurisdictions, however, a need for treatment combined with other factors may permit a court to order a civil commitment. For example, Ohio law allows involuntary hospitalization of a mentally ill person if the person "would benefit from treatment in a hospital for the person's mental illness and is in need of such treatment as manifested by evidence of behavior that creates a grave and imminent risk to substantial rights of others or the person" [Ohio Rev. Code § 5122.01(B)(4)]. South Carolina allows

INFO

Every state permits civil commitment of persons for whom clear and convincing evidence indicates that their mental illness has rendered them physically dangerous to others or to themselves.

INFO

Simply needing treatment can never be the *sole* justification for involuntary hospitalization. In some jurisdictions, however, a person's need for treatment *combined with other factors* may permit a court to order a civil commitment.

for commitment of a "person [who] is mentally ill, needs involuntary treatment and because of his condition . . . lacks sufficient insight or capacity to make responsible decisions with respect to his treatment" [South Carolina Code § 44–17-580(A)(1)].

RISK OF PHYSICAL DETERIORATION

Risk of serious physical deterioration is a variation on the "need for treatment" or "grave disability" justifications described above. Kansas law, for example, permits commitment of a mentally ill person who "is substantially unable . . . to provide for any of the person's basic needs, such as food, clothing, shelter, health or safety, causing a substantial deterioration of the person's ability to function on the person's own" [(Kansas Statute 59–2946(f)(3)]. Wisconsin allows for involuntary hospitalization of a mentally ill person who "evidences behavior manifested by recent acts or omissions" and thereby creates "a substantial probability . . . that death, serious physical injury, serious physical debilitation, or serious physical disease will imminently ensue" without prompt psychiatric treatment [Wisconsin Statute 51.20(1)(a)2.d].

DANGER TO PROPERTY

A few states explicitly include risk of property damage among their criteria for civil commitment. Alaska, for example, permits involuntary hospitalization of a mentally ill person whose "recent behavior" has included "causing, attempting, or threatening harm," and who "is likely in the near future to cause . . . substantial property damage to another person" [Alaska Statutes 47.30.915(10)(B)]. Similarly, Washington law allows for the civil commitment of a person who represents "a substantial risk that . . . (iii) physical harm will be inflicted by a person upon the property of others, as evidenced by behavior which has caused substantial loss or damage to the property of others" [Rev. Code Washington 71.05.020 (23)(a)(iii)].

SUBSTANCE USE AND DANGEROUSNESS

In many jurisdictions, civil commitment statutes expressly preclude a substance abuse disorder from being the sole grounds for involuntary psychiatric hospitalization [e.g., Arizona Statutes 36–501(20)(a); Kansas Statutes Annotated 59–2946(f)(1); Revised Code of Washington 71.05.040]. In some states, however, laws permit judicial commitment of individuals with substance use disorders and no other major mental illness (for a review of the history of this topic, see Hall & Appelbaum, 2002). Some states' civil commitment laws (e.g., those of Indiana, Maine, and Wisconsin) include, in their definition of mental illness or mental disorder, persons who have alcohol and/or drug use disorders. Other states (e.g., Colorado, South Carolina, and Florida) have laws concerning alcohol and drug abuse commitments that are separate from the statutes pertaining to commitment of mentally ill persons. Yet the underlying rationale is similar: a person suffering a severe substance use disorder (in the absence of mental illness) typically may be detained and involuntarily confined or hospitalized if the individual poses a substantial risk of physical harm to himself or others.

Examples of legal language governing commitment of persons with substance use disorders appear in Table 2.1.

In some jurisdictions, special circumstances further permit the commitment of individuals with significant substance misuse to a period of treatment. Excessive alcohol use during pregnancy is an example of such a circumstance. Excessive alcohol consumption during pregnancy is incontrovertibly associated with adverse health consequences for the fetus. Fetal alcohol exposure may be the most common nonhereditary cause of mental retardation, and it can cause many other physical and neurodevelopmental disorders (Warren & Foudin, 2001). A few jurisdictions have responded with laws for involuntary civil commitment of pregnant alcohol abusers. For example, North Dakota, Oklahoma, South Dakota, and Wisconsin have statutes authorizing civil commitment of women who abuse alcohol during pregnancy. These laws function very similarly to more traditional civil commitments for major mental disorders, though the grounds for detention and hospitalization are risk of harm to the fetus.

Table 2.1 | Selected Statutory Language on Civil Commitment for Substance Use Disorders

---

Indiana Code § 12-7-2-130
"Mental illness" means the following:
For purposes of [civil commitment] . . ., a psychiatric disorder that:

(A) substantially disturbs an individual's thinking, feeling, or behavior; and impairs the individual's ability to function.

The term includes mental retardation, alcoholism, and addiction to narcotics or dangerous drugs.

Maine Revised Statute Title 34-B §3801(5)
"Mentally ill person" means a person having a psychiatric or other disease which substantially impairs his mental health, including persons suffering from the effects of the use of drugs, narcotics, hallucinogens or intoxicants, including alcohol, but not including mentally retarded or sociopathic persons.

Wisconsin Statutes 51.15(1)(a), 51.01(8)
A law enforcement officer . . . may take an individual into custody if the officer or person has cause to believe that the individual is mentally ill, is drug dependent, or is developmentally disabled.
"Drug dependent" means a person who uses one or more drugs to the extent that the person's health is substantially impaired or his or her social or economic functioning is substantially disrupted.

Colorado Revised Statutes 25-1-302(1), 25-1-311
"Alcoholic" means a person who habitually lacks self-control as to the use of alcoholic beverages or uses alcoholic beverages to the extent that his health is substantially impaired or endangered or his social or economic function is substantially disrupted.

A person may be committed . . . [if it is established that] the person is an alcoholic and that he has threatened or attempted to inflict or inflicted physical harm on himself or on another and that unless committed he is likely to inflict physical harm on himself or on another or that he is incapacitated by alcohol.
(N.B.: Colorado has similar language concerning commitment of individuals with drug dependence.)

Florida Statutes § 397.675
A person meets the criteria for involuntary admission if there is good faith reason to believe the person is substance abuse impaired and, because of such impairment:
Has lost the power of self-control with respect to substance use; and either

(a) Has inflicted, or threatened or attempted to inflict, or unless admitted is likely to inflict, physical harm on himself or herself or another; or
(b) Is in need of substance abuse services and, by reason of substance abuse impairment, his or her judgment has been so impaired that the person is incapable of appreciating his or her need for such services and of making a rational decision in regard thereto.

Table 2.1 | Selected Statutory Language on Civil Commitment for
Substance Use Disorders (*Continued*)

South Carolina Code of Laws § 44–52-10
"Chemical dependency" means a chronic disorder manifested by repeated
use of alcohol or other drugs to an extent that it interferes with a person's
health, social, or economic functioning.
"Chemically dependent person in need of involuntary commitment"
means a person who is suffering from chemical dependency as
demonstrated by:

  (a) recent overt acts or recent expressed acts of violence;
  (b) episodes of recent serious physical problems related to the habitual
     and excessive use of drugs or alcohol, or both;
  (c) incapacitation by drugs or alcohol, or both, on a habitual and excessive
     basis as evidenced by numerous appearances before the court within
     the preceding twelve months, repeated incidences involving law
     enforcement, multiple prior treatment episodes, or testimony by family
     or by members of the community known to the person relating to a
     lifestyle adversely affected by alcohol or drugs, or both.

2 chapter

RISK OF RELAPSE OR MENTAL DETERIORATION
Around one-third of U.S. states allow commitment for individuals
who risk possible relapse of their illness or mental deterioration.
Some examples include the following:

- Washington state permits civil commitment of
someone whose mental illness is causing a "severe
deterioration in routine functioning evidenced by
repeated and escalating loss of cognitive or volitional
control" and who is not receiving essential care
[Revised Code of Washington 71.05.020(17)(b)].

- In Wisconsin, an individual who cannot understand
or apply information to make informed decisions
about psychiatric treatment may be civilly committed
when recent behavior indicates that "he or she will,
if left untreated, . . . suffer severe mental, emotional,
or physical harm that will result in the loss of the
individual's ability to function independently in the
community or the loss of cognitive or volitional
control over his or her thoughts or actions"
[Wisconsin Statutes 51.20(1)(a)2.e].

- In Alabama, inpatient commitment is permissible
  only if the respondent both "poses a real and present
  threat of substantial harm to self and/or others" and
  "will, if not treated, continue to suffer mental
  distress and will continue to experience deterioration
  of the ability to function independently" (Alabama
  Code § 22–52-10.49a).

Practical Aspects of the Forensic Application of Dangerousness in Civil Commitment

In everyday language, in scientific writing, and in many legal opinions, the noun "danger" refers to "exposure to possible evil, injury,
or harm" or "a source or instance of peril or risk." Similarly, the
noun "risk" refers to the "possibility of suffering harm or loss" or
"a factor, course, or element involving uncertain danger" (*Webster's
II New Riverside University Dictionary*, 1988, pp. 346, 1013).
In other words, "risk" and "danger" refer either to a probability
of an adverse event or to the possible future adverse event
itself. The majority opinion in the well-known *Tarasoff* decision invokes both meanings to justify breaches of therapeutic
confidentiality:

> [W]e can hardly tolerate the further exposure to danger that
> would result from a concealed knowledge of the therapist that
> his patient was lethal. If the exercise of reasonable care to protect
> the threatened victim requires the therapist to warn the endan-
> gered party or those who can reasonably be expected to notify
> him, we see no sufficient societal interest that would protect and
> justify concealment. The containment of such risks lies in the
> public interest. (*Tarasoff v. Regents*, 1976, p. 347)

In a decision that established a *Tarasoff*-type obligation for
Ohio therapists, the Ohio Supreme Court used both definitions in
explaining the duty to protect:

> Society has a strong interest in protecting itself from those
> mentally ill patients who pose a substantial risk [i.e., probability]
> of harm. . . . To this end, society looks to the mental health

profession to play a significant role in identifying and containing such risks [i.e., potential harms to others]. (*Estates of Morgan v. Fairfield Family Counseling Center*, 1997, p. 1324)

In writings on forensic mental health, "risk" usually assumes one of two meanings. The Violence Risk Appraisal Guide (VRAG) ranks evaluees according to their probability of future violent reoffending. In the text describing the VRAG—*Violent Offenders: Appraising and Managing Risk, Second Edition* (Quinsey, Harris, Rice, & Cormier, 2006)—"appraising" refers to assignment of probability levels, and "managing" refers to efforts to avert violent events. In addition to assessing the probability of violent actions (which is what assessment instruments chiefly address), forensic clinicians also consider how frequent violent events might be, how soon they might occur, and the severity or harmfulness of possible violence (Hart, 2001; Heilbrun & Kramer, 2001).

In the civil commitment context, however, "risk" usually refers to actual past events, the relationship between these events and mental illness, and what these events say about the respondent's present "dangerousness"—not possible future events or probabilities. As Table 2.2 illustrates, legal "risk," "danger," and "likelihood of harm" for purposes of civil commitment are often statutorily defined in terms of whether certain things—behavior or symptoms—have actually occurred.

Thus, in civil commitment cases, a key issue before the trial court is whether the respondent has *already done* something threatening or harmful. As is true with criminal prosecution, the fact-finder looks at what has already happened. As a Minnesota ruling puts it:

> The [Minnesota civil commitment] statute clearly requires that the substantial likelihood of physical harm *must be demonstrated by an overt failure* to obtain necessary food, clothing, shelter, or medical care or by a recent attempt or threat to harm self or others. . . . Therefore, speculation as to whether the person *may, in the future*, fail to obtain necessary food, clothing, shelter, or medical care or may attempt or threaten to harm self or others is not sufficient to justify civil commitment as a mentally ill person.

Table 2.2 | Examples of Risk or Dangerousness as Defined in Selected Civil Commitment Statutes

---

Alaska Statutes 47.30.915(10)
"Likely to cause serious harm" means a person who

(A) poses a substantial risk of bodily harm to that person's self, as manifested by recent behavior causing, attempting, or threatening that harm;

(B) poses a substantial risk of harm to others as manifested by recent behavior causing, attempting, or threatening harm, and is likely in the near future to cause physical injury, physical abuse, or substantial property damage to another person; or

(C) manifests a current intent to carry out plans of serious harm to that person's self or another.

Arkansas Code 20–47-207
(1) "clear and present danger to himself or herself" is established by demonstrating:

(A) The person has inflicted serious bodily injury on himself or herself or has attempted suicide or serious self-injury.

(B) The person has threatened to inflict serious bodily injury on himself or herself.

(C) The person's recent behavior or behavior history demonstrates that he or she so lacks the capacity to care for his or her own welfare . . . that there is a reasonable probability of death, serious bodily injury, or serious physical or mental debilitation if admission is not ordered.

(2) "clear and present danger to others" is established by demonstrating that the person has inflicted, attempted to inflict, or threatened to inflict serious bodily harm on another.

Florida Statute 394.467(2b)
[Criteria for involuntary inpatient placement include] substantial likelihood that in the near future [the respondent] will inflict serious bodily harm on himself or herself or another person, as evidenced by recent behavior causing, attempting, or threatening such harm.

New York Mental Hygiene Law § 9.01
"Likelihood to result in serious harm" or "likely to result in serious harm" means

(a) a substantial risk of physical harm to the person as manifested by threats of or attempts at suicide or serious bodily harm or other conduct . . . , or

(b) a substantial risk of physical harm to other persons as manifested by homicidal or other violent behavior by which others are placed in reasonable fear of serious physical harm.

Table 2.2 | Examples of Risk or Dangerousness as Defined in Selected Civil Commitment Statutes (*Continued*)

Pennsylvania Statutes Annotated (2003) 50 Sec. 7301(a)
1. Clear and present danger to others shall be shown by establishing that within the past 30 days the person has inflicted or attempted to inflict serious bodily harm on another.
2. Clear and present danger to himself shall be shown by establishing that within the past 30 days:

   i. the person has acted in such manner as to evidence that he would be unable, without care, supervision, and the continued assistance to others, to satisfy his need for nourishment, personal or medical care, . . . or
   ii. the person has attempted suicide . . . demonstrated by . . . [having made] threats to commit suicide and has committed acts which are in furtherance of the threat to commit suicide; or
   iii. the person has substantially mutilated himself or attempted to mutilate himself substantially.

2
chapter

This is not to say, however, that the person must either come to harm or harm others before commitment as a mentally ill person is justified. The statute requires only that a substantial likelihood of physical harm exists, as *demonstrated by an overt failure* to obtain necessary food, clothing, shelter, or medical care or by a recent attempt or threat to harm self or others. (*In re McGaughey*, 1995, pp. 623–634, emphases added)

This point has significance for the kind of evidence testifying mental health professionals should gather in preparing their presentations to trial courts. Where prospective civil commitment is concerned, the evaluating expert's role is to find out whether certain types of behavior have occurred and to look for connections between that behavior and

INFO

In ordinary speech, the words "risk" and "danger" often refer either to a probability of a future adverse event or to the possible future event itself. In civil commitment cases, however, a key issue before the trial court is whether the respondent has *already done* something threatening or harmful.

the respondent's mental problems in an attempt to identify linkages that justify the preventive detention of civil commitment.

The putative "dangerousness" of mentally ill persons forms the core of current social and legal rationales for involuntary psychiatric hospitalization (Monahan, 1992). Yet "dangerousness" has proved to be an elusive, vexing, and troubling concept for legal authorities and mental health professionals alike (Perlin, 1998). Several decades ago, forensic psychiatrist Melvin Goldzband suggested that dangerousness is "the quality of an individual or a situation leading to the potential or actuation of harm to an individual, community, or social order. It is inherent in this definition that dangerousness is not *necessarily* destructive" (Goldzband, 1973, p. **238**). Although this conception probably captures many features of what people mean when they speak about dangerousness, it may be too amorphous to serve as a useful basis for legal rulings, research, or clinical decision making.

As Monahan and Steadman (1994) point out, the term "dangerousness" confounds the factors on which predictions are based, what type of event is being predicted, and the probability of that event. Ideally, clinicians and researchers should consider each of these notions separately, and legal decision makers should be cognizant of these distinctions. Concerns about future harm should factor in the seriousness of the harm under consideration. Clinicians and legal decision makers must also recognize that a person's dangerousness is not present or absent, but is a probabilistic quantity that admits of degrees and that changes as the individual's circumstances and condition change (Mossman, 2006; Mossman, 2008). Finally, clinicians (and presumably other social institutions such as courts) are not concerned only with identifying dangerous persons, but with intervening to avert harm.

For all these reasons, social science research since the mid-1990s has preferred to study and to speak of "risk assessment," "risk management," and "risk communication" rather than the once-common but infelicitous "prediction of dangerousness." Nonetheless, "dangerousness" persists as a term and as a feature of mentally illness with which courts are concerned. Fortunately, statutes in many jurisdictions define "dangerousness" and related terms in ways that eliminate at least some ambiguity.

In most states, statutes make actions or utterances—that is, *past* behavior—a threshold condition for commitment. This key point—to which we will return several times in this volume—implies that clinicians and evaluators should think of civil commitment as being concerned with judgments about *future* behavior only if specific kinds of *past* behavior have occurred. In most states, commitment statutes direct courts' and clinicians' attention to finding out whether

- the respondent has a serious mental illness,
- the respondent already did something that was threatening, potentially harmful, or actually harmful because of the illness,
- the respondent still has the psychiatric problems that led to the threatening or actually harmful behavior, and
- the problems would continue or worsen without intervening hospitalization and treatment.

Past deeds (including statements) and conditions that continue to be present constitute the primary legal bases for ordering someone's civil commitment.

Least Restrictive Alternative

Even when a respondent clearly poses a risk to self or others, almost all U.S. jurisdictions have statutory language that precludes involuntary hospitalization unless an inpatient placement would be the least restrictive setting for appropriate care (Keilitz, Conn, & Giampetro, 1985). Though *Lake v. Cameron* (1966) originally

CASE LAW
Youngberg v. Romeo
(1982)

● Held that a
patient's civil rights are not
violated if treating clinicians
have exercised professional
judgment when deciding
which treatment to select
from among acceptable
alternatives.

CASE LAW
Olmstead v. L.C.
(1999)

Under the ADA, states
should place mentally disabled
persons in community settings if

● professionals believe such
a placement is appropriate,

● the affected persons do not
object to the community
placement, and

● "the placement can be
reasonably accommodated,
taking into account the
resources available to the
State and the needs of
others with mental
disabilities."

derived this doctrine through statutory interpretation, subsequent decisions also found a constitutional basis for least restrictive placements.

The U.S. Supreme Court has not taken this position explicitly, however. Indeed, the high court's decisions in *Youngberg v. Romeo* (1982) and *Olmstead v. L.C.* (1999) suggest that the principle does not have constitutional status, nor is it absolutely required under other federal law. In *Youngberg*, a case involving the rights of a man with mental retardation who had been physically restrained, the Supreme Court declared that insofar as a patient's civil rights are concerned, the Constitution requires only that clinicians exercise professional judgment when they make decisions about treatment; it is not the job of courts to specify *which* treatment doctors should select from among several acceptable alternatives. In *Olmstead*, the Supreme Court ruled that under the Americans With Disabilities Act (ADA), states must place mentally disabled persons in community settings (rather than hospitals) only when professionals believe such placement is appropriate, the affected persons do not object to the community placement, "and the placement can be reasonably accommodated, taking into account the resources available to the State and the needs of others with mental disabilities" (*Olmstead*, 1999, p. 11).

Nonetheless, the near-ubiquity of the *"least restrictive alternative" (LRA)* requirement in commitment statutes means that courts and testifying professionals must apply the concept when involuntary hospitalization is proposed. Current statutes that effectuate the LRA approach have different emphases. For example:

- Under Alaska law, LRA means that "conditions of treatment are (A) no more harsh, hazardous, or intrusive than necessary to achieve the treatment objectives of the patient; and (B) involve no restrictions . . . except as reasonably necessary for the administration of treatment or the protection of the patient or others from physical injury" [Alaska Statutes Sec. 47.30.915(9)]. Thus risk, potential intrusion, and physical safety are clear factors for evaluating restrictiveness.

- In Ohio, courts should consider diagnoses, treatment plans, prognoses, and patients' preferences and should "order the implementation of the least restrictive alternative [treatment] available and consistent with treatment goals" [Ohio Rev. Code § 5122.15(E)].

- In Wisconsin, commitments must "provide the least restrictive treatment alternative appropriate to the patient's needs" [Wisconsin Statutes 51.22(5)]. Note that this statutory language appears to endorse a therapeutic (and treatment provider's) perspective on what restrictiveness is, rather than *Lake*'s emphasis on the respondent's wishes and physical, extrahospital freedom.

In Judge Bazelon's 1966 *Lake* decision, the LRA meant "alternative courses of treatment" other than hospitalization, with "[e]very effort . . . be[ing] made to find a course of treatment" that the respondent "might be willing to accept" (*Lake v. Cameron*, p. 661). Thus, LRA placement appeared to require investigation or at least inquiry by the trial court about treatment options, with the respondent having a large say about which option is chosen.

Also (and perhaps because the case involved a seemingly harmless older woman), *Lake* was silent about how or whether least restrictive conditions should be balanced against the possibility of harm to the respondent or others. Overall, applying the LRA concept can be puzzling. Its application has typically involved considering involuntary commitment to a state hospital as one of the most restrictive interventions, though some authors have raised concerns that the application of identifying the LRA for individuals has failed to take into account their preferences (Munetz & Geller, 1993). Moreover, these same authors have noted that alternative placements in which persons with mental illness may find themselves receiving treatment may in fact be more restrictive in some ways (e.g., jails and unstable housing through revolving use of crisis beds). In practice, civil commitment determinations that take into account the LRA must grapple with these factors. In those jurisdictions where the LRA concept applies, an examiner must be prepared to articulate why the commitment setting is the least restrictive for the respondent.

Forensic and Legal Issues for Which Experts Often Must Plan

Most often, treating clinicians are the real proponents of mental health civil commitments, which sometimes is their only way to make sure desperately ill patients get the treatment they need. The attorneys involved often do little or no planning for hearings. This means that to make sure patients receive crucial clinical care, clinicians have to make sure that the court will hear adequate evidence regarding mental disorder and dangerousness. Thus, clinicians often have to plan for dealing with the legal constraints under which trial courts hear evidence.

Hearsay

In ordinary mental health care, clinicians rely on information obtained from sources other than patients—for example, reports of family members and information in medical records. In legal proceedings, however, such information is "hearsay," the legal term for a "statement, other than one made by the declarant while testifying at the trial or hearing, offered in evidence to prove the truth of the matter asserted" (Fed. Evid. R. 801, 28 U.S.C. App.). In general, courts do not allow hearsay (that is, it is not "admissible" as evidence) because its reliability cannot be scrutinized via cross-examination.

Under certain circumstances, though, courts permit hearsay. For example, the Federal Rules of Evidence allow an expert (for example, a testifying mental health professional) to offer an opinion based on "facts or data . . . made known to the expert at or before the hearing" despite their being hearsay if those facts or data are "of a type reasonably relied upon by experts in the particular field in forming opinions" (Fed. Evid. R. 703). Many states have a similar exception for civil commitment cases, which means that a professional may testify about information related by family members to support an opinion about involuntary hospitalization [e.g., Iowa Code § 229.12(3)]. Also, in some jurisdictions, special hearsay exceptions allow use of medical records in hearings without the record custodian's testimony (e.g., Wash. Rev. Code § 71.05.360).

In states without such hearsay exceptions (e.g., Ohio), a treating mental health professional who believes a patient needs hospitalization will have to think about how pertinent information will be introduced at the commitment hearing. The clinician may wish to inform family members or other persons who witnessed what the patient-respondent did before undergoing emergency hospitalization that, without their testimony, the trial court may not learn the facts that support commitment.

Privilege Exceptions
TREATING DOCTOR

Most states' statutes on doctor–patient privilege contain an exception that allows treating clinicians to testify at civil commitment hearings. In states that do not have such an exception [e.g., Ohio, *In re Ratz* (2003)], independent experts must obtain and convey information to courts in forms that comport with evidentiary rules. In jurisdictions without medical records hearsay exemptions, independent experts must perform evaluations and elicit data with an eye toward being able to testify about pertinent phenomena.

For example, if a key fact supporting commitment seen in the medical record involves an interaction between the patient-respondent and the treating doctor that the independent examiner did not personally witness, the examiner will need to anticipate the hearsay problem and obtain information about the interaction that the trial court would deem admissible. One way to do this would be to ask the respondent about the interaction. If the respondent confirms it, that confirmation would be admissible (as in "Mr. Smith told me he punched Dr. Jones").

ADMISSIBILITY OF PRIOR PSYCHIATRIC HISTORY (ALSO HEARSAY)

When a patient has undergone previous psychiatric treatment, obtaining information about that treatment is often a critical part of any subsequent diagnostic and therapeutic evaluation. Despite this, not all states permit the introduction of such information in legal hearings [see, e.g., *In re Miller* (1992)]. In such situations, evaluators must obtain information to justify their conclusions (either about diagnosis or about risk) without adducing past history—that is, they must anticipate what kinds of testimony the Court will ultimately deem acceptable.

Empirical Foundations and Limits

3

Epidemiology and Psychiatric Characteristics of Civil Committees

Little has been written comparing involuntary hospitalization rates across the United States since the mid-1980s, when the National Institute of Mental Health reported that 26% of all psychiatric admissions were based on involuntary civil commitments (Rosenstein, Steadman, MacAskill, & Manderscheid, 1986). A report on the use of involuntary psychiatric examinations in Florida indicated that about three of every 1000 people were subject to the initiation of an involuntary examination each year (McGaha, Stiles, & Petrila, 2002).

Comparing the frequency of involuntary hospitalization across jurisdictions is difficult because states vary considerably in how they categorize inpatients. For example, at one point in 2009, approximately half of all Massachusetts public sector long-term care inpatients were hospitalized on some kind of commitment status, either as civil committees or under criminal courts' jurisdiction (i.e., a "forensic" legal status). Also, service delivery systems exhibit great variation in the proportions of acute versus chronic and public versus private sector beds used for civil committees, in the frequency of outpatient commitment interventions, and in the use of alternatives to hospitalization (such as crisis stabilization beds and respite residential care).

Major organizations such as the Substance Abuse and Mental Health Systems Administration (SAMHSA) gather data to help compare systems and their effectiveness. A report of National Mental Health Statistics (Manderscheid, Atay, Male, & Maedke, 2002) notes significant changes over 30 years related to the number and operation of organizations providing mental health services in the United States. Decreases in state hospital occupancy have resulted from preferences for community-oriented care combined with tightening budgets, which together have led to a simultaneous shift toward shorter hospitalizations and increased residential community supports and placements (see Figure 3.1 for trends in state hospital occupancy).

SAMHSA reported that in 2007, state psychiatric hospital residents ranged from a minimum of 3.5 to a maximum of 41 per 100,000 members of the general population in each state surveyed (Lutterman, Berhane, Phelan, Shaw, & Rana, 2009). On average, of those that were in state hospitals (whose population generally reflects more serious and persistent mental illness), 52% were hospitalized on an involuntary civil status and 32% were hospitalized on a forensic status (see Table 3.1). Yet in some states (including New Hampshire, New Jersey, Alaska, and North Carolina), involuntary commitments accounted for more than 90% of state hospital bed utilization. These data focused only on state hospitals and were based on inpatients' current legal status. Many states closed additional state facilities between 2008 and 2011, and these percentages therefore may have shifted further since those data were collected. Also, rates of involuntary detention and civil commitment in settings outside the public sector are unknown.

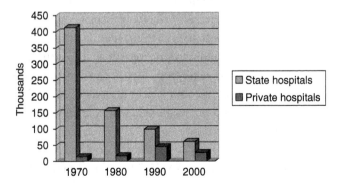

Figure 3.1 Number of State Hospital and Private Psychiatric Hospital Beds over Time. Adapted from Lutterman, Berhane, Phelan, Shaw, and Rana (2009), p. 47.

Table 3.1 Characteristics of U.S. State Hospitals[a]

| | Number of State Hospitals (2007) | Number of Inpatients (Point in Time for 2007) | State Hospital Inpatients per 100,000 Population | Inpatient Categories in State Hospitals (for 2006)[b] | | |
				Voluntary civil	Involuntary civil	Forensic
Total	232	43,601	14.5			
Average per state	5	993	16.8	18%	52%	32%
Minimum per state	0	66	3.5	0%	1%	2%
Maximum per state	27	6,327	41	71%	96%	83%

[a]Adapted from Lutterman, Berhane, Phelan, Shaw, and Rana (2009).
[b]Adapted from the National Association of State Mental Health Program Directors, personal communication via D.P., 2009.

3
chapter

Some individuals who are admitted involuntarily to state hospitals later agree to their hospitalization, which means that some currently voluntary public sector inpatients may have begun their hospitalizations involuntarily. Although data from state hospital admissions in the United States cannot be readily compared to general psychiatric admissions in other countries due to numerous factors, data from England show that between 1996 and 2006, the proportion of overall psychiatric hospitalizations that was involuntary increased from 26% to 36%, with trends toward more cases involving psychosis and substance use disorders (Keown, Mercer, & Scott, 2008).

Because civil committees by definition must have mental conditions severe enough to satisfy jurisdictional requirements, it is not surprising that patients who have high indicators of dangerousness or grave disability also score higher than other psychiatric patients on measures of psychopathology (Segal, Watson, Goldfinger, & Averbuck, 1988b). Nicholson (1986) found that committed patients were generally older, less educated, poorer, more often male, more often nonwhite, and less likely to be married than were voluntary patients.

Research on Assessment Practices

The clinical data concerning which mental health professionals testify in commitment hearings usually differ little from the types of information customarily obtained for purposes of inpatient treatment. But having established that a patient suffers from a serious mental illness that warrants hospitalization, a clinician who wishes to pursue commitment for an unwilling patient must consider and evaluate clinical data in light of the legal criteria that the court will apply.

Some studies have looked at clinicians' abilities to follow legal standards in their civil commitment evaluations. Lidz and colleagues (Lidz, Mulvey, &

BEST PRACTICE
Before pursuing commitment for a patient who suffers from a serious mental illness, consider and evaluate clinical data in light of the legal criteria that the court would apply.

Appelbaum, 1989) examined evaluations of 411 patients by 96 different clinicians to learn whether the clinicians were reliably using legal standards for commitment. They found good agreement regarding assessments of dangerousness as defined by commitment criteria. Situations in which clinicians disagreed involved complex questions, such as whether a patient who desired voluntary hospitalization could still meet commitment criteria, or whether patients who were determined to meet commitment criteria at a transferring facility could be determined not to meet commitment criteria at a receiving facility.

Exploration of suicide and violence risk is a necessary part of the commitment evaluation, and research on assessment of these issues is extensive and complex. Though a full treatment of suicide and violence risk assessment is beyond the scope of this volume [for further reviews, see American Psychiatric Association (APA), 2003; Otto & Douglas, 2010; Pinals, Tillbrook, & Mumley, 2009], several factors relevant to these topics are directly relevant to a civil commitment assessment. Because most jurisdictions permit commitment of individuals who are failing to care for their basic physical needs, clinicians must also form opinions about this capacity— despite the absence of studies that would guide them on how they should assess "grave disability."

With regard to suicide risk assessment, research shows that psychiatric illness is a major correlate of suicide. Additional risk factors include being a man, being older, being white, and having disrupted marital status (American Psychiatric Association, 2003). Knowledge of suicide risk factors has informed clinical interviewing for years. Suicide risk assessment checklists are often seen in clinics and in emergency room settings. More information on the assessment of violence risk and the use of structured assessments appears in Chapter 5.

Reliability of Psychiatric Diagnoses

Diagnoses are practitioners' classifications, and ideally, they satisfy two practical needs: communication and prediction (Goodwin & Guze, 1984). If two clinicians understand what a particular diagnosis is, they should have similar ideas about what ails the person who bears that diagnosis and should make similar, useful statements about the person's expected clinical course.

In diagnostic contexts, "reliability" has two common meanings, both of which may be relevant to mental health practitioners and to courts that hear their testimony. In an informal but practically important sense, the reliability of a psychiatric diagnosis addresses the question, "Can I use this diagnosis to make good treatment decisions and valid judgments about the patient's future course?" "Reliability" also has a statistical meaning that refers to the consistency of a diagnosis across time or across evaluators. That is, reliability refers to whether multiple evaluations of a patient are likely to yield the same diagnosis (analogous to test–retest reliability in psychology), or to the likelihood that multiple independent evaluators examining a patient would give similar diagnoses (interrater reliability). A related concept, "diagnostic stability," refers to the extent to which a patient's diagnosis remains unchanged over time (Whitty et al., 2005).

INFO

"Reliability" has two common meanings:

- Informally, the reliability of a psychiatric diagnosis tells you how well the diagnosis informs treatment decisions and permits valid judgments about the patient's future course.

- Reliability also has a statistical meaning that refers to the consistency of a diagnosis across time or across evaluators.

Psychiatric diagnosis underwent a dramatic transformation in the last quarter of the twentieth century. The third edition of the American Psychiatric Association's *Diagnostic and Statistical Manual of Mental Disorders* ("*DSM-III*," 1980) marked a transition to an atheoretical approach, in which diagnoses depended upon satisfaction of explicit criteria with empirically verifiable relationships to treatment response and prognosis. A hoped-for consequence of this change was better reliability (in both the practical and statistical senses) of psychiatric diagnoses, and research findings tended to show this was true (Spitzer, Forman, & Nee, 1979).

As a result, a huge research literature now addresses these issues. Though several studies (many conducted several years ago) have examined factors contributing to civil commitment, no research to our knowledge looks specifically at diagnostic reliability in civil commitment proceedings. Some studies, however, have touched on closely related topics, and we review some of the recent findings here to help shed light on practice considerations.

Often, forensic examiners have access to information about an evaluee's past psychiatric history. Therefore, a matter of potential relevance in civil commitment hearings is the usefulness of past information, which depends in part on the stability of psychiatric diagnoses. A recent summary (Whitty et al., 2005) of research on diagnostic stability of psychotic disorders suggests that over follow-up periods ranging from 1 year to more than 3 decades, schizophrenia is the most stable initial diagnosis, in that roughly 90% of initial schizophrenia diagnoses are retained at follow-up. Around 80% of diagnoses of affective psychosis persist, and approximately 70% of persons diagnosed with major depression remain so categorized later. Persons diagnosed with schizophreniform disorder, schizoaffective disorder, and psychosis not otherwise specified are more likely to have different diagnoses at follow-up (Whitty et al., 2005; Schwartz et al., 2000). Many persons with psychotic symptoms have comorbid substance abuse problems, and their differential diagnoses should therefore include "substance-induced psychosis." However, about one-fourth of persons who receive this emergency department diagnosis turn out to have a primary psychotic disorder at 1-year follow-up (Caton et al., 2007).

Diagnostic changes may reflect issues other than faulty original assessments. Clinicians may revise diagnoses based on newly revealed information, and the illnesses themselves may evolve (Schwartz et al., 2000). The latter finding may prove useful to clinicians who confront cross-examination questions about why diagnostic conclusions do not agree with conclusions rendered during previous treatment episodes or earlier in the current episode of treatment.

Courts may be more likely to deem diagnostic impressions credible when experts faced with the same information come to the same conclusions. Studies examining interrater reliability have yielded mixed findings. In their comparison of patients' emergency room diagnoses with diagnoses rendered during subsequent hospitalizations, Lieberman and Baker (1985) found fairly good agreement in three broad categories that are relevant to civil commitment—psychotic disorders (kappa = 0.64), major depression (kappa = 0.62), and alcohol abuse (kappa = 0.77). They speculated that high interrater reliability reflected the relatively high base rates of these conditions and clinicians' heightened levels of suspicion. However, they found only fair agreement for other broad categories, and specific diagnoses (e.g., schizophrenia) showed low levels of agreement. A subsequent study (Warner & Peabody, 1995) found even higher levels of agreement between psychiatric emergency service and discharge diagnoses for schizophrenia and schizoaffective disorder (kappa = 0.82), substance use disorders (kappa = 0.87), bipolar disorder (kappa = 0.72), and depression (kappa = 0.64).

Way and colleagues (Way, Allen, Mumpower, Stewart, & Banks, 1998) showed videotapes of 30 patient assessment interviews conducted in a psychiatric emergency service to eight other psychiatrists with emergency room experience, who rated each videotape on severity of depression and psychosis. Intraclass correlation coefficients (a measure of agreement) among the raters was highest for psychosis (ICC = 0.64) and substance abuse (ICC = 0.65), but lower for danger to self (ICC = 0.32) and ability to care for self (ICC = 0.28). Also, the raters' recommendations for disposition did not match the assessing psychiatrist's actual disposition very well. The authors concluded that "[p]sychiatric emergency service assessments need improvement" (Way et al., 1998, p. 1423).

In most medical specialties, clinicians "back up" or verify clinical diagnoses with results from laboratory tests, biopsies, and other "objective" information. Psychiatric diagnoses, by contrast, usually depend entirely on clinicians' observations and patients' reports about

INFO

Courts may be more likely to deem diagnoses credible when experts faced with the same information come to the same conclusions.

their experiences. As a result, psychiatric diagnosis seems "subjective" and therefore implicitly suspect. But if one uses reliability as the index of diagnostic objectivity and legitimacy, a different perspective emerges. Studies of diagnoses in pathology, neurology, and radiology show that interrater reliability is far from perfect, and often is only poor to medium (Andrion et al., 1995; Visvanathan et al., 2006; Johnson et al., 1995; Vobecky, Leduc, Devroede, & Madarnas, 2006; Weidow, Cederlund, Ranstam, & Karrholm, 2006; Alphons Wierema, Kroon, & de Leeuw, 2007; Pies, 2007). By contrast, several studies demonstrate moderate to excellent concordance of psychiatric diagnoses rendered either via direct interview or with the use of a structured diagnostic tool (Warner & Peabody, 1995; Ruskin et al., 1998; Simpson et al., 2002; Jakobsen et al., 2005).

In civil commitment cases, most jurisdictions do not require testifying clinicians to establish specific diagnoses. Very often, however, clinicians will use diagnoses from clinical assessments to establish whether respondents meet commitment criteria and then translate symptoms of these diagnoses into the legal criteria for mental illness. When clinicians introduce diagnoses into their opinions, they should be ready to respond to questions by cross-examining attorneys regarding diagnostic reliability. Pies (2007) suggests that current psychiatric diagnoses appear to be as reliable as diagnoses in "most other medical specialties"; although psychiatric data are different from those used by other specialists, all diagnosticians "must make difficult judgments based on imperfect knowledge" (Pies, 2007, p. 22). As diagnostic nomenclature evolves with new editions of the *Diagnostic and Statistical Manual* or *International Classification of Disease*, clinicians would do well to stay current on any pitfalls related to reliability, validity, and concerns about particular new diagnostic labels. (For a review of current developments in the

BEST PRACTICE

Clinicians often use their clinical diagnoses to help establish whether respondents meet commitment criteria. If you do this, you should be ready to respond to cross-examination questions regarding diagnostic reliability.

revisions of the *Diagnostic and Statistical Manual* slated to be released in May 2013, see www.dsm5.org.)

Research on Decisions for Commitment

Laws codify the criteria used for civil commitment, but a decision to initiate and pursue a petition for commitment involves human judgment, as does a court's judgment about whether a respondent meets commitment criteria. A multitude of factors might affect clinicians' decisions about commitment, only some of which are directly related to legal criteria. Nonlegal factors that might influence clinical judgment include the following:

- patients' socioeconomic and familial situations (Hattori & Higashi 2004; Segal, Laurie, & Segal, 2001),

- geographic location (Roessler & Reicher-Roessler, 1992; Faulkner, McFarland, & Bloom, 1989),

- patients' race and ethnicity (Morgan et al., 2005; Pinals, Packer, Fisher, & Roy, 2004),

- having experienced a malpractice action for failure to commit (Knapp & VandeCreek 1987),

- concerns about being sued for committing someone without cause (Appelbaum, 1995),

- being able to identify a treatment alternative less restrictive than compulsory hospitalization (Lorant, Depuydt, Gillain, Guillet, & Dubois, 2007; Dworkin, 1998), and

- the availability of "holding beds" (Engleman, Jobes, Berman, & Langbein, 1998).

Law enforcement personnel also make complex decisions that affect whether someone goes to a hospital and becomes the subject of a commitment effort. In one study, peace officers were found to civilly detain people with characteristics similar to persons who came to emergency rooms under other emergency commitment petitions, though many fewer of the individuals on peace officer detention were ultimately recommended for commitment hearings (Faulkner et al., 1989). When police officers anticipate having to go through procedures that are time-consuming or unwieldy, they may avoid the commitment process altogether (Faulkner et al., 1989; Miller & Fiddleman, 1983).

Dispositional decisions that rely upon officer discretion leave room for "extrapsychiatric" variables—rather than symptom presentation alone—to influence the decision-making process (Teplin & Pruett, 1992). Police find it hard to bring persons with mental illness to hospitals when they engage in potentially criminal acts that would also justify an arrest (Green, 1997). In one Massachusetts jurisdiction, a verdict of police officer liability in the handling of a person who was being brought to the hospital on an involuntary commitment petition (*McCabe v. City of Lynn*, 1995) inhibited officer involvement in signing such petitions for some time thereafter—which illustrates how liability concerns can influence decisions by emergency personnel and why clinicians should be concerned about their own liability when working with police in crisis situations (Zealberg, Santos, & Puckett, 1996). Other nonclinical factors—the greater emphasis on individual autonomy and patient recovery, elimination of many state psychiatric beds, fiscal constraints, emergency room overcrowding, statutory efforts to abolish commitment, and jail diversion initiatives (see, e.g., Faulkner et al., 1989; Advocates, Framingham Jail Diversion Program, 2008; Massachusetts Department of Mental Health, 2009)—have also diverted patients who once would have been hospitalized away from inpatient commitment.

3
chapter

Studies examining commitment decision making of clinicians have used hypothetical vignette reviews, surveys, or interview questions to inquire about their thought processes. For example, Kumaska and colleagues showed that even when need for treatment was an

INFO

Liability concerns can influence how emergency personnel manage a mental health crisis.

acceptable reason for commitment, psychiatrists tended toward relying on harm to self or others as the justification for involuntary hospitalization (Kumaska, Stokes, & Gupta, 1972). They also noted that psychiatrists' decisions in other settings (e.g., whether to admit patients to the hospital from the emergency room) reflected factors that were beyond the scope of criteria for hospitalization, including personal feelings about the patient, a desire to minimize harmful outcomes, and beliefs about what alternatives to hospitalization may or may not be available.

As statutes shifted toward making dangerousness the sole criterion for commitment, Appelbaum and Hamm (1982) further explored the question of whether psychiatrists make commitment-related decisions for reasons that would be outside the statutory provisions. They found that statutory criteria were among the most important determinants of the decision to seek commitment. Nonstatutory clinical factors—e.g., having a place to live, having support outside the hospital, and whether the patient was "crazy or sane"—also influenced decisions. Yet Appelbaum and Hamm noted that these nominally clinical factors were closely related to legal criteria for commitment, in that the statute's language permitted involuntary hospitalization if not doing so might lead to serious harm—a provision that implicitly invites mental health professionals to consider the clinical risks associated with allowing a patient to leave the hospital.

In an important study of commitment decisions, Lidz and colleagues (1989) placed observers in an emergency room to watch and make verbatim notes on interviews between clinicians and patients. Patients' medical records were also reviewed, and evaluating clinicians provided Likert-scale ratings of the patients they saw concerning dangerousness to others, inability to care for self, suicidality, and committability. In judgments related to whether an individual patient met commitment criteria, reliability between clinicians was found to be high (R in the 0.66–0.68 range for all but ratings of ability to care for self, where the R was 0.44), and the commitment opinions generally seemed to hew closely to the jurisdiction's statutory language. Those cases in which clinicians disagreed about commitability were often ones in which patients wanted voluntary admission but met the standard for involuntary hospitalization. This raised questions about the appropriateness of using commitment when a voluntary hospitalization could have been a viable alternative solution—for example, when commitment may have made it easier for staff to implement treatment without worrying that the patient might quickly request discharge, or to facilitate access to cost reimbursement mechanisms. Disagreement regarding commitment opinions also occurred when a different hospital had already approved emergency commitment. Because these patients had brought themselves to the second facility and were willing to be hospitalized, some clinicians believed that the legal "least restrictive alternative" requirement barred imposing a civil commitment.

These studies suggest that in general, clinicians follow the intent of commitment statutes and do not try to get around dangerousness-based legal standards simply because they want to treat the patient. Studies from other countries yield similar findings. For example, a Canadian study showed that variance in decisions to commit was largely explained by the presence or absence of psychosis and dangerousness (which were part of the commitment criteria), and not other factors such as clinical treatability or availability of alternative resources (Bagby, Thompson, Dickens, & Nohara, 1991).

How experience and clinician characteristics affect commitment decisions was the focus of a study (Sattar, Pinals, Din, & Appelbaum, 2006) that asked psychiatric trainees whether they would pursue commitment for patients described in ambiguous patient vignettes. Residents' decisions were related to their level of training and their own risk-taking behavior. In another study, Engleman and colleagues found that a clinician's probability of deciding to detain a patient was predicted by the proportion of patients detained by the clinician

INFO

Studies suggest that most clinicians follow the intent of the commitment statutes and do not try to subvert dangerousness-based legal standards simply because they want to treat the patient.

3
chapter

in the prior 3 months, along with the setting of the evaluation and the availability of beds in the community. Several patient characteristics—including diagnosis, sex, age, or insurance status—did not predict detention decisions (Engleman, Jobes, Berman, & Langbein, 1998).

Research on the Effectiveness of Involuntary Hospitalization

Stone's "Thank You" Theory

The philosopher John Rawls (1971) argues that rational individuals who accord liberty a paramount status among governing principles would want society to create legal mechanisms and institutions that would "insure themselves against the possibility . . . that through some misfortune or accident they are unable to make decisions for their own good, as in the case of those . . . [who are] mentally disturbed" (pp. 248–249). In Rawls's theory, wanting such legal protections is a logical consequence of being rational rather than a matter for empirical verification. But the *"thank you" theory* offered by psychiatrist Alan Stone (1975) suggests that civil commitment can be justified *empirically* by showing that persons who need involuntary hospitalization but cannot currently recognize or think rationally about their needs will, once they have recovered, *in fact* recognize that they needed treatment and be grateful that treatment had been forced on them. Many clinicians have had patients who feel this way, and a few studies have tried to examine systematically how often the "thank you" phenomenon actually occurs:

- Kane and colleagues (1983) found that patients who had been civilly committed and were interviewed prior to discharge displayed significant changes in attitudes about and recognition of their original need for treatment, with those patients who had responded best to treatment being most likely to view hospitalization positively.

- Edelsohn and Hiday (1990) found that 6 months after discharge, a majority of formerly committed patients thought they should have been hospitalized and that involuntary hospitalization had been necessary.

- Beck and Golowka (1988) found that at discharge, several patients—though not a majority—who had previously doubted whether they needed hospitalization perceived their hospitalization as helpful.

- In a comparison of committed and voluntarily admitted patients in Sweden, Kjellin and colleagues (1997) found that three-fourths of both patient groups reported having improved, but committed patients were more likely to report ethical costs and fewer benefits.

- Gardner and colleagues (1999) found that in follow-up interviews that took place 4–8 weeks after discharge, 52% of 64 patients who had previously said they did not need hospitalization subsequently believed they had needed it. However, patients' attitudes about hospitalization did not become more positive: contrary to the premise of the "thank you" theory, coerced patients were not grateful for having been hospitalized even if they later thought they had benefited.

- In a study across 11 European countries, Priebe and colleagues (2010) found that 1 month after admission, 39% to 71% of involuntarily admitted patients thought their hospitalization had been proper; after 3 months, 46% to 86% of the patients thought hospitalization proper. Difference rates across countries suggested that legislative and practices affected patients' perceptions.

INFO

The "thank you" theory hypothesizes that civil commitment can be justified empirically by showing that persons who need involuntary hospitalization will, once they have recovered, be grateful for having had treatment forced on them.

Thus, if the "thank you" is a measure of the helpfulness of involuntary hospitalization, it appears that many—but certainly not all—civilly committed persons benefit from the experience and recognize that they do so.

Alternatives to Hospitalization

As we noted in Chapter 1, courts may order commitment to inpatient psychiatric care only upon finding that a hospital is the "least restrictive alternative setting" for treatment. In many locales, service arrangements and funding patterns often make hospitalization the *only* "alternative" when severely ill psychiatric patients urgently need treatment. However, a few studies have evaluated the relative benefits of inpatient care and treatment in more open settings. Marshall and colleagues (2001) reviewed nine randomized controlled trials that compared inpatient treatment to day hospitalization in persons with acute psychiatric disorders. They concluded that day hospitalization was suitable for at least one-fourth of persons who currently undergo hospitalization. Neither group tended to get rehospitalized more often, and day hospitalization appeared to be less costly overall. In a subsequent analysis, Marshall and colleagues (2003) found that among patients deemed suitable for day hospitalization, symptoms appeared to improve more quickly than if they had received inpatient treatment.

A recent, multicenter, European trial involving 1117 voluntarily admitted patients who were randomized after admission showed that day hospitalization equaled inpatient care in addressing symptoms, satisfaction with treatment, and quality of life; patients who underwent day hospitalization had better social functioning during a 1-year follow-up period (Kallert et al., 2007). Other studies of patients who are willing to accept *voluntary* treatment suggest that residential community treatment is an alternative to hospitalization that costs less and is just as effective (Fenton, Mosher, Herrell, & Blyler, 1998; Hawthorne et al., 2005).

Greenfield and colleagues (Greenfield, Stoneking, Humphreys, Sundby, & Bond, 2008) compared "medical model" care administered at a locked psychiatric facility (LPF) to care provided in an unlocked, consumer-managed, crisis residential program that included medication management and subsequent assertive community treatment (CRP-ACT). Eligible participants were medically healthy adults who were civilly committed as gravely disabled or dangerous to self under California legal criteria; patients committed as dangerous to others were not eligible. Researchers then followed the nearly 400 participants for a year after admission. CRP-ACT participants were much more satisfied with the services they received, and (not surprisingly) their attrition rate during the follow-up period was lower. The CRP-ACT group did at least as well as the LPF patients on interviewer-rated and self-reported measures of psychopathology.

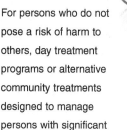

INFO

For persons who do not pose a risk of harm to others, day treatment programs or alternative community treatments designed to manage persons with significant mental illness may be effective and less restrictive interventions.

These studies suggest that for patients who would otherwise meet commitment criteria but do not pose a risk of harm to others, alternatives to traditional locked psychiatric facilities may be effective. However, in a given region, concerns about overall risks of harm, funding, and resource limitations may preclude arranging nonhospital placements for individuals who need acute treatment.

Research on Values and Limitations of Coerced Treatment

Coercion is, by definition, a core feature of *involuntary* civil commitment. Its moral and political justifications include protecting society from dangerous individuals and protecting persons with mental illness from harm they might do to themselves. In addition, coercive treatment serves the coerced person's medical best interests (Sjöstrand & Helgesson, 2008). Ethical debates about the justification of coercion continue, especially in an era that recognizes the importance of emphasizing patient recovery and the value associated with autonomy (Kogstad, 2009; Prinsen & van Delden, 2009).

Given that involuntary civil commitment is a major means of applying coercive psychiatric treatment, investigators have studied *perceived coercion*, that is, the feelings respondents have about how much they were coerced and how the "forced" nature of their treatment affects them. Perceived coercion is not easy to measure, however. One might think that an inpatient's legal status (i.e., having been admitted either as a committed patient or voluntarily) would serve as a simple, clear marker for coercion for purposes of scientific investigation. Things turn out to be more complicated, however (Monahan et al., 1995). For example, a patient's legal status can change during a hospitalization, and many patients who end their hospitalizations on a voluntary status begin hospitalizations involuntarily. Some "voluntary" patients are actually incompetent patients whose guardians have admitted them to the hospital. Furthermore, some patients whose hospitalizations are ostensibly voluntary may actually perceive and have experienced as much or more coercion than involuntarily admitted patients. In demonstration of this last point, Gilboy and Schmidt (1971) found that many "voluntary" patients had experienced explicit coercion because they were under some other official custody that made involuntary commitment their only alternative to signing in "voluntarily."

Nevertheless, many studies have examined the admission process and a patient's legal status to ascertain patient perceptions of coercion. Early studies of this type found that patients who perceived coercion were less likely to view the hospital as a place that could help them and more likely to view it as a place of confinement (Shannon, 1976). Many patients believed they were not given an opportunity to sign into the hospital on a voluntary basis (Bradford, McCann, & Merskey, 1986).

Patients have been asked after discharge how much they felt that they had participated in the admission process and whether they thought their involuntary hospitalization had helped them. Some formerly involuntarily committed patients have reported feeling hurt or embarrassed by the involuntary nature of the process (Edelsohn & Hiday, 1990; Toews, el-Guebaly, & Leckie, 1981) even if they believed that hospitalization had helped them.

In a more recent Swiss study (Bonsack & Borgeat, 2005), 74% of patients believed that they had been under pressure to come into the hospital, whether they were hospitalized involuntarily or not. Though 70% thought that their admission was necessary, more of the involuntary patients in this study felt that they had not improved. Summarizing the findings of many such studies, Monahan and colleagues (1995) found that patients expressed increasingly positive attitudes about the hospitalization by the time of discharge. Yet many patients were unaware of their legal status, many involuntary patients (up to 30%) said they would have come to the hospital voluntarily, and many voluntary patients (about 50%) indicated they felt they had little choice in coming into the hospital.

The fact that coercion overrides wishes about what people want done for their health care may affect their subsequent attitude toward treatment. Perceived fairness of a procedure may influence how a person understands coercion and its meaning afterword. Lidz and colleagues interviewed 157 psychiatric inpatients (of whom 42% were involuntary) within 48 hours of admission (Lidz et al., 1995). For both voluntary and involuntary patients, feelings of having been treated respectfully through a decision-making process that seemed fair—what is known as "procedural justice" in social science literature—were related to the perception of coercion. When patients believed that they had received respectful treatment, had experienced a sense of validation, and had a voice in the process, they were less apt to feel coerced, even if they were ultimately involuntarily committed. A recent study from Dublin showed that although a quarter of those interviewed experienced negative effects on relations with family and physicians, most patients admitted involuntarily to a

3
chapter

INFO

Research suggests that hospitalized patients who feel they have been treated respectfully, have experienced a sense of validation, and have had a voice in the process are less apt to feel coerced, even if they were ultimately involuntarily committed.

psychiatric hospital felt positively about their treatment (O'Donoghue, Lyne, Hill, Larkin, Feeney, & O'Callaghan, 2010).

Does involuntary hospitalization affect future treatment adherence? An 825-patient study found that 10 weeks after discharge, patients with high coercion scores and those with low coercion scores did not differ significantly in self-reported adherence to medication and outpatient treatment sessions (Rain, Williams, Robbins, Monahan, Steadman, & Vesselinov et al., 2003). In a British cohort, compulsory admission was associated with perceived coercion, though one-third of the voluntarily hospitalized patients also felt highly coerced and two-thirds were not sure they were free to leave (Bindman, Reid, Szmukler, Tiller, Thornicroft, & Leese, 2005). Nevertheless, perceived coercion did not predict whether the patients engaged with follow-up treatment. A 2-year follow-up study of persons with first-episode psychosis revealed no difference in treatment adherence between persons who had been admitted voluntarily or those admitted involuntarily (Opjordsmoen, Friis, Melle, Haahr, Johannessen, Larsen et al., 2010), despite the fact that involuntarily admitted patients had more severe symptoms and worse functioning at the outset.

Taken together, these studies suggest that coercion does not result in a greater likelihood of treatment nonadherence, as some patient advocates have insisted it must. Also, involuntary patients do not necessarily feel more coerced than do voluntary patients. Both voluntary and involuntary patients often feel "pressured" to enter a psychiatric hospital, so patients' legal status may not reflect the degree of perceived coercion. Attitudes toward the perceived benefits of an involuntary hospitalization often improve between admission and discharge. A sense of having received fair, respectful treatment often reduces the perception of coercion, even among involuntarily committed individuals.

INFO
Studies suggest that coercion does not result in poorer treatment nonadherence.

Impact of Coercion on Treatment Outcome

Some recent European studies have looked at how coercion might affect psychiatric care. Steinert and Schmid (2004) evaluated 88 consecutively hospitalized, psychotic, voluntary and involuntary patients, examining their participation in five aspects of hospital treatment—admission, hospital stay, medication, discharge, and intention to continue treatment after discharge. Outcome, measured as changes in Positive and Negative Syndrome Scale (PANSS; Kay, Fiszbein, & Opler, 1987) and Global Assessment of Functioning (GAF; American Psychiatric Association, 1987) scores, did not vary with voluntariness of participation in any aspect of treatment.

Wallsten and colleagues (Wallsten, Kjellin, & Lindström, 2006) examined subjective perceptions of outcome and GAF scores in 233 involuntarily and voluntarily hospitalized patients who were evaluated within 5 days of admission and again either at discharge or after 3 weeks of care. Positive views of outcome were strongly related to patients' feeling that they were treated well by staff members; having a mood disorder and having a low admission GAF score predicted improvement on follow-up GAF ratings. Involuntary status was *not* related to GAF-measured outcome.

These two studies suggest that if one uses objective criteria to assess effectiveness, involuntary treatment works as well as voluntary care. However, as previous sections indicate, patients may well view psychiatric care more positively if they have more of a say in what happens to them. These findings related to coercion research are important to consider in light of increasing emphasis on shared decision making (Deegan & Drake, 2006) and person-centered care (Borg, Karlsson, Tondora, & Davidson, 2009; Power, 2009) in psychiatric treatment.

Research on Outpatient Commitment

In an *outpatient civil commitment*, a court orders a person to get mental health care while living in the community [Group for the Advancement of Psychiatry (GAP), 1994]. Consequences for not following the court order vary

INFO

In an outpatient commitment, a court orders a person to get mental health care while living in the community.

across jurisdictions, but most commonly, they involve involuntary hospitalization.

The earliest use of outpatient commitment appears to have been in the District of Columbia in 1972 (GAP, 1994). Most jurisdictions have outpatient commitment statutes (Bazelon Center, 2004), though legal standards for this type of commitment vary greatly. Statutes often require that the subject of the commitment order present a likelihood of serious harm to others if not so committed, a likelihood that the subject will not continue with treatment absent a court order, and/or have a history of repeated hospitalizations. In some jurisdictions (e.g., New York), criteria for inpatient and outpatient civil commitment differ somewhat, whereas other jurisdictions (e.g., Kentucky, North Dakota, Rhode Island, and Pennsylvania) use the same or similar criteria but allow commitments to settings less restrictive than a hospital if clinically appropriate.

Geller (2006) describes three "generations" of research on outpatient commitment. The first two generations involved case studies and quasi-experimental designs. For example, a before-and-after study by Munetz and colleagues of outpatient civil commitment in Summit County (Akron), Ohio reported reductions in emergency room visits, psychiatric hospital admissions, and inpatient lengths of stay (Munetz, Grande, Kleist, & Peterson, 1996). These early but less-than-conclusive studies suggested that outpatient commitment was a promising but little-used intervention.

In the third generation of studies, investigators have used more sophisticated research designs to evaluate effectiveness of outpatient commitment under various state statutory schemes. The RAND corporation reviewed outpatient commitment in eight states (Michigan, New York, North Carolina, Ohio, Oregon, Texas, and Wisconsin) and published findings in 2001 (Ridgely, Borum, & Petrila, 2001; available at www.rand.org). The RAND review found that outpatient commitment seemed to be a helpful intervention, though it was used more commonly as a vehicle to provide for additional supervision *after* a patient's discharge from a hospital than as a preventive, community-based disposition to *avoid* hospitalization.

Many states had adopted additional statutory criteria—which the RAND corporation called "preventive criteria"—related to risk of grave disability rather than using recent behavior to determine a patient's committability. An earlier study had shown that states often did not use outpatient commitment statutes that were on the books (Torrey & Kaplan 1995). In findings consistent with this, the RAND review showed that many states were trending away from using existing statutes, or allowing patients to agree voluntarily in court to comply with treatment as an alternative to going through an involuntary commitment hearing. In many cases, statutes for outpatient commitment seemed outdated.

Research on outpatient commitment in North Carolina (Swartz, Swanson, Hiday, Wagner, Burns, & Borum, 2001) included a randomized trial of effectiveness among persons with severe mental illness. Patients who had longer outpatient commitment periods and intensive outpatient treatment had fewer hospital days, fewer hospital admissions, a greater likelihood of community treatment adherence, and a lower likelihood of violence and victimization.

Despite these finding, the Cochrane group (Kisely, Campbell, & Preston, 2011) concluded that available data do not show that outpatient commitment improves outcomes related to health service use, social functioning, mental state, quality of life, or satisfaction with care. Their analysis of two randomized studies (Swartz, Swanson, Wagner, Burns, Hiday, & Borum, 1999; Steadman, Gounis, Dennis, Hopper, Roche, Swartz, & Robbins, 2001) found little difference in readmissions or arrest rates of those receiving compulsory outpatient treatment compared to community care. As an indication of how modest the effect of outpatient commitment was, the review found it would take 85 outpatient commitment orders to avoid one admission to the hospital and 238 commitments to avoid a single arrest. Though people subject to involuntary outpatient commitment were less likely to be the victims of crime, the Cochrane reviewers questioned the value of an intervention that curtails individual liberty without proven effectiveness or cost efficiencies. They also suggested that future study of the issue should measure a wide variety of outcomes.

Although the Cochrane review raises questions about the merits of outpatient commitment, one of the influential lines of additional research on outpatient civil commitment followed enactment of New York state's Kendra's law (New York State Office of Mental Health, 2006). This law encompasses provisions for what is known as "Assisted Outpatient Treatment" or AOT, the state's term for services provided pursuant to an outpatient commitment order. The law is named for a young woman who was killed when a man with mental illness pushed her into the path of a New York City subway train. A report of the New York State Office of Mental Health (2005) indicated that in the first 6 months of AOT, subjects showed increased engagement in case management services, increased adherence to psychiatric medication, improved community and social functioning, and a reduction in harmful behaviors. Longer-term outcomes included decreased rates of arrest, incarceration, psychiatric hospitalization, and homelessness compared to subjects' pre-AOT experience.

Though Kendra's Law apparently improves several outcomes for AOT patients, some have suggested that these results may simply reflect the enhanced financial resources that pay for services required under the law (Geller, 2006). This issue is partially addressed in the most recently released report regarding the New York AOT experience, which is one of the most comprehensive studies examining AOT interventions with significant follow-up intervals (Swartz, Swanson, Steadman, Robbins, & Monahan, 2009). This study showed that AOT as implemented in New York did prevent future relapse for some patients, reduced hospitalizations, reduced days in hospital, and reduced arrests. Persons subject to AOT received more intensive case management, took their medication more regularly, and experienced subjective improvements in outcomes related to self-care. Recipients of AOT services did not report any greater sense of coercion than non-AOT service recipients. Sustained improvement after AOT was greater for individuals who had received AOT for longer than 6 months. Though the court order likely helped shape service providers' efforts toward recipients, the AOT order itself was a factor in achieving better outcomes, over and above the additional services that patients received. Subsequent data analyses of the New York AOT program show similar benefits (Swartz et al., 2010; Van Dorn et al., 2010). Given the cost of these programs and the challenges in making them operational, further study of their effectiveness will undoubtedly be important. Data related to their effectiveness in a particular jurisdiction may be critical for evaluators who are asked about AOT-type interventions as alternatives to inpatient civil commitment.

3
chapter

APPLICATION

Preparation for the Evaluation 4

Evaluations for civil commitment take several forms and may occur in varied contexts. The setting, locale, source of the referral, and the evaluator's relationship to the evaluee all affect one's preparation for the assessment.

Typical forensic evaluations involve conferring with the retaining attorney, spending lots of time examining records, conducting detailed interviews, and writing reports. Preparing and doing a civil commitment evaluation are very different. In the authors' experience, civil commitment hearings themselves are often quick and perfunctory, with little attention paid to the legal, clinical, and forensic issues at stake. In many settings, treating clinicians participate in civil commitment processes as part of their daily work routine, and evaluations do not involve assessments by experts with special forensic expertise.

In most civil commitment proceedings, fundamental liberty issues and the moral significance of involuntary commitment are not foremost in the minds of the participants. In part, this may reflect the fact that civil commitment offers an opportunity for treatment intended to avert harm and limit the impact of a serious psychiatric illness. Also, a desire for efficiency can affect how legal procedures intended to protect patients' rights are actually carried out. Prolonged adversarial proceedings would both delay treatment and extend a respondent's confinement. Occasionally, however, testifying professionals encounter cases—ones that have generated unusual controversy or are managed by particularly engaged legal representatives—in which zealous legal advocacy and vigorous cross-examination occur. In this chapter, we describe the structure of and preparation processes for civil commitment evaluations undertaken with the expectation that cross-examination and fact-finder decision making will subject clinical findings and opinions to careful scrutiny.

Relationship between Evaluator and Evaluee

We begin by noting the two possible relationships between evaluator and evaluee: (1) the evaluee is the evaluator's patient, or (2) the evaluator is examining someone else's patient. The latter relationship may result when the court appoints an "independent examiner," when a mental health expert is retained either by one of the parties to the adversarial commitment process, or when a hospital implements a system of having specific mental health professionals assume the responsibility for providing commitment evaluations and testimony.

In general, mental health professionals should avoid serving as expert witnesses concerning their own patients because the ethical obligations of courtroom witnesses often conflict with the obligations of treating clinicians (Strasburger, Gutheil, & Brodsky, 1997; Greenberg & Shuman, 1997, 2007). In certain circumstances, however, providing expert testimony about one's patient may be appropriate, expected, and accepted practice (American Academy of Psychiatry and the Law, 2005; Heltzel, 2007). In civil commitment hearings, giving expert testimony about one's patient may well be consonant with one's therapeutic duties because the aim of such testimony is therapeutic: to ensure that a seriously ill patient gets needed treatment.

Of course, testifying about patients can create practical problems for treatment providers. Patients may resent or get angry with doctors whose testimony led to outcomes—confinement in a hospital—that they do not want. Patients may feel stigmatized by public notification of their mental illness. Court processes also expose personal matters to those present, even in jurisdictions where hearings are private. Not surprisingly, then, many patients view the commitment process negatively (Längle et al., 2003; Edelsohn & Hiday, 1990), and testimony about one's own patient may adversely affect one's subsequent therapeutic relationship (American Academy of Psychiatry and the Law, 2005).

In some jurisdictions, courts occasionally or regularly appoint independent examiners to conduct commitment evaluations and provide testimony. This role gives examiners a certain amount of "emotional" distance and may make it easier to feel and stay "neutral." Or, as noted above, occasionally one party—most often, the respondent—retains its own expert. The obligation to strive for objectivity always applies to forensic examinations and testimony, but being selected and paid by one party can create a desire—not always fully conscious—to provide an opinion pleasing to the retaining party.

Occasionally, independent experts have some latitude in the input they provide and in what they can accomplish. Take, for example, the following case:

Ms. B had a long history of setting fires, assaulting others, and hurting herself at times when interpersonal stress made her emotionally fragile and nearly delusional in her thinking. She underwent a 5-year hospitalization marked by episodic aggression (hitting staff and starting physical fights with other patients) and setting a fire about a year before her commitment was due to expire. Though several behavioral treatments had been recommended, she had not agreed to these. She sought to be discharged and to live in the community with a new boyfriend who could not provide financial support. Her behavior had been stable for about 9 months while she had been dating this boyfriend during her hospitalization. Nonetheless, the treating psychiatrist thought that hospital discharge would create a risk of serious harm to Ms. B and others.

Counsel for Ms. B retained Dr. C, an independent evaluator. Dr. C's evaluation led him to believe that Ms. B did not meet the criteria for commitment, and he was prepared to testify accordingly. But Dr. C recognized that Ms. B might decompensate without adequate community supports, which would create a risk of harm to Ms. B or others. Being retained by Ms. B's defense gave Dr. C the opportunity to explain this to Mr. B's attorney and to help Ms. B grasp the importance of getting treatment. The attorney arranged for several continuances of the commitment proceeding to allow Ms. B time to engage in services in the community while still hospitalized. In this case, the retained expert provided much more than forensic assessment services and enabled Ms. B to broker an arrangement that addressed concerns that the hospital had about her and others' safety. No testimony was heard, and no reports were written. The hospital discharged Ms. B, who subsequently remained stable in the community.

Typically, a forensic evaluator is engaged to render an opinion, and if the opinion is not helpful to the retaining party, the retaining attorney may elect not to further use the evaluator's opinion in resolving the legal matter. The case of Ms. B is somewhat complicated and perhaps atypical for a forensic expert in that the expert felt some obligation (with the agreement of the defense attorney) to function in two usually separate capacities—those of evaluator and services broker. Evaluators who encounter situations similar to the case of Ms. B must carefully weigh the pros and cons of taking on dual roles. On one hand, dual roles often generate ethical problems; on the other hand, an evaluator can sometimes use clinical knowledge to facilitate helpful resolutions of both legal and treatment issues. Whenever one feels tempted to assume responsibilities beyond providing an opinion, one should carefully consider case facts and circumstances with the knowledge that one's opinion may shift concerning the commitment question and that any appearance of or actual bias may compromise one's ability to serve as an expert witness. Furthermore, evaluators may wish to consult with colleagues to help them consider the situation

INFO

Dual roles (acting both as evaluator and services broker) may generate ethical problems, but sometimes an evaluator can use clinical knowledge (with the attorney's permission) to bring about helpful resolutions of legal and treatment issues.

thoroughly before embarking on activities related to these types of dual roles.

Statutory and Case Law Constraints

In clinical practice, treatment providers use data from many sources other than patients themselves (e.g., records of past treatment, information from family members) to make management plans. Were a clinician to testify about such data in court, however, it would constitute "hearsay," which (as we explained earlier in this volume) is the legal term for a statement, other than one made by the declarant while testifying at the trial or hearing, offered in evidence to prove the truth of the matter asserted. In the United States, hearsay evidence is usually inadmissible. Many states have *"hearsay exceptions"* for civil commitment hearings, however, so that experts may testify about relevant matters beyond what they have personally witnessed—for example, a statement in the chart or from a family member that the respondent threatened someone a few days before the hearing [see, e.g., *In re Melton* (D.C. 1991)]. Not all jurisdictions permit such exceptions, however [see, e.g., *In re Miller* (Ohio, 1992) and *In re Mental Health of D.L.T.* (Mont., 2003)].

Planning one's data collection requires that one think about the introduction of evidence, to ensure that the methods one uses will allow the results to be admissible in court. This kind of reasoning is what attorneys—not clinicians—are supposed to do. Often, however, attorneys involved in commitment hearings, such as those who represent facilities seeking the commitment, may do little or no preparation and may elicit information from expert witnesses by reading routine lists of questions. Professionals involved in providing commitment testimony thus should be prepared to independently consider matters

INFO

Many states have "hearsay exceptions" for civil commitment hearings, so that experts may testify about relevant matters beyond what they have personally witnessed.

from a legal perspective and to think, for example, about whether key clinical data obtained by various means will be admissible.

In cases where courts "rubber stamp" what doctors want, technical legal constraints may not pose an obstacle to commitment. But in some situations, judges and opposing attorneys take patients' rights very seriously and rigorously challenge professional experts. Professionals who encounter cases where these challenges are more likely must plan their evaluations so that crucial information (and, perhaps, their entire opinion) will not be excluded at the commitment hearing. To do this, examining clinicians need to become familiar with pertinent background documents and others' allegations about recent behavior, and then ask evaluees themselves about these matters. Experts may always testify about things they have seen or heard, so they can tell courts what evaluees have told them about recent behavior. Of course, addressing such matters with evaluees also fulfills the obligation to be fair: it's only reasonable to ask evaluees for their "side of the story." Very often, respondents will frankly explain what they did and why, and experts can then relate respondents' accounts in their courtroom testimony.

Matters of Attorney Representation

Attorney Involvement in the Assessment Process

Attorney involvement in commitment cases varies substantially. In cases in which the respondents' counsel retains the expert, retaining attorneys may ask to be present for the evaluation. Such a request may simply be an attorney's way of learning about the respondent's background and psychiatric problems through the assistance of a clinician trained in mental health assessment. But the attorney may also have a separate agenda related to legal strategy. Some professionals do not let retaining attorneys be present during an evaluation for fear that they may influence or taint the evaluation. Other professionals do not mind or actually like

having attorneys present because
this allows everyone to hear directly
the information that will form the
basis of the expert's opinion. When
an attorney will be present during an
evaluation, the evaluator should try
to arrange interview seating so that
the respondent cannot see the attor-

BEST PRACTICE
When an attorney will be present
during an evaluation, have the
attorney sit outside the evaluee's
field of vision so the attorney
cannot easily signal a client to
withhold or modify information.

ney during the interview (e.g., placing the attorney behind the
respondent). Doing this limits the attorney's ability to signal a
client to withhold information that would hurt the respondent's
case for release.

If a patient's attorney asks to sit in on evaluations by a treating
psychiatrist and the patient consents, the hospital probably should
not deny the request. However, treatment providers should recognize that notwithstanding attorneys' cordial behavior, they will
listen to information with a particular legal goal in mind, and they
will be listening *all the time*. The sorts of statements about uncertainty that clinicians often share with each other—e.g., "Mr. Jones
has not hit anyone since he got here and probably won't do so
again now that he's medicated, but now that the unit social worker
is back from vacation, having Mr. Jones stay here a few more days
will let us make sure he's stable and receives the right community
placement"—provides great ammunition for cross-examination.

Respondents' attorneys can exert control over scheduling
hearings by either acceding to or contesting requests for continu-
ance by the hospital. Attorneys also have access to treatment
records that they can use to support their clients' positions. As the
case of Ms. B above illustrates, attorneys also may be in a position
to counsel patients to agree to voluntary hospitalizations or to
waive their rights to a hearing.

For indigent respondents, courts typically assign counsel from
a list of local attorneys willing to take commitment cases. Like
experts, these attorneys' livelihoods may depend on being asked to
represent respondents, which creates incentives to provide representation in such a way as to increase the likelihood of being called

again in the future. In some instances, this may mean refraining from offering vigorous cross-examination or refraining from filing motions that might annoy the court or referral source. Also, indigent respondents' attorneys usually receive their assignments very shortly before a scheduled hearing and have little time to prepare cases.

In a few jurisdictions, attorneys who wish to take on civil commitment proceedings must undergo certification and take special continuing legal education courses on mental health law (Committee for Public Counsel Services, 2011). Most jurisdictions do not have such requirements, however, and attorneys who take commitment cases have varying knowledge about psychopathology and mental health law. Attorneys looking for independent experts usually ask colleagues for recommendations or consult lists of experts kept by courts or public defenders' offices.

Attorneys as Zealous Advocates or Gatekeepers for Treatment

In the majority of cases, courts' commitment decisions follow the position taken by treating and testifying clinicians. In one early study, judicial decisions correlated strongly with recommendations of physicians, state attorneys, and witnesses (Miller, Ionescu-Pioggia, & Fiddleman, 1983). A more recent study found that although patients' acute psychiatric symptoms decreased during hospitalization, commitment hearings became shorter and less adversarial as the length of hospitalization increased, probably as a reflection of problems associated with chronic mental illness (Parry & Turkheimer, 1992). Publications from the 1980s and 1990s often report a lack of zealous advocacy for respondents by attorneys (Hiday, 1983; Parry, Turkheimer, & Hundley, 1992). Though no formally gathered data provide information about current practice, our observations and those of colleagues suggest that not much has changed in recent years.

Several factors contribute to the dearth of vigorous legal advocacy in most jurisdictions' commitment hearings. As we noted earlier, attorneys may not want to annoy the referring court by lengthening hearings, and they usually have little time or financial incentive to prepare cases. Attorneys may respect the opinions of mental health professionals, believing—as do appellate courts—that clinicians know what's best for persons with mental illness. Also, representing clients with serious mental illness at commitment proceedings creates ethical challenges for attorneys. Because they have a duty to look out for their clients' best interests as well as to advocate for what their clients want, attorneys may feel uncomfortable arguing vigorously for the release of clients who clearly and desperately need inpatient psychiatric treatment. Empirical evidence of these factors comes from a study by Poythress (1978), who taught attorneys the mechanics of effectively challenging experts in commitment proceedings. Despite the training, attorneys did not subsequently provide more zealous representation for their clients. The reasons, Poythress found, stemmed from concerns that successful advocacy might mean that their clients would not get needed hospitalization; attorneys were also reluctant to defy judges, who typically preferred to decide cases in accordance with clinical recommendations.

Strong advocacy against commitment is uncommon in most jurisdictions, but treating clinicians should always prepare for it. Occasionally, attorneys succeed in getting courts to deny commitment of clients who, clinicians believe, need care. Thus, reasonable preparation for a commitment hearing may well include (1) planning for the possibility that the respondent will prevail and (2) thinking about what a patient might do if released from the hospital after a hearing. This is something a treatment team and an independent evaluator should discuss with the patient-respondent, because doing so can yield valuable data relevant to the commitment question. For example, the patient who responds, "I plan to

INFO

Representing clients with serious mental illness at commitment proceedings can create ethical challenges for attorneys, who may recognize that clients who want to be released desperately need inpatient treatment.

get some crack and stop my medications" will have provided information about the likely consequences of failure to hospitalize him or her further. Still, when courts reject the petition for involuntary commitment, reasonable options include offering voluntary hospitalization and providing a referral for community care if the patient insists on leaving the hospital.

Issues in Identifying the Specific Questions within the Referral

One should not conduct an independent evaluation for civil commitment or plan testimony about one's patient without knowing the commitment criteria in one's jurisdiction. Evaluators should also make sure they know what matters will be at issue related to the evaluation and upcoming hearing. For example, medication refusal may result in a combined hearing that will address a patient's competence to consent to or to refuse treatment if the court first finds adequate evidence to issue a commitment order. Assessing competence to refuse treatment calls for lines of inquiry different from those related to civil commitment. To know exactly what is being sought, retained nontreating evaluators should ask the retaining attorney; court-appointed independent experts should get a copy of any relevant court orders. Retained experts may also wish to ask counsel for copies of relevant case law in instances in which a special legal issue has given rise to the referral. Similarly, in preparation for an evaluation, the evaluator may need to know whether the respondent's capacity to consent to hospitalization was explored sufficiently before embarking on the commitment proceedings. This can sometimes help an evaluator understand the context of an emergency detention and whether treating clinicians considered alternatives to involuntary hospitalization. Anticipating this issue in advance of an evaluation allows the evaluator to plan an examination that permits testimony (if the question arises) about the respondent's willingness and capacity to accept voluntary hospitalization.

BEWARE
Do not conduct an independent evaluation for civil commitment or plan testimony about your patient without knowing the commitment criteria in your jurisdiction.

Locating "Collateral" Data

Chapter 5 describes the use of *collateral data* information obtained from sources other than the patient-respondent, such as legal documents, medical records, and the reports of acquaintances and relatives. Here, we talk about obtaining and arranging for *access* to such data.

Current Records

The "supporting materials" that evaluators use in civil commitment evaluations include emergency room records, police records, ambulance records, and current medical records from the facility that is holding the evaluee. When the evaluator is an attending physician or treating clinician, access to these records usually poses little problem, as they generally accompany emergency department materials sent to the inpatient unit with the patient. In some instances, treatment providers or nontreating experts will wish to examine additional records (e.g., of previous treatment episodes). If the evaluator has been retained privately, the retaining attorney may get appropriate releases of information and obtain these records for the evaluator. Otherwise, however, the job of obtaining such records falls to the evaluator, who—if the patient-respondent will consent and sign releases of information—must send releases to the appropriate facilities or parties. Of course, respondents often do not and/or cannot give consent, and the timing of civil commitment proceedings often leaves little opportunity to request and receive documents. Thus, it is not uncommon for hearings to proceed without an evaluator's having received some desired records. However, the fact that the evaluator made the request may be included in testimony to demonstrate appropriate diligence in conducting the evaluation.

4
chapter

Prior Records

Use of records from prior treatment poses several problems for evaluators, whether they are patients' treating clinicians or independent examiners. Examining prior

BEWARE Time constraints often mean that hearings take place without an evaluator's having received some desired collateral data.

treatment records is standard mental health practice, but (as we discussed above) records may not be available in time for the hearing. When records are available, portions of them may be of questionable validity. Often, diagnoses in records have been rendered hastily, sometimes with an eye to obtaining reimbursement rather than to maintaining fidelity to accepted diagnostic criteria, and usually without any thought that they might one day be used and scrutinized in court. Data about prior behavior may not be delineated in detail—for example, an episode in which a patient told clinicians he had set fire to his neighbor's car might simply be summarized as "described recent property destruction." Finally, as we noted above, some jurisdictions restrict the admissibility of information from past records through hearsay rules or privilege statutes that permit litigants to exclude from court most data generated during medical care. Where this is true, testifying clinicians have to express conclusions about diagnoses and risks based on recent information only—something they would never do in ordinary clinical care. In preparing for the evaluation, the evaluator must consider available data with these possibilities in mind.

Interviews

In many cases, evaluators wish to interview persons other than the patient and caregivers—for example, friends or family members who witnessed the mental deterioration or behavior that led to the initiation of the commitment process. Often, such contacts occur via telephone, but they may also take place face-to-face usually at the treating facility. At the outset of such contacts, the evaluator (whether treating clinician or independent examiner) should explain that the contents of the conversation may not remain confidential. Of course, telling informants in advance that nothing is "off the record" may cause them to withhold information from the evaluator, including information crucial to the outcome of a commitment proceeding—for example, the threats and assaultive acts of a husband that led his wife to call police. Depending on what informants are willing to say and on the jurisdiction's handling of hearsay evidence, evaluators may also need to tell informants that they might be called to testify directly as fact witnesses at the commitment hearing.

Contours of the Evaluation: Access to the Respondent and Obtaining Consent

BEST PRACTICE
When you make initial contact to do an interview, explain to the interviewee that the contents of the conversation may not remain confidential because you may have to testify about the interview during subsequent courtroom proceedings.

Civil commitment examinations typically occur on inpatient psychiatric units unless the evaluation concerns an outpatient commitment or an emergency detention order. Independent evaluators who do not have privileges at the hospital where the patient is staying may have limited access to both the evaluee and to current or past medical records. Therefore, before coming to the facility, it is worthwhile to make advance arrangements to examine the evaluee and see records (or to have the retaining attorney make the necessary advance arrangements). In facilities that use computerized medical records, independent evaluators need to make sure that systems will allow them to review current information. Independent evaluators may be able to speak with nursing staff members who can provide information about the evaluee's behavior at the hospital. In providing such information, staff members become collateral informants who could be called to testify in court. In the authors' experience, however, calling these staff members to testify directly rarely occurs.

As noted above, access to treatment records usually requires the patient's consent. An evaluator who is retained by the respondent's attorney can ask the attorney to obtain such consent before the examination. A patient may or may not choose to release prior records to treating clinicians who will testify or to court-appointed examiners, but a court order may facilitate

4
chapter

INFO

Before you travel to a facility, try to make arrangements through the retaining attorney to get access the respondent and to review treatment records.

release of records without patient consent. Generally, family members and other nontreating informants may provide information about the patient without the patient's having given consent. However, contacting a patient's family may require the evaluator to share information about the patient—at the very least, informing family members about the current hospitalization and upcoming hearing. Therefore, evaluators may need to obtain a respondent's written consent to contact collateral sources. This is especially true when the evaluator is also a treating clinician.

Many patients ill enough to require psychiatric hospitalization also lack the capacity to consent to releasing medical records. Treating clinicians set a low capacity "threshold" for accepting a patient's signature as valid consent, even if clinicians have doubts about the patient's overall capacity. Of course, patients under guardianships may not give such consent—their guardians have the authority to sign the consent forms and should be asked to do so. In cases in which doubts arise about the patient's capacity to sign consent forms, a court order authorizing release may resolve the matter.

Gathering information for an evaluation can be time-consuming. Yet commitment proceedings in most jurisdictions must occur soon after emergency detention has occurred or affidavits are filed. Though cases can be continued, the seriousness of patients' problems often limits the desirability of postponing proceedings. This fact distinguishes civil commitment evaluations from other forensic evaluations. Assessment interviews and data-gathering thus must take place rapidly and efficiently because often, the expert will need to testify within hours to days of the evaluation. Some hearings, however, involve recommitments of longer-stay patients, or of patients transitioning from forensic statuses or on forensic legal statuses. For example, some civil commitments arise after dismissal of charges for a former defendant who was incompetent to stand trial or after a prisoner committed for

INFO

Though gathering information for many forensic evaluations can be time-consuming, commitment proceedings in most jurisdictions must occur soon after emergency detention.

treatment comes to the end of his or her sentence. These cases may allow more time for preparation, but they also may involve a higher likelihood of a contested hearing requiring thorough preparation.

Additional Comments on Collateral Information

Collateral information is essential to most forensic evaluations, and civil commitment assessments are no exception. Respondents might be too psychotic, thought disordered, or cognitively impaired to give meaningful information about what happened before they came to the hospital. An evaluator preparing to testify in a civil commitment proceeding needs this information because very often, the process of confinement, medication, or the hospital's structured setting alters the behavior and clinical status of the respondent. An accurate sense of the respondent's recent community functioning is critical to gauging the impact of mental illness and the risks that releasing the respondent might create.

When an evaluator is retained by the respondent's attorney, the attorney may provide an account of what led to the hospitalization. Though this may be helpful, the evaluator should keep in mind that the attorney might be relating information in ways that favor the client. Similarly, collateral informants have their own nonclinical perspectives of and biases about respondents. Therefore, additional collateral information obtained from disinterested sources—such as emergency detention paperwork, ambulance reports, acquaintances, and community treatment providers—can help evaluators verify information and get a clearer grasp of what happened before detention and hospitalization.

Ethical Issues

Confidentiality Considerations

The nonconfidentiality of information revealed by the respondent raises some ethical concerns. If the

> **BEST PRACTICE**
> Try to obtain collateral information from disinterested sources—such as emergency detention paperwork, ambulance reports, acquaintances, and community treatment providers—to verify information and get a clear grasp of what happened before detention and hospitalization.

examiner interviews only the respondent and provides appropriate warnings (see Chapter 5), then the examiner has satisfied the obligation to inform the respondent about the fact that the evaluator may testify about information revealed. Respondents will generally have no privacy or perhaps limited privacy concerning the very personal and sometimes embarrassing matters that led to the commitment proceeding. Some jurisdictions hold commitment proceedings in private [either in the judge's chambers (i.e., *in camera*) or in another nonpublic setting], but civil commitment proceedings in many jurisdictions take place in open court, where persons unconnected with the proceedings—including members of the news media—may attend. This can make civil commitment proceedings uncomfortable and awkward, especially when the clinician providing expert testimony is also the respondent's treating clinician. Nevertheless, testifying experts should prepare themselves to answer questions frankly and directly—both because doing so is what the law requires and to provide information needed for the trier of fact (i.e., the judge, magistrate, or jury making the commitment decision).

Contact with Collateral Sources

An examiner who contacts a collateral source (e.g., a family member or neighbor) must convey the reason for the contact and the parties with whom information will be shared. As we noted earlier, making the contact and explaining the reason for it—"This is Dr. Smith, and I am calling you as part of my independent assessment of Mr. Jones to see whether he must be psychiatrically hospitalized"—will usually enable a collateral informant to figure out that the respondent has serious mental problems, though this fact has not been revealed explicitly. Such revelations may have ramifications for future social relationships (if one calls friends or family members who later shun the respondent) or employment (if ones speaks with persons who know first hand about the respondent's functioning at work). Moreover, collateral informants—who usually are under no obligation to maintain confidentiality—may share with other persons the things they learn or surmise from their contact with the evaluator.

Civil commitment evaluations may be distinct from other forensic assessments in

BEWARE
You should hesitate before contacting anyone other than those individuals identified in legal documents as having made allegations against the respondent or those persons that you know are already aware of the respondent's situation.

that the evaluator must balance the aspirational goal of obtaining "complete" information with sensitivity to an evaluee's situation and interest in maintaining privacy. Evaluators should hesitate before contacting anyone other than those individuals identified in legal documents as having made allegations against the respondent or those persons who the evaluator knows are already aware of the respondent's situation. Other individuals may be contacted, but the decision to do so should be done thoughtfully. The purpose of the evaluation can guide evaluators in deciding who to contact and when collateral information is sufficient. For evaluators, the two main reasons for collateral information are (1) to verify the presence and severity of mental illness and (2) to verify predetention dangerous behavior. Making collateral contacts beyond what is necessary to address these aims may lead to disclosures that needlessly embarrass or harm evaluees. As a matter of respect for persons, evaluators should elicit information from collateral sources, but reveal to those persons as little as possible about the respondent, especially in cases in which the respondent has not given consent to share information.

4
chapter

Data Collection | 5

In Chapter 4 we discussed preparation for civil commitment evaluations. In this chapter, we discuss aspects of data collection used in these types of assessments. We begin with a discussion of "collateral data," the phrase we use to designate written or verbally communicated information obtained from sources other than the respondent.

Collateral Data Sources

Gathering and reviewing collateral data enable the evaluator to plan what to discuss with the respondent beyond those topics usually covered in a mental health assessment. Information provided with the referral usually allows evaluators to identify which collateral sources of information will be important for their assessments. Evaluators usually need not seek information beyond what will directly assist them in conducting their personal examinations of respondents.

In cases in which the commitment hearing is to follow a recent emergency hospitalization, the evaluator should read the documents that supported the initial detention—applications for admission, police records, affidavits, or court records that justified the warrant to apprehend. The evaluator should also examine the clinical record covering the hours to days between the detention and the commitment proceeding. A hospital chart usually contains documentation of the respondent's treatment history plus accounts of recent statements or behavior that the evaluator might discuss with the respondent during the interview. In a continued commitment case involving a respondent who has undergone institutional care for months or years, documentation of behavior that happened long ago or only intermittently over several years may be relevant to whether the respondent still meets commitment criteria. Knowledge of the jurisdiction's criteria for commitment will help the evaluator to anticipate how much (if any) consideration remote historical facts will receive in a commitment hearing.

Other potential collateral sources include interviews (often by telephone) with friends or family members who saw the respondent before detention. Prior treatment providers may also yield helpful information. As noted in Chapter 4, evaluators should consider what persons to contact and should be mindful of what information they share with collateral contacts. In addition to these preparations, the evaluator should consider whether to obtain a release of information from the evaluee or to get a court order authorizing a release of information before making the contact. Obtaining such releases or permission is necessary at times, though this may vary depending on the case, the collateral information being sought (e.g., from a treatment provider versus a family member), and jurisdictional practices. The evaluator may need to seek guidance from retaining counsel as to how to approach this issue. At the outset of phone calls or in-person interviews, an evaluator should tell collateral contacts that any information they reveal may not remain confidential and that they may receive a subpoena to testify about what they have witnessed concerning the respondent.

Table 5.1 contains a list of potential collateral data sources that an evaluator might pursue. Unlike most forensic assessments, civil commitment evaluators usually work under time and confidentiality constraints

Table 5.1 │ Common Sources of Collateral Information

1. Initial detention papers
2. Ambulance records
3. Police records
4. Medical records from emergency room contact prior to hospitalization
5. Medical records from current and past hospitalizations
6. Family members
7. Neighbors

that limit who they may contact and the amount of information they can obtain before a scheduled hearing. Evaluators therefore often must make clinical decisions about whether their collateral data are *adequate*, while being fully aware that more data would be desirable. As noted in Chapter 4, evaluators who frequently conduct civil commitment evaluations become accustomed to balancing time constraints and respect for the respondent's privacy against their desires to be thorough and to make sure their opinions will withstand cross-examination.

Interviewing the Respondent

Cultural and Language Barriers

Before beginning examinations, evaluators should be confident that they can communicate adequately with evaluees (U.S. Department of Health and Human Services Office of Minority Health, 2000). An evaluator may need to arrange for an interpreter to facilitate evaluations of hearing-impaired respondents who communicate using standard sign language or of respondents who do not speak languages in which the evaluator can communicate well. Qualified interpreters are generally adept at their jobs, but they may encounter difficulties in translating the statements of persons who suffer from severe mental illnesses. For example, a well-intentioned interpreter may rearrange an evaluee's disorganized thoughts to provide the examiner with a *farteytcht un farbessert* ("translated and

BEST PRACTICE
You may need to arrange for an interpreter to facilitate evaluations of hearing-impaired respondents or of respondents who do not speak languages in which you can communicate well.

improved") rendering that unintentionally obscures key evidence of a thought disorder. In one instance familiar to the authors, an evaluator listened to an interpreter—who had been struggling at some points—while the interpreter and respondent talked for several moments during the interview. When the evaluator later asked for an explanation of what had happened, the evaluator learned that the interpreter had been trying to understand and translate the evaluee's neologisms. To avoid such problems, evaluators may need to educate interpreters about what is needed (i.e., faithful, verbatim renditions) and the importance of conveying the structure as well as the meaning of respondents' communications.

Informed Consent and Warnings of Nonconfidentiality

INFO
Consent for an evaluation is not legally required when undertaking a court-ordered assessment. Nonetheless, evaluators should attempt to identify themselves and to inform the respondent about (1) why the evaluation is occurring, (2) the limits of confidentiality, (3) the potential uses of information revealed, and (4) the respondent's option not to answer questions.

Consent for an evaluation is not legally required when undertaking court-ordered assessments. However, ethical guidelines (American Academy of Psychiatry and the Law, 2005; Committee on Ethical Guidelines for Forensic Psychologists, 1991) recommend that evaluators try to identify themselves and explain to the respondent why the evaluation is occurring, the limited confidentiality of the evaluation, the potential uses of information revealed, and the respondent's option not to answer questions. Evaluators may also explain that they will provide the court with any information they gather about the respondent, even if the respondent refuses to participate. In some jurisdictions, statutes, case law, or local policies delineate rules about what evaluators must tell respondents (e.g., *Commonwealth v. Lamb*, 1974; *Matter of Laura L*, 2002).

When the testifying "expert" is also the treating clinician, providing notice about or obtaining consent for a specific civil commitment assessment at the outset of contact with the individual is not possible because every treatment interaction could produce information relevant to later testimony. However, treating clinicians who know their patients will soon face a commitment hearing may wish to tell or formally remind their patients that information revealed in clinical contacts may be related in court in upcoming testimony. In some jurisdictions, treating psychiatrists provide notice of the potential for information to be used in court at the outset of treatment and document that this was given. In addition, a later reminder of the notice given before a known hearing date should be recorded in the medical record, depending on local practice. Whether such reminders have occurred may be raised in court hearings. In those jurisdictions that require notice to respondents even in treatment contexts, giving patients such explanations will increase the likelihood that information from clinical contacts will not be disallowed because the patient did not have a chance to waive participation.

The Interview

To the extent that a respondent's mental condition and level of cooperation will permit, an interview should elicit information that will permit the evaluator to reach a well-founded opinion concerning whether the respondent has a mental disorder and has displayed recent behavior that satisfies the jurisdiction's commitment criteria. The American Psychiatric Association's Practice Guideline for the Psychiatric Evaluation of Adults (American Psychiatric Association, 2006) lists several domains for clinical evaluations (see Table 5.2) that provide a useful framework for civil commitment assessments. We assume that readers know how to interview and diagnose patients; therefore, the following sections focus primarily on how elements of standard mental health assessments inform judgments about eligibility for civil commitment. While reading

Table 5.2 | Domains of a Clinical Evaluation

1. History of present illness
2. Past psychiatric history
3. Substance use history
4. Medical history
5. Developmental, psychosocial, and sociocultural history
6. Occupational and military history
7. Legal history
8. Family history
9. Review of symptoms
10. Physical examination
11. Mental status examination

Adapted from the American Psychiatric Association (2006).

the following sections, readers may find it helpful to refer occasionally to the Sample Data Collection Sheet presented in Figure 5.1.

HISTORY OF PRESENT ILLNESS

As with almost any mental health assessment, an examiner should explore the recent course of the evaluee's problems, with special emphasis on current symptoms and the events that led to the respondent's detention. If the respondent does not spontaneously mention the events or behavior listed in the commitment documents (e.g., the affidavit), the examiner can show or read the contents of those documents to the respondent and then ask for the respondent's account of what happened ("It says here that [such and such happened], but I want to hear your side of the story"). In the context of a civil commitment evaluation, a key goal is to sort out the causes and consequences of any aberrant behavior that led to the initiation of commitment proceedings. Evaluators should keep in mind that commitment criteria require a finding not only that risk-creating ("dangerous") behavior occurred, but also that the behavior that created the risk *stemmed from a substantial mental disorder*. As examiners mentally generate respondents'

Independent Examination for Civil Commitment

Location		
Respondent	Birth date	Age
Resident of	Race	Sex
Case No.	Exam Date	
Examiner	Agency Info	
Info Sources		

Precipitants (from records)

Precipitants (evaluee's version)

Previous Hospitalizations			
Admitted	Discharged	Hospital	Comments

Current Hospital Record
Treating Physician
Treating Physician's Diagnosis
Medications
Use of restraints or PRN Medications
Other information concerning hospital course
Interview of Examinee: Pertinent History and Course of Treatment

Figure 5.1 Sample Data Collection Sheet, Based on Ohio's Commitment Criteria.

Evidence of Statutorily Defined Mental Illness				
Thought	Form *logical, coherent* *loose associations* *tangential* *flight of ideas* *disorganized* *blocking* *poverty*		Content *delusions*	
Mood	Self-harm		Affect	
	Other-harm			
Perception	Hallucinations		other	
Orientation	☐ person	☐ place	☐ time	☐ circumstances
Memory	Recent		remote	
Speech (pace, clarity)		Insight		

Independent Examiner's:	
Diagnosis	Prognosis

Evidence of Gross Impairment of ...	
Judgment	
Behavior	
Recognize Reality	
Meet Demands of Daily Living	

Salient Risk Factors

Evidence of Risk: Criteria for Involuntary Hospitalization		
Harm to self	Acts	threats
Harm to others	Behavior	threats
Basic needs	inability to provide ...	
Benefit from treatment	Need	behavior affecting substantial rights of others or self

Meets commitment criteria?	☐ yes	☐ no

Least restrictive setting:	☐ Inpatient ☐ Inpatient to outpatient (court ordered) ☐ Outpatient (court ordered) ☐ No commitment (will sign in voluntarily)

Figure 5.1 Continued

differential diagnosis and elicit data to sort out diagnostic possibilities, they should also think about how clinical data will translate into their jurisdiction's legal definition of "mental disorder" for civil commitment purposes.

In many cases, respondents will not tolerate or cooperate with even a cursory exploration of current symptoms. At the very least, however, evaluators should try to learn whether respondents believe they *have* a mental illness and what respondents understand about their current situation.

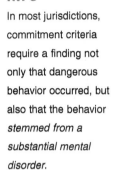

INFO
In most jurisdictions, commitment criteria require a finding not only that dangerous behavior occurred, but also that the behavior *stemmed from a substantial mental disorder.*

As *Zinermon v. Burch* (1990; see Chapter 1) illustrates, respondents sometimes do not recognize that they are ill or being held in a hospital. If this is the case, "signing in voluntarily"—which some patients do when told that they face commitment—is not really possible. When evaluating very confused respondents, examiners should consider asking direct questions about where the respondents are and whether they realize they are undergoing treatment. Knowing a respondent's responses to these questions may help an examiner provide information crucial to deciding whether to let a respondent sign in "voluntarily" rather than hold a hearing on commitment.

PAST PSYCHIATRIC HISTORY

Not all jurisdictions permit testimony about a respondent's previous treatment [on grounds of privilege, see, e.g., *In re Miller* (1992)], but evaluators should still learn what they can from respondents about their psychiatric history. A comprehensive mental health assessment features a chronological summary of previous episodes of mental illness, substance use, and treatment for these conditions (American Psychiatric Association, 2006) and plays a key role in helping the evaluator understand the current presentation and make diagnostic conclusions. For many psychiatric patients (not just civil commitment respondents), the best

5
chapter

sources of *facts* about their treatment history are *records* of treatment, not what patients remember or choose to reveal. However, in a civil commitment assessment, asking about the treatment history may help evaluators learn how a respondent understands his illness and its impact on functioning.

As evaluators explore the history, they can look for patterns of treatment outcomes—successes, failures, how many hospitalizations the respondent has undergone, what difficulties the respondent has had living in the community—and indications of "worst case scenarios," all of which will clarify what risk the respondent's current problems really pose. Asking about previous suicide attempts—including the outcome of any attempts and subsequent need for medical hospitalization—can help the examiner develop a sense of the respondent's current severity of suicide risk (American Psychiatric Association, 2003). Similar considerations apply for questions about past violence while experiencing symptoms of mental illness, or questions about previous times when the respondent's inattention to personal wellbeing during episodes of mental illness—e.g., previous patterns of dressing too lightly by a respondent who was recently found wandering outside in cold weather in his underwear—created a risk of grave disability. Often, a respondent will deny or minimize previous problems when asked about past treatment. When contradicted by written documentation of serious mental illness, such responses suggest that the respondent is unlikely to continue psychiatric care if left alone—an important datum in gauging the respondent's current level of risk and the "least restrictive" but most appropriate setting for care.

MEDICAL HISTORY

Persons with severe mental illness suffer from serious nonpsychiatric medical problems—problems that create a significant risk of harm without proper care—at rates far higher than persons drawn from the general population (Osborn, Levy, Nazareth, Peterson, Islam, & King, 2007).

BEST PRACTICE
Asking about previous suicide attempts can help you develop a sense of the respondent's current severity of suicide risk.

Medical problems can be independent sources of functional impairment or can interact with psychiatric problems (American Psychiatric Association, 2006). Past trauma, sexual functioning, endocrinological illnesses, infectious disease (including HIV and hepatitis C), neurological disorders, sleep disorders, and pain disorders are among the many medical illnesses that can present with mental symptoms, and if these conditions are the sole reason for a respondent's psychiatric impairment, the respondent should not be subject to civil commitment.

As is the case with past psychiatric history, *clinical documentation* is often the best source of *facts* about a respondent's general medical history (Redelmeier, Tu, Schull, Ferris, & Hux, 2001). In civil commitment assessments, asking respondents about medical illnesses, prior procedures, and medical hospitalizations helps evaluators find out how well respondents understand their medical problems and how well they can care for themselves if released. Evaluators can also ask respondents what they know about their current medications, whether they have been taking them, and why they need them.

MENTAL STATUS EXAMINATION

The mental status examination is a standard component of any forensic mental health assessment (American Psychiatric Association, 2006; Patel, Pinals, & Brier, 2008; Heilbrun, Marczyk, & DeMatteo, 2002). Table 5.3 outlines the elements of a mental status examination. Though all aspects of the mental status examination contribute to the assessment process, those aspects that affect a respondent's current risk of harm to self or others are of special relevance in a civil commitment evaluation. To the extent a respondent will allow, evaluators should explore recent suicidal thinking and behavior, violent fantasies and actions, instances of poor judgment, and the respondent's insight into these areas. Cognitive deficits also need to be explored as they may impact the ability to care for self. Other features of current mental status with heightened importance are those with known relationships to risk of violence (e.g., command auditory hallucinations and affective dysregulation) (Pinals,

5
chapter

Table 5.3 | Elements of a Mental Status Examination

1. Appearance and general behavior
2. Motor activity
3. Speech
4. Mood and affect
5. Thought processes
6. Thought content
7. Perceptual disturbances
8. Sensorium and cognition
9. Insight
10. Judgment

Adapted from the American Psychiatric Association (2006).

INFO

Though all aspects of a mental status examination contribute to the assessment process, those aspects that affect a respondent's *current risk of harm to self or others* are of special relevance in a civil commitment evaluation.

Tillbrook, & Mumley, 2009). Insofar as a decision about civil commitment is concerned, data that contribute to diagnostic precision are less important than findings that clearly establish a "substantial mental disorder" and its relationship to recent behavior that has placed the respondent or others at risk of incurring harm.

Special Issues in the Forensic Examination

Competence to Consent to Hospitalization

Civil commitment proceedings are usually unnecessary if a patient can and wants to consent to voluntary hospitalization. Some patients who acquiesce to being admitted cannot validly consent to hospitalization, however, and individuals doing forensic assessments for civil commitment may occasionally encounter such situations.

In response to the Supreme Court's *Zinermon* decision (1990, see Chapter 1), a task force of the American Psychiatric Association prepared a report examining potential standards of competence to consent to psychiatric hospitalization, and suggested that policy interests support requiring patients to display only a modest level of competence (American Psychiatric Association, 1993). Several commentators have agreed with this conclusion because voluntary commitment is essentially a treatment intervention rather than an adverse event (Hoge, 1994; Poythress, Cascardi, & Ritterband, 1996).

Regarding competence to consent to hospitalization, an evaluation should consider basic factors (see, e.g., Hoge, 1994; Poythress et al., 1996) such as whether the patient is aware of (1) being in a hospital, (2) the purpose of the hospitalization, (3) how to ask to be discharged, and (4) the fact that discharge is not automatic. One study (Poythress et al., 1996) suggested that tests for recognition of the facts presented, rather than tests of recall, would be a better mechanism for assessment if one uses the "weak" competence threshold (i.e., a threshold that would more readily allow patients to be admitted voluntarily related to a basic understanding of the hospitalization as exemplified in the factors above) posited by Hoge (1994).

Patients who have competently consented to hospitalization need not undergo assessment of their appropriateness for civil commitment, even if their behavior and mental condition would satisfy criteria for involuntary hospitalization. If such patients later wish to leave the hospital, however, treating clinicians may then need to initiate civil commitment procedures, and an appropriate forensic assessment may subsequently take place.

5
chapter

Examinees Who Do Not Participate Fully in the Assessment

A treating clinician who anticipates testifying at an upcoming civil commitment hearing will usually have no shortage of information

BEWARE
Do not put yourself in harm's way when interviewing a respondent who exhibits violent or threatening behavior. Experts may testify based on their observations of a respondent, and such information may be the only examination data available if a respondent is unable or unwilling to tolerate a formal interview.

about a patient's current mental condition and recent behavior. But independent evaluators will often encounter respondents who are so angry about their detention or so mentally disturbed that they will not or cannot agree to participate in a civil commitment evaluation. Sometimes, respondents' violent behavior, threats, pressured speech, sexual provocativeness, or extreme irritability may limit an evaluator's ability to gather much interview data or may make it unsafe to do so. In the latter circumstances, evaluators should not put themselves in harm's way in order to press for information. After politely attempting to interview some respondents alone, evaluators may conclude that they must end the examination or ask for staff members to be present for safety purposes.

Independent evaluators usually accept specific assignments pursuant to court orders that authorize them to conduct civil commitment examinations. Among the many reasons that such orders may be helpful is that they permit evaluators to explain to uncooperative respondents that the judge has ordered the assessment—which may alter the respondent's attitude toward participation. Similarly, when an evaluator conducts an assessment at the behest of a respondent's attorney, telling this to the respondent may gain the respondent's cooperation, as may asking the lawyer to speak with the respondent before or at the beginning of the examination.

Whenever a respondent appears able to participate but refuses to do so, the evaluator should try to learn the respondent's reason for nonparticipation. Some respondents are forthcoming about their reasons, which can range from psychotic beliefs to rational desires to assert legal rights and protect themselves from an adverse finding. Of course, some respondents will refuse to say why they will not participate, refuse to say anything, or refuse to enter an interview room with evaluators, despite being told of the court order.

If a respondent refuses or cannot participate in a full evaluation, the evaluator may use other available data to form an opinion and to testify to that opinion—but the evaluator should qualify the opinion accordingly during testimony. In these situations, an evaluator can often combine observation while attempting an interview with observations of hospital staff members and other collateral sources to form a coherent picture of the respondent's mental condition, especially the respondent's current mental status. To the extent that the evaluator can glean the reasons for a respondent's nonparticipation (i.e., distinguishing whether the respondent is unable or unwilling to participate), providing these reasons may help the court better understand the respondent's circumstances before rendering a civil commitment decision.

Evaluating Children and Adolescents

As we noted in Chapter 1, the Supreme Court held in *Parham v. J.R.* (1976) that the U.S. Constitution does not require civil commitment proceedings for minors who object to psychiatric hospitalization. States may grant their citizens more rights than the Constitution requires, however, and in some jurisdictions, minors who object to hospitalization enjoy some or all the substantive and procedural rights afforded to adults facing commitment. Evaluating children and adolescents for civil commitment therefore requires an awareness of what laws and criteria govern involuntary hospitalization of minors in the jurisdiction in which one is practicing (Fortunati & Zonana, 2003).

Some mental health professionals obtain specialty training in the assessment and diagnosis of children and adolescents. This training qualifies them to identify specific characteristics in minors—how psychiatric problems present in children, developmental characteristics, issues of personal and family functioning, and the impact of background factors—that are relevant to determining whether psychiatric hospitalization is needed (Tonge, Hughes, Pullen, Beaufoy, & Gold, 2008). Hospitalization patterns (which now feature very short lengths of stay and increased use of community treatments) differ from those provided to adults

(Case, Olfson, Marcus, & Siegel, 2007). Also, child training helps clinicians become comfortable handling legal issues specific to treating minors, including unique concerns regarding confidentiality, assent to evaluation, mandatory reporting of abuse, and consent to release of information. Evaluators who assess minors for civil commitment should have appropriate knowledge or training (especially when the respondent is less than 16 years old), or at a minimum be able to obtain appropriate consultation. Assessing older adolescents may fall within the expertise of both child-trained and adult-trained professionals, depending on the particular features of the clinical case.

Use of Structured Diagnostic Interviews: Pro and Con

Structured diagnostic interviews—e.g., the Structured Clinical Interview of *DSM–IV* Disorders (e.g., SCID; First, Spitzer, Gibbon, & Williams, 1996) and the Schedule for Affective Disorders and Schizophrenia (SADS; Endicott & Spitzer, 1978)—provide evaluators with consistent formats for collecting data and exploring symptoms. Using structured interviews standardizes data collection and improves interrater reliability, which facilitate categorizing evaluees into homogeneous groups of subjects. For this reason, structured interviews are widely used in clinical drug trials, epidemiological studies, and academic research. Professionals occasionally use structured interviews in clinical and forensic practice.

A number of structured interviews have features that are potentially relevant to improving civil commitment evaluations. The SCID, which is organized by diagnosis, has good diagnostic reliability and produces diagnoses in accordance with *DSM–IV*. The SADS, which yields anchored ratings that permit reliable estimates of symptom severity at multiple times during the current episode of illness, has proven to have excellent symptom reliability (kappa > 0.85). The Mini International Neuropsychiatric Interview (M.I.N.I.; Sheehan et al., 1998) allows an examiner to rapidly survey symptoms of several common Axis I disorders, sometimes in under 20 minutes. The M.I.N.I. has been cited or used in more than 250 publications, has excellent interrater reliability (kappas > 0.79), and has good concordance with other structured interviews. Using the M.I.N.I., clinicians with modest training—including nonpsychiatrists—can achieve excellent reliability and accuracy (de Azevedo Marques & Zuardi, 2008).

Diagnoses reached during ordinary clinical care are often inaccurate, incomplete, and inadequate. At least four studies (Ramirez Basco et al., 2000; Miller, Dasher, Collins, Griffiths, & Brown, 2001; Shear et al., 2000; Zimmerman & Mattia, 2000) have shown that structured assessments often reveal comorbid diagnoses that had been missed by the unstructured evaluations that were the usual basis for care. Typical clinical care may identify mood, psychotic, and substance use disorders at prevalences comparable to those established through structured interviews. Anxiety disorders, somatoform disorders, and eating disorders are often overlooked (Zimmerman & Mattia, 1999), however, and these may be the very conditions for which patients really desire treatment.

If the findings of structured diagnostic interviews are treated as the "gold standard," then clinicians often fail to detect comorbid conditions that may affect the need for and impact of care. One possible reason is that even experienced clinicians tend to stop their diagnostic inquiry after they establish a satisfactory (but incomplete) initial diagnosis, a process that Rogers and Shuman (2000) term "premature closure." Also, confirmatory biases may lead clinicians "to . . . seek and overvalue data that are consistent with their hypothesis, and . . . disregard or undervalue data that are inconsistent with their hypothesis" (Rogers and Shuman, 2000, p. 281). A patient's past diagnoses also may contribute to diagnostic inaccuracy in this way (Rogers, 2003).

What do these findings say about optimal practice in a civil commitment evaluation? Real-world clinicians operate under time constraints. Adopting the first diagnosis that fits may be an example of "satisficing," a frugal decision-making heuristic that aims for adequacy rather than ideal results, especially when the costs of obtaining

5
chapter

information are high. Herbert Simon's "bounded rationality" model of human cognition suggests that because people lack the time and cognitive resources to evaluate all relevant alternatives with appropriate probabilistic precision, we search only until we find a solution that seems practically satisfactory (Simon, 1982).

We do not know to what degree missing comorbidities adversely affects patient care. For example, Zimmerman (2008) urges his psychiatric colleagues to improve their diagnostic practices, but he acknowledges that the practical consequences of doing so are uncertain. No research has shown whether the more reliable and comprehensive diagnoses yielded by structured interviews improve clinical outcomes for patients. One reason may be that the pharmacological agents used to treat many disorders have a broad-based impact on a range of conditions. Because of this, comprehensive diagnoses may not be practically important if gross diagnostic class distinctions (e.g., psychoses versus affective disorders) are accurate (Zimmerman, 2008).

Rogers and Shuman (2000) have suggested that structured interviews, particularly the SADS, would improve forensic evaluations related to criminal responsibility and personal injury in tort cases. Note, however, that in these forensic contexts—as in the contexts in which research on the reliability and value of structured interviews has taken place—most evaluees can and will cooperate with thorough, detailed diagnostic evaluations. By contrast, a large proportion of civil commitment respondents cannot participate in brief interviews, and relatively few can tolerate very detailed assessments. We know of no research documenting the potential cooperativeness of civil commitment evaluees with structured diagnostic instruments. However, a study by Pinals, Tillbrook, and Mumley (2006) found that for various reasons, two-fifths of individuals hospitalized as incompetent to stand trial could not undergo evaluation with the MacArthur Competence Assessment Tool–Criminal Adjudication (Poythress et al., 1999).

We also know of no research indicating whether using structured interviews would yield practical improvements in civil commitment determinations. The goal of such evaluations is only to allow the trial court to establish whether evidence satisfies the legal predicate for commitment, viz., that the respondent has a *substantial* disorder fitting one or more of several *broad* categories that causes *gross* impairment in functioning. The legal criteria for involuntary hospitalization imply a mediated relationship between a mental condition and civil commitment, not a direct relationship. If a respondent is clearly psychotic and did something that harmed or created the risk of harm to someone, the presence of a comorbid anxiety disorder, though perhaps significant for long-term treatment, makes *no* difference to the trial court.

INFO

If a respondent is clearly psychotic and did something that harmed or created the risk of harm to someone, the presence of a comorbid anxiety disorder will have little impact on the trial court's commitment decision.

Under these circumstances, we think the following comments about clinical care settings also apply to evaluations of eligibility for civil commitment:

> Clinicians may be forced to draw quick diagnostic conclusions with limited information in busy practice settings or when patients are acutely ill. In these cases, it is important to follow up after patients have been stabilized, to reevaluate diagnoses when patients seem to be nonresponsive to treatment, and to consider the possibility that comorbid problems may be interfering with treatment outcome. (Ramirez Basco, Jacquot, Thomas, & Knack, 2008)

5
chapter

Psychological Testing

Psychological testing is often helpful in diagnostic assessments undertaken for treatment purposes. Though some have argued that psychological tests should be routine in forensic assessments (Borum & Grisso, 1996; Lally, 2003), others have suggested that routine psychological testing would not be the most efficient use of resources in certain forensic contexts, such as competence to stand trial (Mossman et al., 2007).

Results of psychological testing will be *irrelevant* to most civil commitment decisions. In most cases, respondents display gross signs and symptoms of mental illness. The trial court's aim is to establish only whether respondents fit broad diagnostic categories (e.g., having "a substantial disorder of thought, mood, perception, orientation, or memory"). In this context, psychological testing will often yield little beyond what clinical assessment can discern. Moreover, many recently detained respondents do not tolerate even brief evaluations well and cannot cooperate with or focus enough to participate in a valid psychological assessment. Finally, psychological testing may generate hypotheses about diagnoses and personality functioning, but the diagnostic criteria for severe mental disorders are *clinical* manifestations of illness, not the results from psychological testing.

Occasionally, however, diagnostic ambiguities create situations in which psychological testing might address the legal questions at stake in civil commitment proceedings. For example, it is sometimes difficult to decide whether a patient suffers from schizotypal personality disorder or schizophrenia, even after extended clinical contact with the patient. This distinction may be relevant to the evaluator's conclusion about the presence or absence of a substantial disorder or gross impairment (especially in those few jurisdictions that define mental disorder using official diagnostic criteria), and it is the type of distinction for which psychological testing may prove useful.

Many jurisdictions have separate laws governing commitment of persons with developmental disabilities, who generally are not eligible for civil commitment if their problems stem only from their cognitive limitations. If developmentally disabled persons suffer from cooccurring symptoms of mental illness, however, they may be eligible for mental health commitment. Results of intelligence testing may be misleading when a person undergoes evaluation during a phase of severe illness (such as depression or psychosis). However, for persons with longstanding histories of intellectual disabilities, prior testing records, if available, can help evaluators make inferences about baseline intellectual functioning.

In many cases that raise diagnostic questions for which psychological testing is needed, the treatment team will have already undertaken such testing on the inpatient ward. When independent psychological testing is warranted and the independent evaluator is a psychiatrist, arrangements may need to be made through the attorney to obtain an independent psychological consultation to assist with the assessment process.

Rating Scales, Symptom Checklists, and Other Structured Assessment Tools

Though structured interviews and psychological testing have limited utility in mental health civil commitment assessments, rating scales and symptom checklists may occasionally help evaluators identify or quantify pathology in ways relevant to civil commitment. For example, an elderly evaluee's responses on the Mini-Mental State Examination (Folstein, Folstein, & McHugh, 1975) can establish disorientation, and the total score can help an evaluator characterize the severity of dementia. The Alcohol Use Disorders Identification Test ("AUDIT"; Saunders, Aasland, Babor, de la Fuente, & Grant, 1993) and the Rapid Alcohol Problems Screen ("RAPS4"; Cherpitel, 1995, 2000) are examples of easily accessed, quickly administered screens with high accuracy for identifying alcohol-use disorders (Frank, Elon, Naimi, & Brewer, 2008; Kelly, Donovan, Chung, Bukstein, & Cornelius, 2009). These, along with the CAGE questionnaire (Ewing, 1984), may help identify the extent of alcohol use in the respondent and may serve as bases for *lack* of commitment eligibility.

Several other instruments are available that help quantify severity of impairment and psychopathology (American Psychiatric

INFO

The total BPRS score provides an index of overall psychopathology.

Association, 2000). Below, we examine the potential relevance to civil commitment evaluations of two such measures in very common use.

Specific Rating Scales
BRIEF PSYCHIATRIC RATING SCALE

Originally published in 1962 as a 16-item inventory (Overall & Gorham, 1962), the Brief Psychiatric Rating Scale (BPRS) exists in several forms—an 18-item, 1965 revision (Overall & Gorham, 1988), an anchored version (BPRS-A; Woerner et al., 1988), and an expanded, 24-item version (BPRS-E; Lukoff et al., 1986). The BPRS assigns numerical severity levels to several types of psychopathology. Scoring of most items use an evaluee's self-report; the rest can be rated based on observation or collateral information. The BPRS has proven reliability and validity in clinical populations (Lukoff et al., 1986) and is frequently used to quantify psychiatric symptoms (Thomas, Donnell, & Young, 2004). The total BPRS score provides an index of overall psychopathology, and several studies suggest subscales (i.e., combinations of scores from subsets of BPRS items) that may serve as numerical indices of specific types of psychopathology (e.g., mania, depression/anxiety, negative symptoms, and positive symptoms; Ruggeri et al., 2005).

Administering the BPRS typically takes 20–30 minutes for interviewing and scoring and requires some cooperation by the evaluee. A few studies have examined the usefulness of the BPRS in forensic contexts. For example,

- James and colleagues (2001) were able to administer the BPRS to 88% of 479 consecutive British defendants undergoing evaluations of fitness to plead (i.e., competence to stand trial), but particularly relevant to civil commitment assessments was the authors' finding that "the most symptomatic cases may have been those least inclined or able to cooperate with rating" (p. 145).

- McDermott and colleagues (2005) found that BPRS positive symptoms were correlated negatively with Understanding subscale scores of the MacArthur Competence Assessment Tool for Clinical Research (Appelbaum & Grisso, 2001), whereas BPRS negative symptoms were negatively associated with Reasoning Subscale scores.

Other studies have examined the BPRS as a short-term predictor of inpatient violence.

- Yesavage and colleagues (1982) found that the BPRS hostility item was higher in those patients who actually were assaultive during hospitalization.

- Palmstierna and colleagues (1989) found that high hostility and anxiety scores and low grandiosity scores appeared to predict serious violent behavior, but a subsequent, larger (105-patient) study by the same group concluded that other factors (e.g., previous violence and alcohol misuse) were better correlated with inpatient violence (Palmstierna & Wistedt, 1990).

- Troisi and colleagues (2003) found that in a multiple regression model, the hostility and tension-excitement items of the BPRS were predictors of verbal aggression; thought disturbance and suspiciousness-uncooperativeness predicted aggression against objects.

- Amore and colleagues (2008) found that inpatients who were physically violent during hospitalization had higher BPRS scores on several subscales, especially hostility-suspiciousness, but after controlling statistically for other factors (particularly violence during the 30 days before hospitalization) the BPRS elements lost their predictive significance.

GLOBAL ASSESSMENT OF FUNCTIONING

The 1987 edition of the American Psychiatric Association's diagnostic manual included the Global Assessment of Functioning (GAF) as the fifth component of the multiaxial diagnostic scheme (American Psychiatric Association, 1987). The GAF ranks functioning on a 100-point scale, with scores of 10 or less implying "persistent danger of severely hurting self or others" or persistent failure "to maintain minimal personal hygiene," and scores above 90 implying "superior functioning in a wide range of activities." Psychiatric inpatients typically have scores below 40 (Spitzer, Gibbon, Williams, & Endicott, 1994). The reliability and validity of the GAF appear to be acceptable (Patterson & Lee, 1995; Hilsenroth et al., 2000; Söderberg, Tungström, & Armelius, 2005), and scores on the GAF are correlated with other indices of clinical status (Roy-Byrne, Dagadakis, Unutzer, & Ries, 1996; Hilsenroth et al., 2000; Greenberg & Rosenheck, 2005).

Very little research links GAF scores to commitment decisions, and GAF scores are not validated indicators of future harm to self or others. Research suggests that GAF scores are associated with decisions to admit patients to a hospital, but involuntarily admission is linked to other factors, including lack of motivation, symptom severity, time of referral, and danger to self or others (Mulder, Koopmans, & Lyons, 2005). However, a study examining individuals subject to outpatient commitment found that among those with the lowest GAF scores, outpatient commitment brought about a short-term reduction in homelessness (Compton, Swanson, Wagner, Swartz, Burns, & Elbogen, 2003). Thus, low GAF scores suggest problems caring for oneself, which may be relevant to some civil commitment decisions. Future editions of the *DSM* may offer more updated guidance relative to measuring functioning.

PROBLEMS WITH APPLYING RATING SCALES

The preceding paragraphs suggest that the BPRS, GAF, and similar scales might allow evaluators to quantify functioning numerically and provide this evidence to courts that adjudicate civil commitment petitions. For example, a testifying expert might refer to a respondent's high BPRS score as evidence confirming the presence of a "substantial" mental disorder. However, we do not recommend routine use of such scales in civil commitment evaluations, for the following reasons:

- As the findings of James and colleagues (2001) suggest, many respondents will not be amenable to or cooperative with systematic evaluation.

- Though studies may suggest associations between certain scores on psychopathology scales (e.g., the BPRS) and involuntary status, there is no necessary link between the legal criteria for commitment and any BPRS score. Put differently, a high BPRS score implies severe psychiatric symptoms and need for treatment; high scores do not imply satisfaction of other criteria needed to justify involuntary hospitalization.

- GAF scores *are* related to several legal criteria for commitment. The clinical findings that yield GAF scores below 40 refer explicitly to gross functional impairment—being unable to work, "considerably influenced by delusions or hallucinations," "suicidal preoccupation," "suicidal attempts," "frequently violent," etc. Notice, however, that it is specific types of behavior—not a score—that justify civil commitment. At best, a GAF score only provides a numerical summary of the specific actions and clinical findings that support a respondent's need for hospitalization.

Standardized Instruments to Assess Suitability for Commitment
ABSENCE OF INSTRUMENTS
For many types of forensic assessment, examiners may avail themselves of structured instruments designed for the specific evaluation task. For example, mental health professionals have created more than a half-dozen *forensic assessment instruments (FAIs)* to assist evaluations of adjudicative competence. Though scores or

other results produced by FAIs are not dispositive of any psycholegal matter, proper use of FAIs ensures systematic assessment and often provides a basis for comparing individual evaluees to a normative or relevant population (Jacobs, Ryba, & Zapf, 2008; Mossman et al., 2007).

No one has designed FAIs for use in civil commitment evaluations, however, and no one is likely to do so, for the following reasons:

- Though one can often make useful generalizations about U.S. commitment criteria (as we have tried to do in this volume), legal standards differ significantly enough across U.S. jurisdictions to make development of a "national" instrument impractical.

- The chief tasks that mental health professionals perform in civil commitment evaluations are diagnosing mental illness and deciding where treatment should take place. These are fundamental clinical skills that all psychologists and psychiatrists who treat seriously ill patients should possess.

- Witnesses at civil commitment hearings usually include the respondents' treating clinicians, who have knowledge about and familiarity with their patients' conditions and histories that amply satisfy a trial court's needs.

- Most civil commitment hearings are brief and contested half-heartedly (if at all), which makes the practical need for assiduously administered instruments minimal.

- Legal criteria for commitment focus the trial court's attention primarily on the respondent's actual *past* events and actions, rather than on the types of entities—such as intelligence, functional capacity, or probabilities of future acts—that psychological and forensic assessment instruments typically measure.

POSSIBLE CANDIDATES

Though the just-mentioned factors militate against using FAIs in civil commitment assessments, some authors have suggested that FAIs might be appropriate for use in these evaluations (Stefan, 2006; Heilbrun & Erickson, 2007). We review and comment on three candidate FAIs here related to violence risk assessment, recognizing that violence is only one concern of a civil commitment evaluation. Other areas of civil commitment assessment, such as assessment of suicide risk, may benefit from following the numerous suicide risk assessment checklists, guidelines, and tools (see, e.g., American Psychiatric Association, 2003) that may be utilized in routine clinical practice in local settings (such as emergency rooms) and are not typically referred to as FAIs. In the review below, we discuss one instrument that was developed to include assessments of other aspects of a civil commitment evaluation, such as suicide risk and grave disability. Readers interested in more information regarding violence risk assessment may wish to consult another volume in this series, *Evaluation for Risk of Violence in Adults* (Heilbrun, 2009).

INFO

Cross-jurisdictional variations in legal standards and the focus of hearings on actual past events make it unlikely that anyone will develop FAIs for civil commitment.

Classification of Violence Risk™ (COVR™). The COVR™ (Monahan et al., 2005a) is a commercial software product designed to help mental health practitioners quickly implement the findings of the MacArthur studies (Monahan et al., 2001) on community violence by psychiatric patients. These studies assessed more than 100 potential risk factors in 1100 acute psychiatric inpatients who were then followed in the community for several months after discharge. In using the COVR™, an evaluator conducts a short record review and a 10-minute interview focusing on the risk factors that proved most useful in assigning probabilities of violence in the study group (Monahan et al., 2000). The COVR™ software implements a "classification tree method" (Steadman et al., 2000)

5
chapter

for gathering and prioritizing information, such that the questions asked and the order of questions depend on the evaluee's previous answers. This approach to assigning risk allows consideration of many potential combinations of risk factors, in contrast to traditional regression methods, which use a single set of factors and weights to calculate risk estimates.

The COVR™ output is a percentage and confidence interval for the likelihood of violence over the next several months. A problem with these estimates and intervals, however, is that the authors simply tested bootstrap samples (a statistical technique for cross-validation) from the *full* study population only on the single classification tree that they developed for the full study population. A better approach would have been to draw multiple bootstrap samples from the full population to construct multiple classification trees, with each of these multiple trees then used to classify the full population and to produce bootstrap estimates of predictive accuracy. Given the approach that the COVR™ creators used, the published accuracy estimate [area under the receiver operating characteristic (ROC) curve = 0.81] is probably overly optimistic, and the risk percentage outputs are too extreme—that is, the percentages for low-risk groups are too low, and the percentages for high-risk groups are too high. A follow-up study of the COVR™ (Monahan et al., 2005b) produced results indicative of this over-optimism. A further problem with using the risk percentages relates to possible selection effects in the COVR™ administration, e.g., selectively evaluating patients independently suspected to be at heightened risk for violence (McCusker, 2006). One study, however, showed the COVR™ had some utility in assessing risk of future violence among forensic patients in the United Kingdom (Snowden, Gray, Taylor, & Fitzgerald, 2009). Over time, we may see more research related to the COVR™ that will help us understand its utility in civil commitment cases.

HCR-20. The HCR-20 (Webster, Douglas, Eaves, & Hart, 1997) is another FAI designed to gauge the risk of violence in psychiatric patients. The instrument's name reflects its three-part structure and 20 items: 10 items about the evaluee's personal *h*istory, five items about current *c*linical status, and five items relevant to *r*isk management. Inclusion of each item is backed by research showing an association between the item and a heightened probability of future violence. The currently available second edition of the HCR-20 manual briefly summarizes published research support (as it existed in the mid-1990s) for each item, and a *Companion Guide* (Douglas, Webster, Eaves, Hart, & Ogloff, 2001) discusses strategies for managing risk.

One of the first tests of the HCR-20 (Douglas, Ogloff, Nicholls, & Grant, 1999) used information about 193 British Columbia involuntary psychiatric inpatients followed for 2 years (on average) after discharge. The HCR-20 scores of the 73 former patients who had violent incidents were considerably higher than the scores of the others (ROC area = 0.76); the HCR-20 also performed well at "predicting" violent crimes (ROC area = 0.80). Studies in other countries and other clinical contexts have found that violent individuals consistently score higher on the HCR-20 than nonviolent individuals do (see generally Douglas, Guy, & Weir, 2007). For example, the HCR-20 was modestly accurate in sorting violent from nonviolent psychiatric inpatients (ROC area = 0.65) on a short-stay unit (McNiel, Gregory, Lam, Binder, & Sullivan, 2003).

Unlike the COVR™, the HCR-20 does not yield risk percentages, and the authors of the HCR-20 intend the numerical score to be only a first step in evaluating risk. The 20-item list is meant to be an "*aide-mémoire*" (Webster et al., 1997, p. 5) to help evaluators assemble data about salient, well-known risk factors. Evaluators should then consider other factors about evaluees—for example, information about potential victims, amenability to treatment, recent threats, and the "fit" between particular evaluees and the populations in which the HCR-20 has shown predictive validity—to reach an ultimate global judgment ("low," "medium," or "high") about violence potential.

A clear problem in attempting to use the full HCR-20 for civil commitment evaluations is the time (often more than 2 hours) and extensive background information needed for scoring the historical items (particularly "psychopathy"). The five clinical

5
chapter

items—insight, attitudes toward treatment, presence of symptoms, impulsiveness, and treatment response—can often be assessed quickly, however, and the clinical subscale by itself has some predictive validity for inpatient violence (McNiel et al., 2003). However, studies have also shown that this type of instrument may not be as useful as clinical symptoms in predicting institutional aggression (McDermott, Quanbeck, Busse, Yastro, & Scott, 2008), and this should be borne in mind if using this instrument to further a civil commitment evaluation.

Three Ratings of Involuntary Admissibility (TRIAD). In the 1980s, sociologist Steven Segal and colleagues described the performance and results of the TRIAD, an instrument designed to assess whether psychiatric emergency service (PES) clinicians used a shared, reliable professional standard in applying California's civil commitment criteria. The TRIAD has three checklists and 84 total items that are relevant to a clinician's assessment of suicide risk, risk of violence to others, and grave disability. The items can be combined into 146 patterns of behavior and circumstances. Each potential pattern, in turn, leads to assigning a severity score of 1 to 4 concerning dangerousness to self, dangerousness to others, and danger from disability. The TRIAD also has a fourth scale, the total admissibility score (Segal, Watson, & Nelson, 1986).

In a triad of articles (Segal, Watson, Goldfinger, & Averbuck, 1988a, 1988b, 1988c), Segal and colleagues found that decisions about hospitalization reflected a shared conception of dangerousness that could be behaviorally defined. They also found that patients rated as most dangerous were also those who were most severely ill, that perceived dangerousness was associated with severe symptoms (especially impulsiveness), and that these factors were clearly correlated with admission decisions. A major barrier to using the TRIAD for civil commitment evaluations, however, is that the instrument is not published or available anywhere (S. P. Segal, personal communication, November 20, 2008).

Brøset Violence Checklist. The Brøset Violence Checklist (BVC) (Almvik & Woods, 1999; Almvik, Woods, & Rasmussen, 2000) is designed to help hospital staff members assess risk of violent acts by psychiatric inpatients. The checklist consists of six traits—confused, irritable, boisterous, physically threatening, verbally threatening, and attacking objects—scored either present (1 point) or absent (0 point). The sum of item ratings indicates the level of violence risk.

In a study of ratings concerning 109 consecutively admitted patients, Almvik, Woods, and Rasmussen (2000) found that each BVC item was correlated with violent behavior; interrater reliability was good for individual items and the scale overall, and the ROC area was 0.82 + 0.04. Another study (Björkdahl, Olsson, & Palmstierna, 2006) showed that a score of 0 correctly identified almost all nonviolent patients, and a study of the BVC in psychogeriatric patients yielded a ROC area of 0.940 + 0.015 (Almvik, Woods, & Rasmussen, 2007).

The BVC has a limited empirical database, but given where (psychiatric units) and on whom (psychiatric inpatients) the BVC has been evaluated, this instrument may be relevant to persons subject to potential commitment. The BVC has the advantage of being quick to administer, easy to understand, and based on readily observable behavior. Note, however, that at least three BVC items (verbal threats, physical threats, and attacking objects) are "overt acts" that by themselves might justify civil commitment.

ADDITIONAL COMMENTS

Four other factors limit the use of the COVR™, HCR-20, TRIAD, BVC, and similar instruments in civil commitment evaluations:

- Most studies evaluating FAIs for violence risk have focused mainly on patients who had undergone treatment (that is, were already hospitalized) and (for the COVR™ and HCR-20) had been discharged to the community. The instruments' performance

5
chapter

might be different for persons possibly subject to civil commitment.

- Existing evidence suggests that judges, mental health professionals, and other populations do not agree on what probability of future violence justifies involuntary hospitalization. Monahan and Silver (2003) found that some probate judges thought a 1% risk was sufficient; others thought the odds of violence should be at least 3:1. In studies that examined attitudes about balancing the costs of false-positive and false-negative errors in predicting violence (Mossman & Hart, 1993; Mossman, 2006), subjects exhibited differences covering *five orders of magnitude*. Thus, even if assessment instruments are good at sorting levels of risk, applying their results to civil commitment determinations remains problematic.

- Available FAIs focus on violence toward other persons; they do not assess suicide risk or grave disability.

- As Table 2.2 shows, what jurisdictions mean by risk of harm to others varies considerably. The modal concern is risk of "serious" physical harm or injury, which arguably is the same as "substantial" physical harm (Kentucky's phrase). In several jurisdictions, however, any physical harm or injury would suffice; in others, the concern could include emotional injury (Hawaii) or any harm that is "substantial" (Alabama); in at least six states, any harm or danger appears sufficient.

- FAIs are normed or validated for detection of a specific type of behavior. In some jurisdictions, the fit between the definition of violence used to validate the FAI and the statutory specification of risk to others may fit closely enough to let the FAI findings be relevant to a legal determination of risk to others. But in some jurisdictions, statutes direct courts' attention to emotional harm, any "substantial" harm, or any harm at all. In these jurisdictions, FAIs may not provide relevant information about risk (Mossman et al., in press).

Given all these limitations, should results from structured or actuarial FAIs play any role in civil commitment decisions? The answer may differ depending on the context of the civil commitment, such as whether the respondent's legal status originates as a forensic one in which violence or public safety played a role in the original clinical issue (Mossman et al., in press; *Ecker v. Worcester State Hospital*, 2010). To the extent that the individual components of the FAIs are validated, individual items also may suggest specific areas of inquiry with demonstrated relationships toward violence. For example, it may be helpful for evaluators to point out and for trial courts to know that impulsiveness and severe symptoms are validated risk factors for violence. Establishing the presence of these factors in combination with recent overt actions or statements lends empirical support to testimony that respondents remain at significant risk of harming themselves or others. In the future, even courts in jurisdictions with "overt act" commitment requirements may favor testimony that adduces scientifically demonstrated risk factors to support the expert's contention that a respondent's mental illness is linked to the respondent's risk-generating behavior (Mossman et al., in press).

Medical Diagnostic Tests and Data

Civil commitment evaluations usually concern respondents who have undergone emergency hospitalization. Because admission procedures include a physical examination, "standard" laboratory tests, and other studies needed for medical diagnosis, it would be uncommon for an independent forensic evaluator to need additional medical or laboratory analyses to conduct the civil commitment evaluation. Occasionally, however, independent evaluators may identify tests that would be helpful but that were not done. (A common reason is that the patient refused to cooperate.) In those circumstances, the evaluator may speak with the respondent and the treating psychiatrist to see whether it is possible to arrange for desired laboratory testing.

The potential implications and relevance of nonpsychiatric medical illness to civil commitment are illustrated by the case of a hospitalized respondent who made grandiose claims about her wealth and paranoid comments about harassment by neighbors. Physical examination revealed breast lumps and advanced dental caries that were inflamed and required immediate antibiotic treatment, but the respondent became irritable and agitated when her treating psychiatrist asked her to get further assessment and medical intervention. At her civil commitment hearing, the judge ruled that the respondent met the criteria for involuntary hospitalization: her paranoia regarding medical providers prevented her from getting the care needed to avert further risk of grave disability.

Physical illnesses sometimes first manifest themselves as psychiatric problems (Knutsen & DuRand, 1991), so medical evaluation and laboratory tests can sometimes provide important clues about the source of a respondent's psychopathology. For example, changes in "vital signs" (pulse rate, blood pressure, and body temperature) may suggest early signs of alcohol withdrawal, and abnormal laboratory results (such as elevated liver function tests) may confirm that alcohol dependence is contributing to the clinical picture, even though patients minimize this aspect of their medical history (Spiegel, Dhadwal, & Gill, 2008). In geriatric populations, it is not uncommon to see physical conditions present as psychiatric behavioral problems (e.g., urinary tract infections, pneumonia, etc.). Tests of total protein, albumin, and prealbumin provide indications about nutritional status that are relevant information to deciding whether a respondent is at risk of harm to self through self-neglect of basic needs for food. Neuroimaging [via computed tomography (CT) or magnetic resonance imaging (MRI) scans] is not a standard hospital admission procedure, but psychiatrists use it with increasing frequency to look for causes of psychiatric symptoms.

Assuming that the respondent has permitted treating clinicians to perform a physical examination and indicated medical tests, the evaluator should peruse the results for diagnostic information relevant to an opinion regarding civil commitment. Evaluators who are not physicians may feel unqualified to perform this task, particularly when a respondent's caregivers have identified conditions that require extensive medical intervention. If this problem arises in an evaluation, possible solutions include consulting other portions of the medical record (e.g., those that list or describe treatment for medical disorders) for clarification, asking the respondent's treating physicians about what is going on and how it affects the respondent's psychiatric status or vice versa, or speaking with a psychiatrist colleague. If none of these options seems satisfactory, nonphysicians may withdraw from a particular assignment and recommend that a psychiatrist perform the evaluation.

INFO

Physical illnesses sometimes manifest themselves initially as psychiatric problems, so medical evaluation and laboratory tests may provide important clues about the source of a respondent's psychopathology.

Data Collection Forms

Clinicians and forensic evaluators often develop checklists and data collection tools to help them approach cases systematically and to make sure they remember to gather all the information they need. A sample information gathering tool appears in Figure 5.1.

5
chapter

Interpretation | 6

Having completed an interview, and having gathered data from records and collateral sources, the evaluator must decide whether the respondent seems to satisfy legal criteria for civil commitment. One way to summarize the decision-making process is by using a flow chart (see Figure 6.1) depicting a series of judgments and contingent steps that depend on those judgments.

Another way to interpret data is to think about the how the clinical facts established by an examination pertain to the jurisdiction's legal standard for commitment. Here, the questions to ask oneself include the following:

- How do I know that the respondent has a *substantial* mental disorder?

- Does that disorder cause *gross* impairment?

- How do I know that the respondent poses a risk to self or others due to that mental disorder?

Does the Respondent Have a Substantial Mental Disorder?

The first matter to decide is whether the respondent has the requisite "mental disorder" as defined in applicable statutes and case law. Addressing this question in the context of civil commitment requires approaching the diagnosis differently from the way treating clinicians typically do.

As a first step, the evaluator should delineate the *behavioral evidence* for the disorder. One way for an evaluator to do this is to ask, "What are the *observable behavioral manifestations* of the

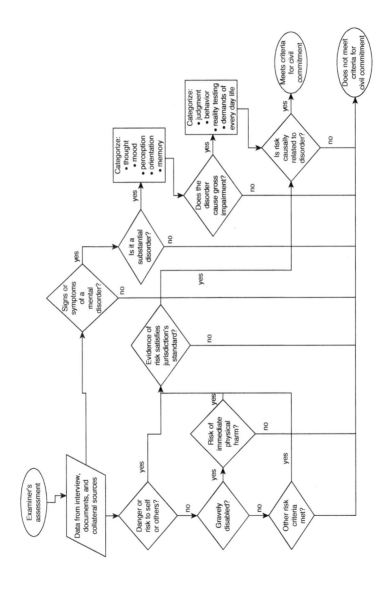

Figure 6.1 Judgments and Decisions toward Determining Commitment Opinions.

disorder?" and "*How* do I know that this respondent's thought, mood, perception, orientation, or memory are disordered?" Posing questions this way forces the evaluator to think beyond typical clinical conclusions and diagnoses—such as "this guy is really psychotic!" or "this woman is halluci-

BEST PRACTICE

Once you complete an interview and gather data from records and collateral sources, you must decide whether the respondent seems to satisfy the legal criteria for civil commitment.

nating and delusional" or even "this patient has schizophrenia"— and to enumerate the specific signs and symptoms that the evaluator or others have observed. Ultimately, the "consumer" of the evaluator's diagnostic formulation is a trial court, and (as we have seen in Chapter 2) trial courts usually care more about the gross manifestations of an illness than precise diagnostic classifications. During testimony, the court's questions about whether (for example) a respondent has a perceptual disorder will be better addressed by testimony that the respondent appeared to talk and respond to individuals who were not physically present than by a *conclusory statement* that the respondent was "psychotic."

A second step involves considering the *sources* of evidence for the mental disorder. Here, we ask the reader to recall earlier discussions in this volume regarding jurisdictions that permit no hearsay exception for civil commitment hearings, where testimony about mental illness must be based on the evaluator's personal contact with and observations of the respondent.

A third step involves considering the *reliability* of evidence for mental disorder. Evaluators should treat what some collateral informants tell them with polite skepticism. Conflicting narratives may make it difficult to sort out what may have actually happened or why it happened in a given situation, which could have a bearing on the civil commitment decision. For example, if a respondent with mental problems is alleged to have assaulted his father but the father has a history of becoming aggressive toward the respondent, it may be difficult for the evaluator to know whether the son's aggression stemmed from psychosis or a desire to defend himself. Collateral sources also may be biased, may embellish facts, or even fabricate stories to achieve some desired goal, such as getting the

6
chapter

BEST PRACTICE

The first matter you need to decide is whether the respondent has the requisite "mental disorder" as defined in statutes and case law. The following three steps can guide your decision:

- Delineate the *behavioral evidence* for the mental disorder.

- Consider the *sources* of evidence for the mental disorder.

- Consider the *reliability* of evidence for the mental disorder.

respondent committed or limiting the respondent's ability to retaliate later. Considering interpersonal contexts and the relationships between respondents and informants will help the evaluator decide how much (or how little) outside information to incorporate into the forensic opinion. Though the reliability and weight of testimony are ultimately for the court to decide, the evaluator also has a duty to evaluate information when forming an opinion to a reasonable degree of medical or scientific certainty.

Having critically considered the types, sources, and reliability of the behavioral evidence for the respondent's mental disorder, the evaluator is ready to formulate an opinion that will be relevant to the court. As noted previously, most jurisdictions' commitment statutes do not refer to official diagnostic classifications. Forensic evaluators usually do think about diagnostic categories, however, because they are also clinicians who have received training in making diagnoses and treating mental illnesses. They bring a clinical perspective to forensic questions and almost automatically think about data by applying their clinical insights. It therefore is natural for evaluators to wonder, "What diagnoses potential qualify as 'substantial disorders' for purposes of civil commitment?"

We agree with Cohen and colleagues that "any psychiatric diagnosis of a major mental disorder that is listed in Axis I of the American Psychiatric Association's diagnostic manual (*DSM-IV-TR*) would" *potentially* meet most statutes' definitions of a substantial disorder (Cohen, Bonnie, & Monahan, 2008, p. 4). So would some personality disorders (especially borderline personality disorder), some manifestations of substance use disorders (e.g., intoxication or withdrawal syndromes), and some manifestations of medical or neurological conditions (e.g., dementia) unless commitment for such conditions is specifically barred by statute.

Being able to place a respondent's mental condition within an official diagnostic scheme goes a long way toward showing that the condition is a "substantial disorder." In current usage, the word "substantial" often refers to size or amount (e.g., "a substantial gift"). But in older dictionaries, this usage appears *after* other definitions, including "real; actually existing" (World Publishing Company, 1951, p. 1699). Mid-twentieth-century dictionaries best reflect the concerns of legislatures when they drafted civil commitment statutes that include the phrase "substantial disorder." To courts hearing testimony, then, the fact that signs and symptoms meet the criteria for a recognized diagnosis helps prove that a respondent's condition is not just a collection of emotions, unusual opinions, or idiosyncratic attitudes—it is a genuine, real, actual, disorder.

INFO

Although many statutes do not refer to official diagnostic categories, being able to place a respondent's mental condition within an official diagnostic scheme goes a long way toward showing that the condition is a "substantial disorder."

Does the Substantial Disorder Cause Gross Impairment?

Whether *any* diagnosis actually justifies civil commitment depends on more than its appearance in a diagnostic manual. The disorder must also be severe enough that it significantly or "grossly" impairs performance of activities that reflect mental functioning. In a typical statutory formulation, these activities include "judgment, behavior, capacity to recognize reality, or ability to meet the ordinary demands of life" [Ohio Rev. Code § 5122.01(A)]. To help address this aspect of the forensic data interpretation, evaluators should ask themselves, "What did the respondent *do* to demonstrate gross impairment?"

6 chapter

INFO

Consider: "What did the respondent *do* to demonstrate gross impairment?"

Many people who undergo involuntary hospitalization have mood disorders. However, most cases of depression—though they may include persistent sadness, hopelessness, cognitive impairment, and thoughts about death—leave individuals capable of managing the tasks of everyday living, albeit with reduced efficiency. Anxiety disorders possibly account for a plurality of psychiatric disability, but rarely do these conditions grossly impair basic judgment, social behavior, daily coping, or reality testing. At some point during their lives, persons with schizophrenia usually *do* suffer gross impairments that justify hospitalization. Yet with currently available treatments, most individuals with schizophrenia are impaired enough to need hospitalization only a small portion of the time.

As was true for the decision about having a substantial disorder, the forensic evaluator should clarify specifically what *behavioral evidence* supports a contention that the disorder grossly impairs functioning and what the sources of this evidence are. To conclude that gross impairment is present, the evaluator should be able to adduce specific events that demonstrate the impairment. Examples include:

- standing naked outdoors in cold weather (evidence of severe problems with judgment);

- shouting insults at total strangers (a gross impairment in behavior);

- laughing aloud at imaginary voices (a gross problem in recognizing reality); and

- failing to eat for days when food was available (a severe impairment in a basic aspect of daily living).

Does the Respondent Pose a Risk?

Risk in This Legal Context

We noted previously that having a mental disorder is the quintessential predicate for civil commitment. Yet most treatment of mental disorders occurs in voluntary settings, and only a small percentage of persons with mental disorders get civilly committed. Persons usually are free to go without medical care, and it is quite permissible legally—and, sadly, quite common—for adults with mental disorders to ignore their problems, refuse to acknowledge their problems, and go untreated. Under current law, what creates an exception to these general rules is some risk-creating behavior that has brought the respondent to the attention of clinicians, law enforcement officials, and, ultimately, the courts that hear civil commitment petitions. Thus, the following are crucial questions in interpreting data from a civil commitment evaluation: "Does the respondent pose a risk?" and "Exactly what statement, action, or other evidence proves that the risk exists?"

INFO

Crucial questions in interpreting data from a civil commitment evaluation are:

- Does the respondent pose a risk?

- Exactly what statement, action, or other evidence proves that the risk exists?

Statutes define what counts as evidence of risk. Mental health professionals know that various forms of psychosis are "risk factors" for deteriorating functioning (Niendam, Jalbrzikowski, & Bearden, 2009) or aggression (Bobes, Fillat, & Arango, 2009), and that severe anxiety and global insomnia are "risk factors" for suicide (American Psychiatric Association, 2003). In many U.S. jurisdictions, however, civil commitment statutes or related case law explicitly requires some actual behavior—often termed an "overt act" [see, e.g., Minn. Stat. § 253B. 02(17); *In re J.P.* (1998)]—just as is required for conviction of a criminal offense (Mossman et al., in press). Depending on the jurisdiction, this may mean that results of statistically validated measures [e.g., the COVR™ (see Chapter 5)] will have limited relevance to a legal decision about whether civil commitment is justified. In jurisdictions (e.g., Massachusetts) where a recent overt act is not required but where a "substantial risk of serious harm" is deemed likely to occur if there is a "failure to hospitalize" (Mass. General Laws c. 123, §§ 7 and 8), courts may accept other types of historical or current evidence of that substantial risk, allowing the evaluator and judges some interpretive leeway.

The criteria for commitment based on grave disability often are less particular about actual behavior. Statutes usually require, however, that the risk of deterioration-related harm be manifested in specific vulnerabilities [e.g., "lack of capacity to protect himself from harm or to provide for his basic human needs," Va. Stat. § 37.2–817C(a)(2)] that are provable by clear and convincing evidence. For example, in some jurisdictions, evidence of abnormal laboratory studies, unattended medical care, and malnutrition may be needed to prove the grave disability. In jurisdictions with additional commitment criteria, the evaluator usually must establish that the respondent has engaged in certain *behaviors* related to those criteria to justify a conclusion that the particular risk is present.

Careful readers may find the preceding paragraphs odd, for two reasons. First, when thinking about whether a recent "overt act" presents a risk, we know that not all *past* aggressive behavior implies a high likelihood of *future* aggression. How, then, should an evaluator decide whether some example of a respondent's past behavior constitutes a risk? Second, it may seem odd to clinicians to use the word "risk"—a term that now suggests concern about a *future* adverse event—to refer to something the evidence for which is a person's *past* conduct or symptoms. We will address these questions in reverse order.

As readers of Wikipedia and recently published dictionaries can confirm, much current usage of the word "risk" relates to inherent uncertainty in financial decisions and investment returns. Here, risk is a quantity susceptible to measurement—"a *measurable* uncertainty" (Knight, 1921, p. 20)—that plays a key role in computations concerning potential outcomes of investment. Now, even in nonfinancial contexts [e.g., occupation safety, see Occupational Health and Safety Management Systems (OHSAS)18001, clause 3.21], notions of likelihood of adverse events combined with the severity of their impact have become core definitions of risk. But in older dictionaries (whose definitions, as we have earlier noted, are relevant to understanding words adopted in mid-twentieth-century statutes), a "risk" is a "hazard; danger; peril; exposure to harm; as, he, at the *risk* of his life, saved a drowning man" (World Publishing Company, 1951, p. 1470). Here, "risk" serves to designate a *currently present feature* of the environment. This is the type of "risk"—not a probability of future event, but something already manifest—that is created by an individual's threats or harmful behavior.

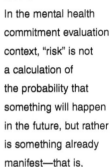

INFO

In the mental health commitment evaluation context, "risk" is not a calculation of the probability that something will happen in the future, but rather is something already manifest—that is, created by an individual's threats or harmful behavior.

This helps us see why many but not all recent violent acts represent current risks. Often, we can identify something about our environment that shows why a previous peril has dissipated—for example, if the rain has stopped, we no longer risk getting wet by going outdoors. A person who has recently acted aggressively has a heightened probability of acting aggressively again. But if something crucial to the person's recent violence has changed—for example, the thing that made the person angry has been resolved, or the person has taken medication that caused psychotic symptoms to diminish—we reasonably conclude that the risk has dissipated, too. On the other hand, if the attitudes, situation, and mental condition of a person who recently made threats or acted aggressively have changed little, then the person's recent behavior reflects a still-present risk of future harm to self or others.

Culture, Ethnicity, and Perception of Risk

Earlier, we identified some challenges encountered when evaluating individuals from other cultures or linguistic backgrounds. In interpreting data, forensic evaluators should be aware of potential biases toward perceiving ethnic minorities as more dangerous than whites, which may render these persons more likely to be involuntarily hospitalized (Hicks, 2004). Data also suggest that in forensic contexts, persons of ethnic or racial minorities are more likely to be admitted to environments of stricter security (Pinals, Packer, Fisher, & Roy, 2004), and that, for a variety of reasons, African Americans are more likely than whites to be subjects of involuntary outpatient commitment (Swanson et al., 2009). Thus, as Griffith (1998) has noted, an evaluator must consider cultural, racial, and related factors when formulating the opinion.

A thorough treatment of how to conduct culturally informed assessments lies beyond the scope of this volume, and we recommend that readers consult some of the many excellent available sources on this topic (e.g., Saldaña, 2001; Group for the Advancement of Psychiatry, 2002; Tseng, Matthews, & Elwyn, 2004; Bhugra & Bhui, 2007). We also refer readers to a short description of cultural considerations that we helped develop for evaluators of adjudicative competence, but that are in large part directly applicable to civil commitment evaluations, too (Mossman et al., 2007). As we noted there (p. S30):

[S]everal areas of knowledge can improve clinicians' efforts to work with persons from difference cultures. Adapted for the forensic context, these include:

- knowledge of the patient's culture, including history, traditions, values, and family systems;

- awareness of how experiencing racism and poverty may affect behavior, attitudes, and values;

- knowledge of how ethnically different evaluees may seek help and express mental distress;

- awareness of how language, speech patterns, and communication styles differ among cultural communities;

- recognition of how professional values may conflict with or accommodate the emotional and legal needs of evaluees from different cultures; and

- awareness of how community and institutional power relationships affect persons in different cultures.

Is the Risk Causally Related to the Mental Disorder?

INFO

Perceiving and articulating the connection between clinical findings and legal criteria are key features of forensic mental health practice.

Perceiving and articulating the connection between clinical findings and legal criteria are key features of forensic mental health practice. As we pointed out in Chapter 2, the only risks that are relevant to civil commitment hearings are risks that stem from respondents' statutorily defined mental disorder. When civil commitment hearings take place before thoughtful fact-finders, establishing a link (or establishing that there is no link) between mental disorder and risk is a crucial point of testimony.

Because the link is often obvious, the best way to explain our point is through hypothetical examples of respondents who pose a clear risk that is *not* related to their mental disorder:

- Since childhood, mobster Tony Soprano has experienced panic attacks during which he sometimes loses consciousness. Once, while he was grilling sausages, Mr. Soprano dropped a container of lighter fluid into the fire, causing an explosion. Mr. Soprano receives psychiatric care from Dr. Jennifer Melfi, who learns in today's session that Mr. Soprano intends to "dispose of" an FBI informant later in the day. Mr. Soprano (1) poses a risk of serious harm to others and (2) suffers from a mental condition (panic disorder) that (3) grossly impairs his behavior (loss of consciousness). But the risk to others does not stem from Mr. Soprano's mental condition, so he does not meet civil commitment criteria.

- Georg Friedrich Händel suffers from bipolar II disorder, and during his current 3-week hypomanic

6 chapter

episode, he has slept 2 hours a night while composing an entire oratorio. Even while hypomanic, Händel is normally a peaceful man (though he writes lots of sixteenth notes). But one evening, Händel gets drunk, starts bragging about his divinely inspired, superhuman compositional prowess, and threatens to kill Bach and Vivaldi, explaining, "Then I'll be the undisputedly greatest composer of the Baroque era!" Examination shows that threatening others is uncharacteristic for Händel: even when hypomanic, he usually just composes a lot and sleeps very little. Händel (1) poses a risk of harm to others and (2) has a mental disorder that (3) grossly impairs his behavior and judgment. The risk to Bach and Vivaldi probably stems from his intoxication, however, and once he sobers up, Händel does not meet commitment criteria.

- Jane Doe suffers from schizophrenia and has experienced hallucinations and delusions when symptomatic, believing radio signals have been sent through her dental implants as a sign that a radio personality loves her. Lately, though, she has taken antipsychotic medication and is symptom-free. Ms. Doe also smokes two packs of cigarettes a day and has a long record of criminal offenses, including robbery charges she incurred when she impulsively snatched things from stores; she also steals from others (sometimes knocking them down and hurting them in the process) to get money for cigarettes. Ms. Doe is out of cigarettes and has no money, and at today's appointment, she tells her therapist that she plans to steal purses from elderly women until she finds one that contains some cigarettes. Ms. Doe (1) poses a risk of harm to elderly women she may encounter, and she (2) has a serious mental illness that (3) has repeatedly impaired her ability to recognize reality. But the risk to elderly women does not stem from Ms. Doe's schizophrenia: the risk is just an aspect of Ms. Doe's criminality. Even if Ms. Doe has nicotine dependence and antisocial personality *disorder*, these conditions do not qualify as a mental illness for purposes of commitment because they are *not* conditions that grossly impair those mental capacities (i.e., thought, mood, perception, orientation, or memory) that are relevant to civil commitment.

What Is the Least Restrictive Available Setting for Treatment?

As we noted in Chapter 1, virtually all U.S. jurisdictions embrace the doctrine of placement in the "least restrictive" treatment setting that is available. No matter what the legal setting for testimony, it is helpful to consider decisions about the locus for *treatment or placement* (and the relevant evidence supporting those decisions) separately from data about mental illness and risk. To accomplish this, forensic evaluators should ask themselves these types of questions as they interpret available data:

- "Has the option for voluntary inpatient treatment been adequately explored?"
- "Would outpatient treatment work now?"
- "Has outpatient treatment ever been attempted? If so, did it work? Why, or why not?"

The following example illustrates the application of the "least restrictive" principle to a hypothetical case.

6
chapter

Mr. A

CASE FACTS AND LEGAL STANDARD
Mr. A, a man who suffered from schizophrenia, had been homeless for 5 months. He often talked to himself.

Mr. A (continued)

He believed he worked for the FBI and occasionally would go to the local FBI office to report for duty. Twice in the last year, FBI staff had called the police to have Mr. A removed, and he was charged with trespassing and disorderly conduct.

An outreach team found Mr. A under a bridge in the winter. He was inadequately clothed and was shouting disorganized phrases about the FBI. He told the outreach workers he had not eaten in 10 days as part of his latest covert FBI assignment. Concerned, the staff arranged for an emergency involuntary inpatient evaluation. During a 4-day hospital stay, Mr. A took antipsychotic medication and appeared less disorganized. He ate well, agreed to go to the soup kitchen if released, and talked less about the FBI. He asked to leave the hospital after the 4 days but agreed to wait in a local respite program that provided a place to sleep and staff support while other services could be arranged.

In the locale where Mr. A lives, a person meets the criteria for inpatient commitment if "failure to hospitalize would create a likelihood of serious harm by reason of mental illness." Likelihood of serious harm may includes suicide, violence toward others, or a "very substantial risk of physical impairment or injury to the person himself as manifested by evidence that such person's judgment is so affected that he is unable to protect himself in the community and that reasonable provision for his protection is not available in the community" (see, e.g., Massachusetts General Laws, c. 123, §§. 1 and 7). Does Mr. A meet these criteria for further involuntary hospitalization?

ANALYSIS

In this case example, Mr. A does not pose much risk of harm by suicide or violence—eligibility for continued involuntary hospitalization hinges on whether he can manage safely in the community. Before the emergency hospitalization, he had not eaten in 10 days for delusional reasons, which raises concerns about physical deterioration. He has eaten for just 4 days, and it is not clear

Mr. A (continued)

whether or how long he would continue eating if left to his own self-care in the community.

Thinking about the questions "Has the option for voluntary inpatient treatment been adequately explored?" and "Would outpatient treatment work now?" should lead an evaluator to consider (1) whether Mr. A might

BEST PRACTICE
As an evaluator, you should be familiar with the array of services in the community and their basic offerings. Questions related to these services may come up in testimony about whether less restrictive settings had been considered.

agree to continuing hospitalization on a *voluntary* status, and (2) whether he might now participate in some available outpatient program. In this case, Mr. A is taking appropriate medication and appears willing to wait at the hospital (i.e., stay there voluntarily) before going to a local respite program. The evaluator is familiar with the local respite program and knows that staff members there can monitor Mr. A's medication, nourishment, and general well-being. Under the circumstances, the evaluator may well conclude that an alternative less restrictive that hospitalization is available, and that Mr. A does not meet commitment criteria.

COMMENT

At times, it may be difficult to delineate what alternative placements are available to the individual respondent, so it helps if an evaluator is familiar with the array of services available in the community and their basic offerings. For example, if a patient is to return to "supported housing," does this mean that someone will check on the patient daily? Will there be medication drop offs and some form of medication monitoring? Will someone assist the patient with getting to appointments and day services? The answers to these questions will affect the evaluator's beliefs about whether a particular alternative is a realistic and appropriate alternative to involuntary civil commitment. In some cases, an evaluator may be in a position to work with the respondent or the lawyer to negotiate options for the respondent that would avoid a commitment.

6
chapter

Some Tough Cases

Many civil commitment cases are very straightforward, their conclusions are obvious, and court hearings do little beyond providing judicial oversight to ensure that the respondents' rights have been respected. Here, we examine some cases in which the respondents' needs for treatment are obvious, but their eligibility for commitment is ambiguous. The cases illustrate how the principles of interpretation described above apply.

Mr. B (Based on *In re Renz*, 2008)

CASE FACTS AND LEGAL STANDARD

Mr. B, who is HIV-positive, was diagnosed with schizophrenia several years ago. At various times, he has denied having HIV and said he had cured himself. He has taken prescribed medication for HIV only intermittently. He has also reported that after telling some sexual partners about his infection, they have not cared whether he used protection. Within the past year, Mr. B has contracted and received treatment for chlamydia, gonorrhea, and syphilis, which suggests he was not using protection during intercourse. When his treating psychiatrist tried to educate him about his HIV infection, Mr. B appeared not to understand the infection or the need for taking HIV medication.

In this jurisdiction, a commitment as "mentally ill and dangerous" [see Minn. Stat. § 253B. 02(17)] requires clear and convincing evidence that because of a mental illness the respondent:

(1) poses a clear danger to others demonstrated by an overt act causing, or attempting to cause, serious physical harm to another; and

(2) has a substantial likelihood of engaging in actions that could do serious physical harm to another person.

Is Mr. B "mentally ill and dangerous" as defined by the statute?

Mr. B (Based on *In re Renz*, 2008) (continued)

ANALYSIS
We first ask whether Mr. B poses a risk under the statute, that is, whether he has (1) caused or tried to cause harm to others and (2) is likely to do things that could cause others serious physical harm. No evidence shows that Mr. B has actually infected or tried to infect anyone with a sexually transmitted disease, so Mr. B may not meet criterion (1), unless the court would interpret (1) as including reckless actions, that is, actions done intentionally and that create a risk. Even if transmitting chlamydia, gonorrhea, or syphilis is not doing "serious physical harm" to someone, transmitting HIV certainly is. The per-contact probability of transmitting HIV during unprotected sex is below 1% (Wawer et al., 2005; Vittinghoff, Douglas, Judson, McKirnan, MacQueen, & Buchbinder, 1999), but any instance of unprotected sex *could* transmit HIV. Presumably, having unprotected sex is an "overt" act within the meaning of the statute, even if the act is done in private. Mr. B has had unprotected sex before, and given his denial of his HIV status and his behavior-justifying statements, he seems unlikely to change this pattern. So he poses a risk as defined under criterion (2). Assuming the diagnosis of schizophrenia is correct, Mr. B is also mentally ill.

Is mental illness the reason Mr. B poses a risk? Though some persons with schizophrenia deny having a mental illness, denial of mental illness is not a diagnostic criterion for schizophrenia. Denial occurs often enough, however, to justify a view that denial and behavior that stems from that denial are "results" or manifestations of the mental illness. But Mr. B's risk stems from not using protection during sex and from denying that he has HIV. Many HIV-positive persons who do not have schizophrenia have unprotected intercourse, take their anti-HIV medication irregularly, and deny the significance of their illness. Without some clearer link between Mr. B's schizophrenia and his sex practices, we cannot attribute those practices to his mental illness.

6
chapter

Mr. B (Based on *In re Renz*, 2008) (continued)

COMMENT
In contrast to our just-outlined reasoning, Mr. B's treating doctor testified that Mr. B's schizophrenia had caused him not to understand his HIV infection and how he could transmit the infection to others. The trial court found that Mr. B was "mentally ill and dangerous" under the statute, and an appeals court confirmed this. Concerning criterion (1), the appeals court cited case law stating that a requisite overt act can occur irrespective of the actor's intent or the outcome of the act: "Just as a mentally ill person who fires a shotgun at another or drives a vehicle into a crowd of people at 100 m.p.h. commits an overt act causing or attempting to cause serious physical harm to another, so too does a mentally ill person with HIV who engages in unprotected sexual activity" (*In re Renz*, p. 5).

Mr. C (Based on *In re Kottke*, 1988)

CASE FACTS AND LEGAL STANDARD
Three weeks ago, an office building security guard saw Mr. C dancing wildly in the foyer. When the guard asked Mr. C to leave, Mr. C announced that he owned the building and punched the guard in the face (leaving red knuckle marks) as the guard escorted him outdoors. Twelve days later, Mr. C uttered racial slurs to a man outside a downtown store. When another man challenged Mr. C to fight, Mr. C ran off, but a few moments later Mr. C struck the man from behind and knocked him to the ground. Police later arrested Mr. C.

After he was in jail for 10 days, Mr. C underwent an evaluation for civil commitment. During the examination, Mr. C voiced paranoid thoughts and had disorganized speech, but he also was polite and mild-mannered. While confined, Mr. C had been very cooperative, had taken the medication prescribed for him, and had even requested medication when he needed it.

Mr. C (Based on *In re Kottke,* 1988) (continued)

The jurisdiction uses the same test for commitment of someone who is "mentally ill and dangerous" as applied in Mr. B's case above. Is Mr. C "mentally ill and dangerous" as defined by the statute?

ANALYSIS

Mr. C's recent actions show that he posed a risk of harm to others before his arrest. The examination suggests, however, that 10 days of treatment while jailed lowered this risk significantly; the risk may no longer be "substantial." Also, Mr. C's violent behavior followed actions by other persons that were understandable but provocative. One could reasonably argue that others' actions, not Mr. C's illness, caused the violent incidents—though Mr. C's responses reflect poor judgment that might be a sign of a mental illness.

Recall (from Chapter 1 discussing *Vitek*) that courts view involuntary psychiatric hospitalization as more stigmatizing and restrictive than mere incarceration. Even if one thought that Mr. C was "mentally ill and dangerous," the success of his current voluntary treatment suggests that he may not need a more "restrictive" setting at this time.

COMMENT

At the hearing, a court-appointed evaluator testified that Mr. C did not meet the statutory standard for dangerousness. The judge disagreed, however, reasoning that Mr. C's "annoying public behavior," "insulting comments," "two unprovoked assaults," and continuing delusional beliefs created a substantial risk of similar future acts. An appeals court reversed and expunged the "dangerous" labeling on the grounds that Mr. C's behavior, "intolerable as it was, neither inflicted nor was intended to inflict the serious physical harm of the type contemplated by the statute."

Ms. D (Based on *In re E.S.*, 2005)

CASE FACTS AND LEGAL STANDARD

Several weeks before hospitalization, Ms. D had stopped taking her medication. Subsequently, Ms. D began walking naked outdoors. She accused her daughters of using "supernatural powers" to play inside her genitalia. She rubbed olive oil on her neighbors' doors "to keep demons inside" and accused her neighbors of "doing witchcraft" to harm her. While walking on a bike trail, Ms. D hit a man's dog on the head with a stick, saying the animal was "possessed with demons." She also took her 2-year-old grandson on a trip out of town without telling his parents, though she returned the boy in good health. Ms. D was arrested for throwing plates at passing cars while she was naked and covered in cooking grease, and soon thereafter underwent emergency hospitalization.

At her commitment hearing, the treating psychiatrist testified that Ms. D was "psychotic" upon admission and that she appeared "very agitated and aggressive." Once Ms. D started taking her regular antipsychotic medication again, however, she began "doing much better." The psychiatrist also testified that Ms. D had a history of noncompliance with medication. Ms. D testified that she was taking her medication, that grease was an inexpensive moisturizer, and that when she took her grandson, she had left his parents a message. Concerning the dog incident, Ms. D said she "had started carrying a stick just to warn dogs off . . . I thought they were demons. I didn't want to get bit by a dog."

Under the statute [see Iowa Code § 229.1(15)], civil commitment may occur only if clear and convincing evidence shows that the respondent has a mental illness, cannot make responsible decisions about treatment, and is likely:

(1) to physically injure herself or others if left
    untreated, or

Ms. D (Based on *In re E.S.*, 2005) (continued)

(2) to inflict serious emotional injury on others if left untreated, or

(3) to suffer physical harm because she cannot satisfy her needs for food, clothing, medical care, or shelter.

To prove (1), the jurisdiction requires an "overt act," i.e., a past aggressive act or threat that makes probable the commission of an act that would likely cause someone physical injury. Does Ms. D meet commitment criteria?

ANALYSIS

Nothing in the vignette suggests that Ms. D cannot meet her needs for food, clothing, or shelter. Her past overt acts include striking a dog and throwing plates at cars, but no injurious behavior or threats to harm herself or other persons. She did fail, however, to meet her medical needs when she did not obtain psychiatric care on her own, and she has risked such failure in the future in virtue of her history of not taking prescribed psychotropic medication. In taking her grandson without his parents' permission, Ms. D showed the potential to cause serious emotional injury, and her other behavior, if it continued, might frighten or traumatize someone. Ms. D appears, therefore, to meet the jurisdiction's definition of risk to inflict serious emotional injury. She also exhibits signs of mental illness. Her standing outside naked reflects poor judgment that could lead to harm to herself by virtue of being victimized. Thus, this action may satisfy the grave disability standard in some jurisdictions. The vignette does not give us definitive evidence about her capacity to make responsible decisions about treatment. Her current acceptance of medication suggests that she can make responsible decisions, but her past behavior (including the history of noncompliance) raises doubts about this.

6
chapter

Ms. D (Based on *In re E.S.*, 2005) (continued)

COMMENT

The trial court found that Ms. D met the statutory criteria for commitment. An appeals court affirmed, commenting that "impulsively taking a 2-year-old child out of state without parental permission, striking a dog with a stick, and throwing plates at passing cars" were "overt acts" showing that Ms. D would "pose a physical danger to herself or others if allowed to remain at liberty without treatment."

Ms. E

CASE FACTS AND LEGAL STANDARD

For many years, Ms. E believed that Martin Luther King's "I Have a Dream" speech formulated new constitutional principles that were binding on U.S. courts. She became inspired to communicate this important revelation to judges in Gevalt County, Ohio, and she called their offices repeatedly to explain her insights and to insist that courts follow the new principles. Eventually, the calls became so repetitive and disruptive that authorities charged her with harassment, a criminal misdemeanor. She was found incompetent to stand trial, but she refused medication (for what psychiatrists concluded was a delusional disorder) and was not restored to competence to stand trial.

The criminal court then referred Ms. E's case to probate court for possible civil commitment. Ms. E had never threatened or tried to harm herself or anyone else; she ate regularly and cared for herself. During the examination, she spoke rapidly as she disjointedly explained her views. She said, however, "I've learned my lesson" about telephoning judges; henceforth, she would spread her message through letter-writing campaigns and the local chapter of the NAACP.

Ms. E (continued)

In Ohio [see Ohio Revised Code §5122.01(B)], civil commitment requires a showing that a substantial mental disorder has caused a person to act in ways indicating at least one of the following:

(1) substantial risk of harm to others;

(2) substantial risk of harm to self;

(3) substantial risk of "serious physical impairment or injury" from self-neglect; or

(4) the person would benefit from treatment and needs such treatment in virtue of behavior "that creates a grave and imminent risk to substantial rights of others or the person."

Does Ms. E meet any of these criteria?

ANALYSIS

Ms. E has done nothing to suggest she would do harm to herself or others or incur serious physical impairment by neglecting her basic needs. Treatment is less likely to bring about remission of a longstanding delusional disorder than might be expected with an acute psychosis (Manschreck & Khan, 2006), but medication and psychotherapy probably would still help Ms. E. Her behavior has been annoying enough to generate criminal charges, and the delusions that led to this behavior remain unchecked. The question of whether making repeated, annoying telephone calls constitutes "a grave and imminent risk to substantial rights of others" ultimately calls for a legal decision rather than the opinion of a mental health professional, though the mental health professional evaluating Ms. E may need to choose whether to bring the case forward for a commitment proceeding.

COMMENT

The facts in the case of "Ms. E" come from a real case, though the authors altered contents and identifying information to

6
chapter

Ms. E (continued)

preserve the original respondent's confidentiality. In the actual case, the judge decided that making annoying phone calls—though potentially a criminal offense—did not violate another person's "substantial right." With the case dismissed, the respondent was released.

In looking at these examples, we see that each case requires close analysis of the facts and circumstances of each respondent's situation. After examining all available data, the evaluator must make interpretations based on the jurisdictional legal definition of commitment, the availability of less restrictive options, and local applications of the law in various settings. In most cases, determining whether an individual would meet the commitment criteria will be more straightforward than these examples. But ambiguous fact situations are common, and when these occur, clinicians should not be surprised if judicial determinations differ from what a purely clinical point of view might dictate is best for patients' care. A sound understanding of commitment criteria and a sensitivity to each case's nuances will help evaluators perform assessments and offer opinions that aid courts, even if courts' rulings conflict with evaluators' opinions.

Report Writing and Testimony | 7

For most types of forensic assessments, independent evaluators prepare detailed reports but rarely get called to testify at hearings or trials. For civil commitment assessments, however, the reverse is true: evaluators usually do not prepare formal reports, but they can count on going to court to testify. In this chapter, we describe elements of good report writing in those rare instances that require it and then offer recommendations for providing testimony. We begin with some comments about preparation of the document that legally initiates civil commitment procedures: the affidavit or petition for commitment.

Affidavit/Petition

From a clinical standpoint, illness creates the need for treatment. But if a person will not accept needed care, a written affidavit (or "petition" in some locales) is the legal mechanism for triggering civil commitment proceedings. The affidavit should state the rationale for the commitment in succinct terms, because it is the first step in invoking an appropriate court's power to impose a form of treatment. In this context, "treatment" typically refers to psychiatric hospitalization, though as Chapter 3 explains, outpatient civil commitment is another possible outcome.

INFO

For most types of forensic assessments, independent evaluators prepare detailed reports and rarely are called to testify. For civil commitment assessments, however, the reverse is true: *evaluators usually do not prepare formal reports, but they often appear in court to testify.*

Affidavits are legal documents, and dealing with legal documents is every attorney's specialty. Many basic mental health concepts (e.g., the differences between psychologists and psychiatrists) are hard for attorneys to keep straight, but attorneys quickly spot inadequacies in the legal paperwork required in civil commitment cases. When inadequacies in affidavits are identified, courts may *have to* dismiss commitment cases even when the clinical justification for imposing treatment is more than ample. The reason is that legally, an improper affidavit fails to invoke the trial court's jurisdiction.

Independent experts do not file the paperwork that initiates commitment proceedings. In most locales, treating clinicians provide "expert" testimony after having previously completed affidavits concerning patients who, based on the clinicians' assessment, need hospitalization. This means that hospital-based clinicians and other professionals who work in settings in which initiation of commitment is a commonly faced task (e.g., community mental health centers) should be familiar with the legal requirements for properly completing affidavits or petitions and the legal purposes that these documents satisfy.

Jurisdictions differ in their requirements about how and when affidavits or petitions must be completed. Yet some general considerations apply to most situations in which U.S. clinicians find themselves:

Timeliness

As we noted earlier, jurisdictions' statutes and court rules set out how long clinicians have to file affidavits when a patient undergoes emergency hospitalization. If affidavits do not meet the legal requirements for timeliness of filing, they are invalid. In some jurisdictions, an affidavit or petition for emergency detention is completed to initiate holding a patient for an emergency hospitalization or a brief evaluation; a second document filed during this brief holding period will trigger a court hearing on the commitment matter. Whenever a patient needs hospitalization, poses significant risk if released, and cannot or will not sign in voluntarily, the treating clinician needs to know the deadline for submitting the affidavit to the court and what submission formats (e.g., by fax) local courts will accept.

Risk Categories

Typically, affidavits or petitions must contain a specific allegation concerning a specific, statutorily permitted risk—e.g., risk of harming self, risk of harming others, risk of physical injury from grave disability—upon which the jurisdiction of the court is based. Many jurisdictions have special colored forms for each stage of the involuntary holding process (with informal names such as "pink slips" or "green sheets") with a checkbox section that directs clinicians to choose the appropriate risk category. Depending on the stage of the process (e.g., emergency detention papers or petitions that will lead to a legal or administrative hearing to commit an individual), sections of these forms require varying levels of detail about the factors that justify the commitment.

Required Facts

Finally, the affidavit or petition for commitment must allege *facts* sufficient to show probable cause (legal jargon meaning "a legitimate reason") to believe that the person described is potentially subject to hospitalization by court order. Note our emphasis on the word "facts," which we use here in its legal sense. From a court's standpoint, a diagnosis ("schizophrenia") or symptom description ("hallucinations") is an *opinion* reached by experts based on facts. Facts are specific actions, incidents, or events that persons (lay individuals and clinicians alike) can observe. Conclusory diagnostic statements do not satisfy the requirements of courts or others who review such documents because the writer's status as an expert has not been legally established. The affidavit therefore must set forth facts that can form the basis for finding probable cause that an individual may be mentally ill and in need of court-ordered hospitalization. To give a concrete example, it is better to write that a patient "states she is 'Queen of the United States' and insists on being called 'Your Majesty'"— actual statements and behavior—than the conclusion that the patient "is grandiose and delusional."

A recent case (*Mitterbach v. Cuyahogo County Probate Court*, 2007) provides an example of an affidavit that was ultimately judged insufficient. After designating the categories of risk posed, the doctor wrote that his patient

> has extensive history of psychiatric illness. She is [illegible word] delusional. Speech is rambling and speech is disorganized as well. Pt has been [illegible word] non-compliant with meds. Needs [illegible word] [illegible word] treatment as [illegible word].

An appeals court found this affidavit invalid because it did not contain facts that would substantiate (1) the extensive history of psychiatric illness, (2) how the patient was noncompliant with medications or whether anyone had prescribed medications for her, (3) what her delusions were, (4) any substantial risk of serious physical impairment, or (5) that the patient could not provide for her basic physical needs.

Mitterbach makes another implicit point about affidavits that initiate involuntary holds, which are often handwritten: documents that contain sound, appropriate, factual statements are useless if their recipients cannot read them. When completing critical legal documents (especially those that must be read after fax transmission), writers should take time to write legibly. Typed petitions (which are typically prepared to continue a commitment after an initial period of detention) have the advantage of legibility. Many courts now accept computerized affidavits.

BEST PRACTICE
When completing critical legal documents, write legibly. Typed or computer-generated petitions usually are readable after faxing.

The Report

Because of time constraints, civil commitment proceedings rarely involve the preparation of a detailed, formal forensic report, even for cases in which independent (nontreating) evaluators undertake assessments. In most jurisdictions, the affidavit mentioned above is the only written "report" filed prior to the hearing on civil commitment. When reports are requested, they can follow general forensic report writing guidelines (see, e.g. Pinals, Glancy, & Lee, 2011) and the principles articulated later in this chapter. In general, however, mental health professionals who are retained as independent evaluators should not generate written reports unless requested to do so by the retaining party.

Because courts usually make involuntary hospitalization decisions based on oral testimony, there are no national standards for reports in civil commitment cases. Some jurisdictions permit or accept written documents prepared by clinicians in lieu of in-person testimony, largely as a time- or money-saving measure. These courts sometimes provide guidelines, specific formats, or fill-in forms for submitting such information. Clinicians should complete these documents legibly, guided by the recommendations we make above concerning preparation of affidavits (e.g., including the respondent's concrete statements

BEWARE
Mental health civil commitment proceedings rarely involve preparation of a detailed, formal forensic report. If you are retained as an independent evaluator, do not generate a written report unless requested to do so by the retaining party.

Table 7.1 | Sample Elements of a Civil Commitment Report

---

1. Identifying information

    a. Information relevant to the patient and his or her circumstances
    b. Information related to the evaluator, the retaining party, and the reason for the evaluation

2. Warning of the limits of confidentiality and informed consent to the evaluation

3. Basic historical background information

    a. Social/Developmental history
    b. Educational history
    c. Relationship history
    d. Work history
    e. Psychiatric history
    f. Substance use history
    g. Criminal and violence history

4. Current mental status examination

5. Hospital course

6. Opinions

    a. Presence of mental illness
    b. Linkage of mental illness to commitment criteria

---

and behavior as evidence of mental illness or dangerousness). For cases in which a report is requested and the court provides no specific guideline, the outline suggested in Table 7.1 provides one way of deciding what material to include and a format for organizing information.

Dilemmas of Construction and Inclusion
POTENTIALLY INCRIMINATING INFORMATION

In many civil commitment cases, the crucial clinical data showing that a respondent poses a risk to others would also represent evidence of a crime (e.g., an assault) if introduced at a criminal trial. Some jurisdictions have statutory provisions that prohibit information introduced at a civil commitment hearing from being used for purposes of a subsequent criminal prosecution [e.g., Rev. Code Wash. § 71.05.390(19)] or that make the contents of a commitment hearing private and confidential, which may have the same practical effect. Such protections may not exist in all jurisdictions, however. Knowing local practices and the legal issues related to these circumstances can help evaluators decide what information to include in reports.

In situations in which criminal charges have already been filed but not adjudicated, evaluators preparing commitment reports to be used in court should usually refer to acts in question as "alleged" (e.g., "Mr. Smith's alleged assault on a bystander") to avoid making the implicit presumption that the respondent is guilty of a criminal offense. Similarly, evaluators' opinions that incorporate the behavior into the risk analysis might use phrasing that is not incriminating, e.g., "if the facts occurred as alleged, then the respondent's behavior and related delusions of [examples] imply an imminent risk of harm to self or others if the respondent were released." Evaluators also need to think about how much information they should include in a report if a respondent's action has given or may give rise to criminal charges. We illustrate these problems and possible solutions in the following examples.

- **Case Example A:** Ms. A and a friend entered a suicide pact together at Ms. A's home. The friend killed herself, but Ms. A, who had overdosed, was found by a third friend who called police. After getting treatment elsewhere for the overdose, Ms. A came to the psychiatric hospital, where her caregivers learned that the police might charge Ms. A with homicide of her friend. Ms. A's doctor thought she remained at high risk to hurt herself and needed commitment, and an independent evaluator agreed. But both clinicians wondered whether details of the Ms. A's suicide attempt and the circumstances of her friend's death, which might include incriminating information, should appear in the documents submitted to the court and in the medical record.

- **Case Example B**: Mr. B heard voices telling him to fondle his 10-year-old niece, and he delusionally believed that his niece was married to him and was pregnant with his child. A relative called the police, and a child abuse investigation determined that Mr. B had fondled the niece several times. At the hospital, Mr. B (who was grossly psychotic) spoke about what occurred with his niece to staff members, who documented this information in the medical record. Hospital staff members learned that the district attorney planned to file charges against Mr. B for indecent assault and battery on a minor. In his psychotic state, Mr. B could not appreciate or understand what the evaluator told him about limits of confidentiality and the potential for in-court exposure of information he revealed. The evaluator wondered whether the report should include details of the sexual acts, which were the primary grounds for justifying a civil commitment based on risk of harm to others.

DISCUSSION OF CASE EXAMPLES

In both these situations, multiple factors affect decisions about what to include in the court report, and decisions about what to put in reports may differ from what a treatment provider should include in a medical record. In Case A, the fact that authorities had not yet charged the patient might be one factor. Understanding the potential uses of the report would be another. The treatment provider in Case A included the information about the suicide pact and the allegations of homicide in the medical record progress note because the data were directly relevant to decisions affecting treatment, such as the need for therapy and decisions related to management and privilege levels in the hospital. The treatment provider also recognized that the data were relevant to the commitment standard and that she may be asked about it at her patient's commitment hearing. The treatment provider understood that the patient's statements would likely be privileged; they had been uttered in the context of a psychotherapist–patient relationship and were in a confidential medical record, though medical records were exempt from this protection if they were needed for civil commitment proceedings. If criminal charges were filed and the prosecutor attempted to use the report as evidence against Ms. A, a criminal defense attorney might invoke the concept of privilege on the defendant's behalf, which would potentially allow for redaction of incriminating information from the medical record in subsequent proceedings.

An independent forensic evaluator of Ms. A who is deciding what to include in a civil commitment report that is going to the court or to the retaining attorney could simply decide not to worry about these issues, because the primary task is to address whether the person meets civil commitment criteria. The forensic evaluator could also reasonably believe that it would be the retaining party's responsibility to redact a report or seek to have information excluded if an attempt was made to use if for other purposes besides commitment. An alternative approach involves the following reasoning: because no criminal charge had yet been filed, to require an evaluator to write a report that anticipates all possible outcomes would be unreasonable. The evaluator recognized that a defense attorney in any subsequent criminal proceeding could seek redaction of information that was gathered for different purposes. From the civil commitment evaluator's standpoint, however, omitting the information would mislead the court—a clear failure to fulfill a moral obligation. Furthermore, not including full information would be a disservice to the respondent, who would have been placed at greater risk of release (and subsequent suicide).

Considering whether a respondent has the capacity to waive privilege may be another factor to consider in deciding what to write in a report. In Case B, criminal charges had already been filed. In situations in which respondents lack the capacity to understand that information might be self-incriminating, evaluators might consult with the hospital attorney or the retaining attorney to review observations about the respondent's capacity to make such decisions. This may help the evaluator develop some sense of how or whether the information might ultimately be used in a criminal proceeding. (Note that a respondent's attorney might have a different view than the hospital's attorney—a respondent's attorney would generally not want information related to risk to be included in written reports.) Including incriminating details in a report ultimately may be necessary and appropriate, however, either to meet a treatment provider's obligation to conduct and document a clinical risk assessment, or to fulfill an independent evaluator's obligation to document factors specifically relevant to civil commitment.

PRIVACY AND CONFIDENTIALITY

Even when future criminal charges appear unlikely, treating clinicians and independent evaluators, just like other forensic evaluators, should be thoughtful about what information they include in reports, though not so guarded that necessary information does not get included. A written report should describe a respondent's present condition and recent events in the respondent's life to the extent that such information is needed to provide an accurate portrayal of the respondent and to support the conclusion about eligibility for commitment. Reports should omit sensitive or personal material not directly relevant to the specific instance of proposed commitment, however. This will mean that in many cases, some categories in Table 7.1 will not be included or will be completed sparsely. If, for example, a respondent has not authorized the release of information about prior psychiatric treatment, past psychiatric history might be limited or not appear at all.

In many cases, respondents, if asked, would not grant permission for the use or release of *any* information about their current clinical condition. A court order authorizing the evaluation and access to necessary materials (e.g., the respondent's medical chart) provides an independent evaluator with justification for both viewing those materials and presenting appropriate information to the court, including "protected health information" (PHI) as defined under the Health Insurance Portability and Accountability Act of 1996 [HIPAA; see 45 C.F.R. § 164.512(e)].

BEST PRACTICE
Be thoughtful but not overly guarded about what information you include in reports. Include what is needed for the civil commitment report and without being misleading, leave out information that is extraneous.

In some states, statutes provide explicit permission or requirements concerning sharing clinical information about respondents [see, e.g., Va. Code § 32.1–127.1:03(D)(12–13); Rev. Code Wash. § 71.05.390(17)(c)], and such laws constitute legitimate bases for releasing PHI under HIPAA [see 45 C.F.R. § 164.512(a)].

Forensic reports typically have fewer privacy protections than do medical records, in part because hearings are public in some jurisdictions and because reports are distributed to several persons and are quoted in court. Out of respect for a respondent's privacy, an evaluator might use nonspecific language in some parts of a forensic report that nonetheless conveys the significance of the respondent's actions or statements. For example, if it were necessary to refer to past sexual behavior, an evaluator might write that "the respondent's behavior reflected his unconventional sexual practices" rather than "the respondent has had several sexual encounters with trash cans and parking meters." Again, however, the clinician should keep in mind that vague or conclusory statements in reports may not satisfy attorneys' or the court's need for specific information. Therefore, the clinician must weigh carefully whether respect for the individual's privacy might obfuscate the data that the court would need to make a commitment determination. For Case B above, the evaluator might write that "the respondent reported engaging in sexual behavior with his niece that reflected his delusion that they were married," which identifies the risk behavior sufficiently without describing in detail what the respondent reported having done. If needed, further details might be verbalized during testimony to make the risk issues clear to the court.

Preparing a report often involves balancing competing values: the desire for thorough documentation of data supporting opinions, the need to avoid unduly prejudicial descriptions in forensic reports (e.g., language that may be derogatory, unbalanced, or overly emotional in tone), and the virtue of writing in a way that still demonstrates respect

BEST PRACTICE
Overly vague or conclusory statements may jeopardize comprehension of the risk data needed for commitment determinations.

for persons. Together, these values make it difficult to formulate "bright-line," easy-to-follow rules about what to include and how to include it. Even very experienced evaluators encounter cases that require examining choices and consulting with colleagues to get other perspectives and resolve doubts regarding report contents.

KEEPING FOCUSED ON THE FORENSIC QUESTION

Thoughtful forensic evaluators sometimes believe that because any fact is potential fodder for direct or cross-examination, they should describe every detail of cases in their reports. But good forensic reports should hew to the psycholegal question at hand and should not include information that is irrelevant to the question of whether the respondent needs civil commitment. This is especially true when personal information about the respondent's friends or family members is involved. For example, it is very difficult to contemplate situations in which the HIV status and sexual preferences of a respondent's brother or the sexual assault history of a respondent's mother would be relevant to civil commitment.

DEALING WITH ETHICAL, LEGAL, AND PRACTICAL LIMITATIONS

As Heilbrun, Marczyk, and DeMatteo (2002) point out, forensic evaluators should describe findings fairly and not cover up weaknesses or limitations in their data—for example, the unavailability of potentially relevant information, the limitations of psychological tests used, or the impact of an evaluee's response style on the accuracy of one's opinion. In many civil commitment evaluations, time constraints limit data gathering, the evaluator cannot speak at length (or at all) to the respondent or cannot verify third-party information. If an evaluator needs to prepare a report under such circumstances, it is only reasonable to acknowledge these limitations and their potential impact on conclusions. Forensic psychologists' and psychiatrists' ethical guidelines both

INFO

Good forensic reports should be written with the psycholegal question in mind and should not include information that is irrelevant to the commitment question.

address these issues in different ways (American Academy of Psychiatry and the Law, 2005; Committee on Ethical Guidelines for Forensic Psychologists, 1991). For example, the ethical guidelines of the American Academy of Psychiatry and the Law (2005) do so by emphasizing honesty and striving for objectivity.

In their recommendations for report writing regarding civil commitment, Heilbrun and colleagues offer the following suggestions about clarifying the sources of data and the reasoning in a report:

- Base diagnoses on data from multiple sources, including self-reports, collateral interviews, relevant records, and testing;

- Include direct quotations from these sources when relevant and illustrative;

- Attribute factual information to its respective source, with limiting language (e.g., "to her knowledge") as needed; and

- Address both the degree and imminence of any risk, rather than using the term "danger" (Heilbrun et al., 2002, p. 381).

ARTICULATING CONCEPTUAL LINKAGES AND THE RATIONALE FOR THE OPINION

Opinions and recommendations are most helpful and persuasive when they spell out *why* a respondent does or does not meet the criteria for civil commitment. In preparing a report, an evaluator should describe such matters with the jurisdiction's statutory provisions in mind. In Massachusetts, for example, commitment may occur when "failure to hospitalize" a respondent "would create a likelihood of serious harm by reason of mental illness" (Mass. Gen. Laws c. 123, s. 7). "Likelihood of serious harm" is defined elsewhere in the statute (Mass. Gen. Laws c. 123, s. 1), and "mental illness" is defined in the state's Department of Mental Health regulations. To express an opinion that addresses the elements of the statute, the evaluator should explain each of the elements in turn and how they fit together.

7
chapter

A study of psychologists conducted to examine the perceived value of different types of risk communication found that the most highly valued style involved the identification of risk factors and recommendations for interventions that might mitigate the risk (Heilbrun, O'Neill, Stevens, Strohman, Bowman, & Lo, 2004).

However, in a civil commitment report, a document that simply lists factors that heighten or mitigate the risk of harm will not be sufficient and could potentially be confusing. For example, a man who, in a serious suicide attempt, set himself on fire and cannot now use his limbs may have numerous risk factors for further suicide. But the mitigating factor—that he is physically disabled—may limit his ability to do further harm to himself and, therefore, his risk. The evaluator could address this with a well-reasoned opinion explaining how the evaluator weighed the risks and reached a particular opinion. As Heilbrun (1997) notes, language that communicates risk related to the decision at hand fits the requirement of a civil commitment report better than the types of risk management language included in a clinical consultation. The reason is that civil commitment is a single-point-in-time decision in which the decision-maker (the court) does not have ongoing involvement with the respondent and is not in a position to act clinically to reduce the ongoing risk.

Statements about the magnitude, imminence, likelihood, and frequency of potentially harmful acts are other key elements of a practically useful violence risk assessment (Resnick, 2008). As Mulvey and Lidz (1984) note, the term "dangerousness" speaks to more than violence—it also connotes a *propensity* for someone to engage in violent acts. Heilbrun and colleagues (2002) suggest that forensic evaluators not use the global term "dangerousness" in their reports. It is more informative and practically useful to identify specific risk factors, risk levels, and the nature of potential harms, along with interventions that might mitigate the risk (Heilbrun et al., 2004). In a report on civil commitment, a concise description of these elements can help readers and the fact-finder understand why the evaluator believes the "intervention" under consideration— involuntary hospitalization—is or is not appropriate.

In Chapter 5, we explained why currently available actuarial risk assessment instruments have limited application to commitment decisions. This does not mean that evaluators need to abjure any use of such instruments. Assessment instruments may help clinicians quantify the severity of psychopathology (as does the Brief Psychiatric Rating Scale, for example), identify patients as being at high risk for self-harm in the hospital (e.g., inpatient suicide screening instruments), or assess the risk for acting violently during the months immediately after a hospitalization (e.g., COVR™). But evaluators should not use results from these instruments as the sole basis for a risk opinion and, if using them, should be cautious in describing results and linking results to commitment opinions. Remember, courts that hear civil commitment cases must attend to statutory criteria, which often make *recent behavior* or a clear sense of why failure to hospitalize would lead to harm the *sine qua non* for ordering involuntary hospitalization.

ULTIMATE OPINION LANGUAGE

At a civil commitment hearing, the court—not the mental health expert—renders the *"ultimate opinion"* about whether the respondent meets civil commitment criteria. Of course, every competent evaluator *ought* to have a well-based opinion about what the conclusion of a civil commitment hearing should be—after all, evaluators are mental health professionals who, by virtue of their data-gathering and educational background, are well suited to make clinical judgments about the need for and importance of someone's undergoing psychiatric hospitalization. But civil commitment takes away

7
chapter

a person's liberty, and the United States vests the authority to deprive liberty (and to make other psycholegal decisions) in courts, not mental health professionals.

Because psycholegal decisions rest with legal fact-finders, forensic mental health professionals are divided about whether they should include explicit opinions about the ultimate issue in their reports and testimony. Were they to do so in the civil commitment context, their reports would include statements such as "the respondent's risk of harm and mental illness meet criteria for civil commitment" or "the respondent is civilly committable." The potential usefulness of such statements is that they inform the court about what the evaluator thinks the clinical data mean. The potential problem with such statements is that the evaluator may appear to usurp the court's role by providing a judgment that may seem entirely clinical, but that also involves a justification for detaining someone against involuntarily.

Much of the debate around ultimate issue testimony has centered on criminal cases (see, e.g., Buchanan, 2006; Slovenko, 2006). Judges and lawyers appear to prefer testimony on the ultimate issue (Redding, Floyd, & Hawk, 2001), and forensic clinicians are often asked their opinions in questions that include ultimate issue language. In preparing written documents for civil commitment proceedings, clinicians typically *must* answer questions that expressly ask whether the requisite level of mental illness and certain types of risks are present.

In those situations that call for civil commitment reports that are more detailed than the customary affidavit, we suggest that evaluators do something equivalent to saying "2 + 2" without saying "4." Concerning a suicidal inpatient who appears to meet the criteria for commitment, for example, the evaluator would describe the signs and symptoms of illness and state that these demonstrate the presence of a "substantial disorder" with "gross impairment"; the evaluator would also enumerate risk factors, recent behaviors, and other relevant findings. The evaluator might conclude with a statement (couched in the statutory phrasing from the local jurisdiction) that these findings prove the presence of an immediate risk of serious harm or death if hospitalization does not continue. In a sample commitment report, Heilbrun and colleagues (2002) state, "Mr. W. appears to present as a high risk for self-injurious behavior and is, therefore, a 'clear and present danger' to himself under § 7301 of the Mental Health Procedures Act" (p. 385). The report then describes the elements of behavior satisfying legal criteria using more clinical and descriptive terminology. This approach conveys unambiguously to the court what the evaluator believes without appropriating the court's prerogative to determine whether the respondent "meets the commitment criteria."

Testimony

Why Bother Doing a Good Job?

As we have previously noted, civil commitment cases commonly eventuate in courtroom testimony. In many locales, however, commitment hearings are quick and perfunctory. Attorneys for both the respondent and the proponent of commitment usually do little or no preparation for hearings, and when prehearing consultation between attorneys and witnesses does occur, the time spent can often be measured in seconds. Many attorneys for respondents are as eager as anyone else to see that their clients receive the treatment their doctors recommend. Under these circumstances, devoting much care or thought to one's expert testimony will usually seem pointless. Moreover, thoughtful testimony sometimes annoys legal personnel because it seems needlessly time-consuming.

Nonetheless, we think that mental health professionals should strive to provide cogent, relevant, thoughtful, and effective testimony whenever they testify. Here's why:

- Even in locales where the court usually rubber stamps what the doctors want, cases occasionally arise in which a respondent's attorney will sincerely contest commitment or in which the trial court will carefully scrutinize evidence before reaching a conclusion. Such cases occur unexpectedly and without warning. Especially when a respondent has a serious, treatable mental illness and really poses a risk, failure to provide evidence in a form that "makes the case" for commitment does the respondent (and potentially the community) a disservice. So it is best to be prepared, even if the preparation is pointless 95% of the time.

- When testifying in court, mental health professionals provide evidence not just about the respondent, but also about several other matters: the types of clinicians they are, their own competence, their attitudes, and their profession's virtues. Lousy or clumsy testimony may convince a court to order commitment but leave a bad impression (for the respondent who is still to receive care, along with everyone else present) about the skills, knowledge, and services of mental health professionals.

- Good testimony can have a beneficial (and even therapeutic) impact on respondents who do not acknowledge that they are ill. First, participants view as fair and satisfying legal proceedings in which their positions have been heard and treated respectfully, even when the decision goes against them (Tyler & Blader, 2003). Second, respondents may learn something about themselves. For example, one of our patients acknowledged that she was ill only after she attended her commitment hearing and found that her auditory hallucinations interfered with her ability to process her treating doctor's testimony.

- Civil commitment is *always* a serious matter. It temporarily deprives respondents of their most precious right: freedom. Sometimes, commitment is the only morally acceptable course for society and for persons who care about individuals with mental illness. Moreover, as we noted earlier in this volume, involuntary hospitalization is justifiable even under ethical systems that give liberty the highest value (Rawls, 1971). Nevertheless, mental health professionals should care about their patients' rights, even when they act to curtail those rights. We display our concern for patients' needs and remind ourselves of our respect for our patients' rights and humanity by clearly and thoughtfully providing the evidence that courts use to make decisions about restricting freedom.

- Thoughtful, cogent, credible testimony sometimes shows—in contrast to what legal personnel often expect to hear—that a respondent should *not* undergo involuntary placement for treatment. Though many people believe otherwise, having a serious mental illness or needing intensive psychiatric care does not, by itself, justify confinement or the imposition of treatment. Not infrequently, circumstances, conditions, or beliefs that justified emergency detention or the good-faith filing of an affidavit change in a few days, and by the time a hearing takes place, civil commitment is no longer supportable. Just as good testimony helps a fact-finder understand that clear and convincing evidence supports involuntary hospitalization, good testimony can also help a fact-finder to see that clear and convincing evidence for commitment does not exist in a particular case.

In preparing to testify, evaluators (whether independent examiners or treating clinicians) need to consciously divorce their evaluation findings and conclusions from considerations of what would be *best* for respondents. Sometimes, dedicated clinicians have a hard time doing this. But we need to remember that although very few respondents do not need psychiatric treatment of some sort,

7
chapter

their need for treatment is not a sufficient condition for involuntary commitment (despite what mental health professionals often wish in circumstances where the value of hospital treatment seems clear).

Clinicians (whether treatment providers or independent evaluators) usually want their testimony to be effective, and effective testimony usually requires planning. In addition to thinking about how to present evaluation data and clinical observations, an evaluator should consider when using reliable information from other sources—e.g., treatment history, records, or collateral interviews—might be helpful. The attorneys involved ideally should make the necessary arrangements for introducing such information and having additional witnesses appear, but when attorneys do not do much preparation, evaluators often have to do so. The best information supporting dangerousness often comes from sources other than the evaluation interview, and testimony by fact witnesses (e.g., family members) might be necessary to support a proposed commitment. Clinicians may realize that family members' evidence ought to be heard and their testimony would usually come before the expert testifies. Treating clinicians may have opportunities to let family members know that they might need to testify as they may meet with family on the inpatient units in the course of patient care. In almost all cases, a testifying clinician will have a few moments before a hearing to meet with an attorney, explain the situation, and discuss options for presenting evidence.

When possible of course, advance preparation with the attorney for whom one will provide direct testimony can be invaluable. Describing one's findings and opinions aloud can be a good way to recognize and to inform the attorney about the strengths and weaknesses of the case. Because commitment criteria are written in legal language, it can be challenging for clinicians, especially those with less forensic training, to translate their clinical observations into the legal commitment criteria.

Challenges to Expertise

Before hearing an expert's opinion, a trial court is supposed to determine whether the proposed testimony is "admissible" under legal rules that govern what fact-finders are allowed to consider. In some cases, this determination will require the court to evaluate the basis for and grounding of the testimony. Each jurisdiction has its own guidelines for this inquiry.

For most purposes (including those of this volume), U.S. jurisdictions can be grouped according to whether they follow evidence rules propounded in the *Frye* (1923) or *Daubert* (1993) decisions, or in some hybrid of these. Under the *Frye* rule (followed by roughly two-fifths of states), expert evidence is admissible only if "the thing from which the deduction is made" (i.e., the basis or method by which the proposed expert has reached his conclusions) is "sufficiently established to have gained general acceptance in the particular field in which it belongs" (p. 1014).

In 1993, the U.S. Supreme Court held, in *Daubert v. Merrell Dow Pharmaceuticals*, that because Congress had rewritten the federal rules of evidence in the 1970s, the *Frye* rule no longer applied in federal courts. Instead, courts faced with a proffer of scientific evidence should conduct a flexible inquiry, considering factors such as (1) whether the theory or technique that is the basis for the proposed evidence has been tested, (2) whether the theory or technique has undergone peer review or publication, (3) the known or potential rate of error, and

CASE LAW

Frye v. United States
(1923)

● Introduced the concept that expert evidence is admissible only if it is based on matters that are generally accepted in the relevant field.

7
chapter

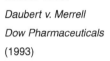

CASE LAW

Daubert v. Merrell Dow Pharmaceuticals (1993)

● Held that the *Frye* rule no longer applied in federal courts. Instead, courts should conduct a flexible inquiry into the basis of any proposed scientific evidence.

(4) whether the theory or technique is generally accepted within the relevant scientific community. Thus, under *Daubert*, "general acceptance" (the essence of the *Frye* rule) is just one factor a court should consider.

In a subsequent case (*Kumho Tire Co. v. Carmichael*, 1999), the Supreme Court held that federal courts should conduct *Daubert*-type inquiries before admitting nonscientific types of evidence, too. Although *Daubert* and *Kumho* apply to federal courts, most U.S. states have adopted *Daubert*-like rules concerning the admissibility of expert testimony, either by statute or through case law. Also, a huge amount of legal scholarship (including scholarship that touches on the admission of forensic mental health testimony) has considered the impact that *Daubert* could or should have on expert testimony.

Several commentators (e.g., Schopp & Quattrocchi, 1995; Heilbrun et al., 2002; Litwack, Zapf, Groscup, & Hart, 2006; Slobogin, 2006) have suggested that *Daubert*, *Kumho*, and related decisions and evidence rules should affect the type, presentation, and quality of evidence allowed in civil commitment hearings. Actual decisions have gone otherwise, however. In several published decisions, for example, courts have addressed *Daubert*- or *Frye*-based challenges to evidence introduced in *sex offender* commitments. In these cases, "expert testimony on risk assessment . . . is rarely excluded, and the *Daubert* and

CASE LAW

Kumho Tire Co. v. Carmichael (1999)

● The Supreme Court held that federal courts should conduct *Daubert*-type inquiries before admitting nonscientific types of evidence.

Kumho decisions appear to have exerted little effect on its admission" (Litwack et al., 2006, pp. 508–509).

Though *Daubert*-related questions about admissibility questions have arisen in other cases (see, e.g., Gottstein, 2008), our search of the legal literature suggests that just one appellate decision has examined evidence from a mental health commitment case from a *Daubert* perspective. In *State ex rel. L.C.F.* (2003), the respondent appealed his commitment to inpatient treatment on grounds that expert testimony at his hearing was unreliable. The testifying physician had been in just the second month of his psychiatry residency. The trial court had allowed the testimony after establishing that the resident, who had done his medical studies in Pakistan, had passed his licensing examinations. The resident also had done a 1-year psychiatry rotation in Pakistan, had done research on psychotropic drugs, and had been certified more than 100 times by Pakistan courts to testify on psychiatric matters. The appeals court held that although some psychiatric residents may not have adequate knowledge and credentials to testify as medical experts, the trial court's acceptance of this resident as an expert was not an abuse of discretion.

Challenges to the foundations of expertise are rare in civil commitment hearings. Still, *Daubert* and *Kumho* provide a useful rubric for thinking about the quality and groundings of one's conclusions. The topics and content of earlier chapters in this volume summarize the scientific bases of expert testimony relevant to civil commitment.

Some Style Tips

Clinicians interested in improving the quality and effectiveness of their testimony can attend many regularly offered courses on the subject or can consult books that cater to varying levels of experience from novice (e.g., Brodsky, 1991; Gutheil, 2009) to seasoned (e.g., Gutheil & Simon, 2002; Brodsky, 2004). Here, we confine ourselves to a few tips specific to commitment hearings that may prove helpful to individuals during their first few experiences as expert witnesses.

7
chapter

Civil Commitment Checklist

Meeting the statutory requirements for civil commitment in your state.

Y N
☐ ☐ Did you read the Affidavit/Statement of Belief to the patient?
☐ ☐ Did the patient tell you his/her version of the events reported in the Affidavit?
☐ ☐ ♦ Does the patient have mental illness?
☐ ☐ ♦ Is there evidence of dangerous behavior(s)?
☐ ☐ ♦ Was the respondent's behavior because of mental illness?
☐ ☐ ♦ Is inpatient hospitalization the least restrictive setting for treatment?

Legal parameters regarding dangerous behaviors and hearsay.
☐ ☐ ♦ Did the dangerous behaviors happen recently (if recency is in criteria)?
☐ ☐ ♦ Would failure to hospitalize lead to likelihood of serious harm (for some jurisdictions that do not require recency of behavior)
☐ ☐ Is all your evidence based on your own firsthand experience? If not, in this jurisdiction will the court allow you to testify about hearsay?

Testimony.
☐ ☐ Have you rehearsed or practiced what you will say?
☐ ☐ Have you anticipated likely cross-examination questions?
☐ ☐ Have you gathered important information such as the admission date, medications, age, sex, relevant lab/imaging studies, and psychiatric history?

*If you answer "yes" to all questions relevant to your jurisdiction you are ready to testify about the need for civil commitment. If you answer "no" to any ♦items, civil commitment may be inappropriate. If you answer "no" to any of the other questions, you're not ready to go to court.

Figure 7.1 Preparing to Testify. Reprinted with permission from Thatcher and Mossman (2009).

BE PREPARED WITH THE FACTS

It is okay to use notes while you testify, but you should be familiar with the content of those notes and with the clinical case generally. Thatcher and Mossman (2009) provide a checklist of items concerning a respondent that clinicians can review to ensure they are ready to testify (see Figure 7.1), and in Figure 7.2, we provide a sample "testimony cheat sheet" that translates clinical facts from a hypothetical case into statutory criteria. Readers may find that the "cheat sheet" helps them condense key clinical information into a document that they can bring to the stand for easy reference to case facts as they relate to statutory commitment requirements.

Joe Smith

Patient DOB: 2/7/65
Date of Admission: 1/5/09 via emergency detention after broke window at home
Dates of contact with respondent: 1/5/09, 1/6/09, 1/8/09
Dates of major events in hospital (e.g. seclusion, restraint, assaults, non-adherence, etc):
1/6/09 assaulted peer, restraint for two hours, 1/8/09 spat on nurse
Mental Illness Definition
    <u>Substantial disorder of mood</u>: Pressured speech, mood lability, euphoric laughing, lack of need for sleep for 3 weeks; long history of bipolar d/o-hospitalized in 1998, 2001, 2007, receives PACT services
    <u>Disorder of thought</u>: flight of ideas, clang associations ("bang-sang the doctor"), believes he is Mayor
    <u>Disorder of perception</u>: hearing voices, talking to self as if responding to voices
    <u>Disorder of orientation</u>: N/A
    <u>Disorder of memory</u>: N/A
****
    <u>Gross impairment of judgment and behavior</u>: broke window at home, spat on nurse, sitting in hallway for hours singing, intrusive with peers
    <u>Gross impairment of capacity to recognize reality</u>: thinks he is Mayor and does not need to eat
    <u>Gross impairment of the ability to meet the ordinary demands of life</u>: Little sleep for three weeks, poor nutrition and hygiene, labs showed anemia
Dangerousness criteria:
    <u>Suicide risk</u>: N/A
    <u>Danger to others</u>: Easily agitated and angered, hostile on approach at times, broke window, frightens others by unpredictable laughing, crying, and excessive movements, spat on nurse, assaulted peer
    <u>Grave disability</u>: not eating or sleeping well, medical needs not attended to with anemia
Least Restrictive Alternative
    <u>Inpatient</u>-evicted from home, hospital needed to attend to medical issues, observe improvements, nursing staff to monitor progress and provide medications, risk to others in community or other settings

---

Figure 7.2 Sample Summary Data Aid to Testimony Preparation. This sample reflects data related to a patient who was admitted via emergency detention. Police escorted him to the hospital. The patient had a history of bipolar disorder, had not been taking his medication, and had been wandering the city for several weeks as he became increasingly irritable. The data are presented and designed to correspond to the local commitment statutory requirements and are an example of a "cheat sheet" that someone might bring to the witness stand to assist in testimony.

BE PREPARED TO DEFEND YOUR OPINION

In clinical work, mental health professionals value consensus, agreement of all parties, and minimization of conflict. But legal hearings are intentionally adversarial. Attorneys for the side opposed to your position will challenge you—even when they personally *agree* with you—because it is their job to represent their client's positions. Conceding the genuine limitations or weak points in your position is part of being a scrupulous expert witness. But interests of justice

7
chapter

require you to defend your position during cross-examination, and that will usually mean disagreeing openly with the opposing position.

BE PREPARED TO ANSWER WITHIN THE CONSTRAINTS OF THE QUESTIONS POSED

Court witnesses are constrained to respond to questions they are asked. Therefore, during testimony you should not expect to "present the patient" as you would in a clinical context (e.g., during hospital rounds). You should answer questions fully, and you may elaborate on answers to make their meaning clear. But if the attorney fails to ask you questions about an area or event that you think is important, there may be nothing you can do about it. Once again, preparation with the retaining attorney in advance of the testimony can be helpful in avoiding this problem.

WHEN OPPORTUNITIES ARISE, STATE OBSERVATIONS

One important way to elaborate on answers is by describing the concrete findings and observations that led to your conclusions. Suppose, for example, that you are testifying about Ms. Jones, a respondent with schizophrenia who has been hallucinating and has struck people. The attorney asks you whether Ms. Jones "has a substantial disorder of thought or perception." You could just answer, "Yes." But if you fear that the attorney would not follow up with a question about the basis for that conclusion, you might continue, "and I concluded this because Ms. Jones told me she was hearing voices of several dead people, and she looked around the room and spoke back to them when we met."

INFO

Helpful tips for commitment hearings:

- Be prepared with the facts

- Defend your opinion

- Answer within the constraints of the questions posed

- When opportunities arise, state observations

FOR RESPONDENTS WHO MEET COMMITMENT CRITERIA

If you have concluded that the respondent meets commitment criteria:

- Explain the ways in which your clinical observations constitute signs or symptoms of a mental disorder. For example, you could say, "The 'voices' Ms. Jones 'heard' were auditory hallucinations, and these are symptoms of schizophrenia."

- Earlier (Chapters 2 and 6), we pointed out that for legal purposes, "substantial" disorders of thought or mood need not be only those disorders that are labeled "thought disorders" or "mood disorders" in official diagnostic manuals. When a respondent's condition satisfies official diagnostic criteria, stating this helps to support the general point that the respondent is mentally ill. Invoking a recognized diagnosis also shows that you are using widely shared professional concepts rather than idiosyncratic views.

- Having symptoms, even serious ones, is not the same as being impaired by them. When attorneys' questions provide appropriate opportunity, you should give specific, *behavioral* examples of the respondent's gross impairment. For example: "Mr. Smith is not taking care of himself. He won't bathe. He doesn't dress unless staff members tell him to. Police brought him to the hospital because he was standing outdoors in freezing weather wearing only an undershirt."

- Recall (from Chapters 1 and 6) that the cause of a respondent's risk must be the mental illness. Thus, testimony should link the respondent's clinical condition to recent behavior by explaining how that behavior arose from the mental illness. For example, the psychotic motive is clear in this testimony:

7
chapter

"Ms. Jones displayed a risk of harm to others when she struck a nurse yesterday; Ms. Jones told me the reason she did that was because the nurse was trying to control her by beaming microwaves into her brain."

FOR RESPONDENTS WHO DO NOT MEET COMMITMENT CRITERIA

If you have concluded that the respondent does not meet the commitment criteria, you may need to convince nonclinicians and mental health colleagues alike that this is true, despite the respondent's recent behavior or obvious mental illness. There are several reasons why this can be difficult but important.

- Many persons (especially physicians) believe that a medical condition that compromises insight should occasion intervention to override foolish choices by patients. But as we have emphasized at many points, modern commitment law states that the presence of a disorder and the need for treatment do not, by themselves, make an individual eligible for commitment.

- Sometimes poor judgment leads to dangerous situations, but not all behavior that reflects poor judgment constitutes dangerous behavior for purposes of civil commitment. Moreover, not all bad judgment emanates from mental illness. A person with mental illness who hitchhikes at night could get assaulted or hit by a car—but so might a hitchhiker without mental illness. Risky behavior by someone with mental illness sometimes stems from poor judgment, not from the person's psychiatric disorder.

- Criminal behavior is not necessarily dangerous behavior (recall Ms. D from Chapter 6).

- Some respondents who might have come to hospitals during personal crises settle down quickly and would, if permitted, obtain outpatient treatment voluntarily and safely. Though legitimate concerns led to their emergency detention, these persons might not qualify for civil commitment after a few days of inpatient care.

- For some respondents, an emergency detention gives concerned relatives an opportunity to mobilize resources to safeguard their loved ones and arrange treatment. As *O'Connor v. Donaldson* (1975) held, when responsible persons will care for a nondangerous mentally ill person, commitment may not be permissible.

Conclusions

Writing reports and testifying in civil commitment proceedings are opportunities for mental health professionals to serve both respondents and the legal system. To the extent that mental health professionals can translate into the court's language what the respondent is presenting clinically, the court benefits from having the best possible information to render a legal decision. Despite the casual and perfunctory approach to civil commitment of some courts, what is at stake at a commitment hearing are an individual's liberty and personhood and society's legitimate need to protect persons with mental illness from experiencing or doing harm. Clinicians can take pride in carefully evaluating respondents and in providing courts with testimony that is thoughtful, well-grounded, and respectful of everyone involved.

References

Advocates, Framingham Jail Diversion Program: Program Summary. (2008). Retrieved April 22, 2010 from http://www.advocatesinc. org/index-BIG.htm.

Almvik, R., Woods, P., & Rasmussen, K. (2007). Assessing risk for imminent violence in the elderly: The Brøset Violence Checklist. *International Journal of Geriatric Psychiatry, 22*, 862–867.

Alphons Wierema, T. K., Kroon, A. A., & de Leeuw, P. W. (2007). Poor performance of diagnostic tests for atherosclerotic renal artery stenosis—discrepancies between stenosis and renal function. *Nephrology Dialysis Transplantation, 22*, 689–692.

American Academy of Psychiatry and the Law. (2005). American academy of psychiatry and the law ethics guidelines for the practice of forensic psychiatry. Retrieved from http://www.aapl.org/ethics.htm.

American Psychiatric Association. (1980). *Diagnostic and statistical manual of mental disorders* (3rd ed.). Washington, DC: American Psychiatric Association.

American Psychiatric Association. (1983). Guidelines for legislation on the psychiatric hospitalization of adults. *American Journal of Psychiatry, 140*, 672–679.

American Psychiatric Association. (1987). *Diagnostic and statistical manual of mental disorders* (3rd ed, Revised.). Washington, DC: American Psychiatric Association.

American Psychiatric Association. (1993). *Consent to voluntary hospitalization* (Task Force Report No. 34.) Washington, DC: American Psychiatric Association.

American Psychiatric Association. (1999a). *Mandatory outpatient treatment resource document* (Reference No. 990007). Washington, DC: American Psychiatric Association.

American Psychiatric Association (1999b). *Task Force on Sexually Dangerous Offenders: Dangerous sex offenders: A Task Force Report of the American Psychiatric Association.* Washington, DC: American Psychiatric Association.

American Psychiatric Association. (2000). *Handbook of psychiatric measures.* Washington, DC: American Psychiatric Press.

American Psychiatric Association. (2003). *Practice guideline for the assessment and treatment of patients with suicidal behaviors.* Retrieved from http://www.psychiatryonline.com/pracGuide/pracGuideTopic_14. aspx.

American Psychiatric Association. (2006). Practice Guideline for the psychiatric evaluation of adults (2nd ed.). *American Journal of Psychiatry, 163*, 1–36.

American Psychiatric Association Task Force Report No. 26 (1987). *Involuntary commitment to outpatient treatment.* Washington, DC: American Psychiatric Association.

Amore, M., Menchetti, M., Tonti, C., Scarlatti, F., Lundgren, E., Esposito, W., & Berardi, D. (2008). Predictors of violent behavior among acute psychiatric patients: Clinical study. *Psychiatry and Clinical Neurosciences, 62,* 247–255.

Andrion, A., Magnani, C., Betta, P. G., Donna, A., Mollo, O., Scelsi, M., Bernardi, P., Botta, M., & Terracini, B. (1995). Malignant mesothelioma of the pleura: Interobserver variability. *Journal of Clinical Pathology, 48,* 856–860.

Anfang, S. A., & Appelbaum, P. S. (2006). Civil commitment—the American experience. *Israel Journal of Psychiatry and Related Sciences, 43,* 209–218.

Appelbaum, B. C., Appelbaum, P. S., & Grisso, T. (1998). Competence to consent to voluntary psychiatric hospitalization: A test of a standard proposed by APA. *Psychiatric Services, 49,* 1193–1196.

Appelbaum, K. L. (1990). Civil commitment: The role of the mental health professional. *Expert Opinion, 3*(1), 4–7.

Appelbaum, P. S. (1984). Is the need for treatment constitutionally acceptable as a basis for civil commitment? *Law, Medicine and Health Care, 12,* 144–149.

Appelbaum, P. S. (1985). Special section on APA's model commitment law: An introduction. *Hospital and Community Psychiatry, 36,* 966–967.

Appelbaum, P. S. (1994). *Almost a revolution: Mental health law and the limits of change.* Oxford: Oxford University Press.

Appelbaum, P. S. (1995). Civil commitment and liability for violating patient rights. *Psychiatric Services, 46,* 17–18.

Appelbaum, P. S. (2000). The Draft Act Governing Hospitalization of the Mentally Ill: Its genesis and its legacy. *Psychiatric Services, 51,* 190–194.

Appelbaum, P. S., & Gutheil, T. G. (2007). *Clinical handbook of psychiatry and the law* (4th ed.). Philadelphia: Lippincott, Williams, & Wilkins.

Appelbaum, P. S., & Hamm R. M. (1982). Decision to seek commitment: Psychiatric decision making in a legal context. *Archives of General Psychiatry, 39,* 3447–3451.

Appelbaum P. S., & Kemp K. N. (1982). History of commitment laws in the 19th century. *Law and Human Behavior, 6,* 343–354.

Appelbaum, P. S., & Rumpf, T. (1998). Civil commitment of the anorexic patient. *General Hospital Psychiatry, 20,* 225–230.

Appelbaum, P. S., & Grisso, T. (2001). *MacArthur Competency Assessment Tool for Clinical Research (MacCAT-CR).* Sarasota, FL: Professional Resource Press.

Bagby, R. M., Thompson, J. S., Dickens, S. E., & Nohara, M. (1991). Decision making in psychiatric civil commitment: An experimental analysis. *American Journal of Psychiatry, 148,* 28–33.

Bazelon Center. (June 2004). Involuntary outpatient commitment: Summary of state statutes. Washington, DC: Author. Retrieved from http://www.bazelon.org/LinkClick.aspx?fileticket=CBmFgyA4i-w%3d&tabid=324, accessed February 13, 2011.

Beck, J. C., & Golowka, E. A. (1988). A study of enforced treatment in relation to Stone's "thank you" theory. *Behavioral Sciences & the Law, 6,* 559–566.

Bhugra, D., & Bhui, K. (Eds). (2007). *Textbook of cultural psychiatry.* New York: Cambridge University Press.

Bindman, J., Reid, Y., Szmukler, G., Tiller, J. Thornicroft, G., & Leese, M. (2005). Perceived coercion at admission to psychiatric hospital and engagement with follow-up—a cohort study. *Social Psychiatry and Psychiatric Epidemiology, 40,* 160–166.

Björkdahl, A., Olsson, D., & Palmstierna, T. (2006). Nurses' short-term prediction of violence in acute psychiatric intensive care. *Acta Psychiatrica Scandinavica, 113,* 224–229.

Bobes, J., Fillat, O., & Arango, C. (2009). Violence among schizophrenia outpatients compliant with medication: Prevalence and associated factors. *Acta Psychiatrica Scandinavica, 119,* 218–225.

Bonnie, R. J. (2001). Three strands of mental health law: Developmental mileposts. In L. E. Frost & R. J. Bonnie (Eds.), *The Evolution of Mental Health Law* (pp. 31–54). Washington, DC: The American Psychological Association.

Bonsack, C., & Borgeat, F. (2005). Perceived coercion and need for hospitalization related to psychiatric admission. *International Journal of Law and Psychiatry, 28,* 342–347.

Borg, M., Karlsson, B., Tondora, J., & Davidson, L. (2009). Implementing person-centered care in psychiatric rehabilitation: what does this involve? *The Israel Journal of Psychiatry and Related Sciences, 46,* 84–93.

Borum, R., & Grisso, T. (1996). Establishing standards for criminal forensic reports: An empirical analysis. *Bulletin of the American Academy of Psychiatry and the Law, 24,* 297–317.

Bradford, B., McCann, S., & Merskey, H. (1986). A survey of involuntary patients' attitudes towards their commitment. *Psychiatric Journal of the University of Ottawa, 11,* 162–165.

Brill, H., & Patton, R. E. (1959). Analysis of population reduction in New York state mental hospitals during the first four years of large-scale therapy with psychotropic drugs. *American Journal of Psychiatry, 116,* 495–509.

Brodsky, S. L. (1991). *Testifying in court: Guidelines and maxims for the expert witness.* Washington, DC: American Psychological Association.

Brodsky, S. L. (2004). *Coping with cross-examination and other pathways to effective testimony.* Washington, DC: American Psychological Association.

Brooks, R. A. (2007). Psychiatrists' opinions about involuntary civil commitment: Results of a national survey. *Journal of the American Academy of Psychiatry and the Law, 35,* 219–228.

Buchanan, A. (2006). Psychiatric evidence on the ultimate issue. *Journal of the American Academy of Psychiatry and the Law, 34,* 14–21.

Burt, R. A. (2001). Promises to keep, miles to go: Mental health law since 1972. In L. E. Frost & R. J. Bonnie (Eds.), *The evolution of mental health law* (pp. 11–30). Washington, DC: The American Psychological Association.

Case, B. G., Olfson, M., Marcus, S. C., & Siegel, C. (2007). Trends in the inpatient mental health treatment of children and adolescents in US community hospitals between 1990 and 2000. *Archives of General Psychiatry, 64,* 89–96.

Caton, C. L., Hasin, D. S., Shrout, P. E., Drake, R. E., Dominguez, B., First, M. B., Samet, S., & Schanzer, B. (2007). Stability of early-phase primary psychotic disorders with concurrent substance use and substance-induced psychosis. *British Journal of Psychiatry, 190,* 105–111.

Chambers, D. L. (1972). Alternatives to civil commitment of the mentally ill: Practical guides and constitutional imperatives. *Michigan Law Review, 70,* 1107–1200.

Cohen, B. J., Bonnie, R. J., & Monahan, J. (2008). Understanding and applying Virginia's new statutory civil commitment criteria. Retrieved from http://www.dbhds.virginia.gov/OMH-MHReform/080603Criteria.pdf.

Committee for Public Counsel Services. (2011). *Certification requirements.* Retrieved from http://www.publiccounsel.net/Practice_Areas/Mental_Health/certification/certification_index.html.

Committee on Ethical Guidelines for Forensic Psychologists. (1991). Specialty guidelines for forensic psychologists. *Law and Human Behavior, 15,* 655–665.

Compton, S. N., Swanson, J. W., Wagner, H. R., Swartz, M. S., Burns, B. J., & Elbogen, E. B. (2003). Involuntary outpatient commitment and homelessness in persons with severe mental illness. *Mental Health Services Research, 5,* 27–38.

de Azevedo Marques, J. M., & Zuardi, A. W. (2008). Validity and applicability of the Mini International Neuropsychiatric Interview administered by family medicine residents in primary health care in Brazil. *General Hospital Psychiatry, 30,* 303–310.

Deegan, P. E., & Drake, R. E. (2006). Shared decision making and medication management in the recovery process. *Psychiatric Services, 57,* 1636-1639.

Deutsch, A. (1945). *The mentally ill in America: A history of their care and treatment from colonial times.* New York: Columbia University Press.

Dix, Dorothea, Memorial to the Legislature of the State of Massachusetts, 1843, Massachusetts State House Library, reference number 973–044 v. 6.

Douglas, K. S., Guy, L. S., & Weir, J. (2007). *HCR-20 violence risk assessment scheme: Overview and annotated bibliography.* Retrieved from http://kdouglas.wordpress.com/hcr-20/.

Douglas, K. S., Ogloff, J. R. P., Nicholls, T. L., & Grant, I. (1999). Assessing risk for violence among psychiatric patients: The HCR-20 violence risk assessment scheme and the psychopathy checklist: Screening version. *Journal of Consulting and Clinical Psychology, 67,* 917–930.

Douglas, K. S., Webster, C. D., Eaves, D., Hart, S. D., & Ogloff, J. R. P. (Eds.) (2001). *HCR-20 violence risk management companion guide.* Burnaby, BC, Canada: Mental Health Law and Policy Institute, Simon Fraser University and Louis de la Parte Florida Mental Health Institute, University of South Florida.

Durham, M. L. (1985). Implications of need-for-treatment laws: A study of Washington state's involuntary treatment act. *Hospital and Community Psychiatry, 36,* 975–977.

Dworkin, J. (1998). To certify or not to certify: Clinical social work decisions and involuntary hospitalization. *Social Work in Health Care, 13,* 81–99.

Edelsohn, G. A., & Hiday, V. A. (1990). Civil commitment: A range of patient attitudes. *Bulletin of the American Academy of Psychiatry and the Law, 18,* 65–77.

Engleman, N. B., Jobes, D. A., Berman, A. L., & Langbein, L. I. (1998). Clinicians' decision making about involuntary commitment. *Psychiatric Services, 49,* 941–945.

Failer, J. L. (2002). *Who qualifies for rights? Homelessness, mental illness and civil commitment.* Ithaca, NY: Cornell University Press.

Faulkner, L. R., McFarland, B. H., & Bloom, J. D. (1989). An empirical study of emergency commitment. *American Journal of Psychiatry, 146,* 182–186.

Fenton, W. S., Mosher, L. R., Herrell, J. M., & Blyler, C. R. (1998). Randomized trial of general hospital and residential alternative care for patients with severe and persistent mental illness. *American Journal of Psychiatry, 155,* 516–522.

Fortunati, F. G., Jr., & Zonana, H. V. (2003). Legal considerations in the child psychiatric emergency department. *Child and Adolescent Psychiatric Clinics of North America, 12,* 745–761.

Foucault, M. (1973). *Madness and civilization: A history of insanity in the age of reason.* New York: Vintage Books, Random House.

Frank, E., Elon, L., Naimi, T., & Brewer, R. (2008). Alcohol consumption and alcohol counselling behaviour among US medical students: Cohort study. *British Medical Journal, 7,* 337, a2155.

Gardner, W., Lidz, C. W., Hoge, S. K., Monahan, J., Eisenberg, M. M., Bennett, N. S., Mulvey, E. P., & Roth. L. H. (1999). Patients' revisions of their beliefs about the need for hospitalization. *American Journal of Psychiatry, 156*, 1385–1391.

Geller, J. L. (2000). The last half-century of psychiatric services as reflected in Psychiatric Services. *Psychiatric Services, 51*, 41–67.

Geller, J. L. (2006). The evolution of outpatient commitment in the USA: From conundrum to quagmire. *International Journal of Law and Psychiatry, 29*, 234–248.

Geller, J. L., Fisher, W. H., & McDermeit, M. (1995). A national survey of mobile crisis services and their evaluation. *Psychiatric Services, 46*, 893–897.

Gilboy, J., & Schmidt, J. (1971). "Voluntary" hospitalization of the mentally ill. *Northwestern University Law Review, 66*, 429–453.

Goldzband, M. G. (1973). Dangerousness. *Bulletin of the American Academy of Psychiatry and the Law, 1*, 238–244.

Goleman, D. (1986, December 9). States move to ease law committing mentally ill. *New York Times*, C1, C4.

Goodwin, D. W., & Guze, S. B. (1984). *Psychiatric diagnosis* (3rd ed.). New York: Oxford University Press.

Gottstein, J. B. (2008). Involuntary commitment and forced psychiatric drugging in the trial courts: Rights violations as a matter of course. *Alaska Law Review, 25*, 51–105.

Green, T. M. (1997). Police as frontline mental health workers: The decision to arrest or refer to mental health agencies. *International Journal of Law and Psychiatry, 20*, 469–486.

Greenberg, G. A., & Rosenheck, R.A. (2005). Using the GAF as a national mental health outcome measure in the Department of Veterans Affairs. *Psychiatric Services, 56*, 420–426.

Greenberg, S. A., & Shuman, D. W. (1997). Irreconcilable conflict between therapeutic and forensic roles. *Professional Psychology: Research and Practice, 28*, 50–57.

Greenberg, S. A., & Shuman, D. W. (2007). When worlds collide: Therapeutic and forensic roles. *Professional Psychology: Research and Practice, 38*, 129–132.

Greenfield, T. K., Stoneking, B. C., Humphreys, K., Sundby, E., & Bond, J. (2008). A randomized trial of a mental health consumer-managed alternative to civil commitment for acute psychiatric crisis. *American Journal of Community Psychology, 42*, 135–144.

Griffith, E. E. (1998). Ethics in forensic psychiatry: A cultural response to Stone and Appelbaum. *Journal of the American Academy of Psychiatry and the Law, 26*, 171–184.

Groff, A., Burns, B., Swanson, J., Swartz, M., Wagner, H. R., & Tompson, M. (2004). Caregiving for persons with mental illness: The impact of outpatient commitment on caregiving strain. *Journal of Nervous and Mental Diseases, 192*, 554–562.

Group for the Advancement of Psychiatry. (2002). *Cultural assessment in clinical psychiatry*. Arlington, VA: American Psychiatric Publishing.

Group for the Advancement of Psychiatry, Committee on Forensic Psychiatry. (1948). *Commitment procedures, report 4*. New York: Group for the Advancement of Psychiatry.

Group for the Advancement of Psychiatry, Committee on Government Policy. (1994). *Forced into treatment: The role of coercion in clinical practice, report no. 137*. Washington, DC: American Psychiatric Press, Inc.

Group for the Advancement of Psychiatry, Committee on Psychiatry and the Law, (May, 1966). *Laws governing hospitalization of the mentally ill*. Vol. VI, Report 61. New York: NY.

Guo, S., Biegel, D. E., Johnsen, J., & Dyches, H. (2001). Assessing the impact of mobile crisis services on preventing hospitalization: A community-based evaluation. *Psychiatric Services, 52*, 223–228.

Gutheil, T. G. (2009). *The psychiatrist as expert witness* (2nd ed.). Washington, DC: American Psychiatric Publishing.

Gutheil, T. G., & Simon, R. I. (2002). *Mastering forensic psychiatric practice: Advanced strategies for the expert witness*. Washington, DC: American Psychiatric Association.

Hall, K. T., & Appelbaum, P. S. (2002). The origins of commitment for substance abuse in the United States. *Journal of the American Academy of Psychiatry and the Law, 30*, 33–45.

Hart, S. D. (2001). Assessing and managing violence risk. In K. S. Douglas, C. D. Webster, S. D. Hart, D. Eaves, & J. R. P. Ogloff. (Eds.), *HCR-20 violence risk management companion guide* (pp. 13–25). Burnaby, British Columbia, Canada: Mental Health, Law, and Policy Institute, Simon Fraser University, and Department of Mental Health Law and Policy, Florida Mental Health Institute, University of South Florida.

Hattori, I., & Higashi, T. (2004). Socioeconomic and familial factors in the involuntary hospitalization of patients with schizophrenia. *Psychiatry Clinical Neurosciences, 58*, 8–15.

Hawthorne, W. B., Green, E. E., Gilmer, T., Garcia, P., Hough, R. L., Lee, M., Hammond, L., & Lohr, J. B. (2005). A randomized trial of short-term acute residential treatment for veterans. *Psychiatric Services, 56*, 1379–1386.

Health Insurance Portability and Accountability Act of 1996 (HIPAA); see 45 C.F.R. § § 164.512(a) and 164.512(e).

Heilbrun, K. (1997). Prediction versus management models relevant to risk assessment: The importance of legal decision-making context. *Law and Human Behavior, 21*, 347–359.

Heilbrun, K. (2009). *Evaluation for risk of violence in adults*. New York: Oxford University Press.

Heilbrun, K., & Erickson, J. (2007). A behavioural science perspective on identifying and managing hindsight bias and unstructured judgment: Implications for legal decision-making. In D. Carson, B. Milne, F. Pakes, K. Shalev, & A. Shawyer (Eds.), *Applying psychology to criminal justice* (pp. 201–210). Chichester, UK: John Wiley & Sons.

Heilbrun, K., & Kramer, G. (2001). Update on risk assessment in mentally disordered populations. *Journal of Forensic Psychology Practice, 1,* 55–63.

Heilbrun, K., Marczyk, G. R., & DeMatteo, D. (2002). *Forensic Mental Health Assessment: A casebook.* New York: Oxford University Press.

Heilbrun, K., O'Neill, M. L., Stevens, T. N., Strohman, L. K., Bowman, Q., & Lo, Y. W. (2004). Assessing normative approaches to communicating violence risk: A national survey of psychologists. *Behavioral Sciences and the Law, 22,* 187–196.

Heltzel, T. (2007). Compatibility of therapeutic and forensic roles. *Professional Psychology: Research and Practice, 38,* 122–128.

Hicks, J. W. (2004). Ethnicity, race, and forensic psychiatry: Are we colorblind? *Journal of the American Academy of Psychiatry and the Law, 32,* 21–33.

Hiday, V. A. (1983). Are lawyers enemies of psychiatrists? A survey of civil commitment counsel and judges. *American Journal of Psychiatry, 140,* 323–326.

Hiday, V. A., Swartz, M. S., Swanson, J. W., Borum, R., & Wagner, H. R. (2002). Impact of outpatient commitment on victimization of people with severe mental illness. *American Journal of Psychiatry, 159,* 1403–1411.

Hilsenroth, M. J., Ackerman, S. J., Blagys, M. D., Baumann, B. D., Baity, M. R., Smith S. R., Price, J. L., Smith, C. L., Heindselman, T. L., Mount, M. K., & Holdwick, D. J., Jr. (2000). Reliability and validity of DSM-IV Axis V. *American Journal of Psychiatry, 157,* 1858–1863.

Hoge, S. K. (1994). On being "too crazy" to sign into a mental hospital: The issue of consent to psychiatric hospitalization. *Bulletin of the American Academy of Psychiatry and the Law, 22,* 431–450.

Illinois Legislation Regarding Hospitals for the Insane. (1869). *American Journal of Insanity, 26,* 204–229, p. 207.

Jacobs, M. S., Ryba, N. L., & Zapf. P. A. (2008). Competence-related abilities and psychiatric symptoms: An analysis of the underlying structure and correlates of the MacCAT-CA and the BPRS. *Law and Human Behavior, 32,* 64–77.

Jakobsen, K. D., Frederiksen, J. N., Hansen, T., Jansson, L. B., Parnas, J., & Werge, T. (2005). Reliability of clinical ICD-10 schizophrenia diagnoses. *Nordic Journal of Psychiatry, 59,* 209–212.

James, D. V., Duffield, G., Blizard, R., & Hamilton, L. W. (2001). Fitness to plead. A prospective study of the inter-relationships between expert opinion, legal criteria and specific symptomatology. *Psychological Medicine, 31,* 139–150.

Johnson, A. B. (1990). *Out of bedlam: The truth about deinstitutionalization.* New York: Basic Books.

Johnson, C. J., Kittner, S. J., McCarter, R. J., Sloan, M. A., Stern, B. J., Buchholz, D., & Price, T. R. (1995). Interrater reliability of an etiologic classification of ischemic stroke. *Stroke, 26,* 46–51.

Kallert, T. W., Priebe, S., McCabe, R., Kiejna, A., Rymaszewska, J., Nawka, P., Ocvár, L., Raboch, J., Stárková-Kalisová, L., Koch, R., & Schützwohl, M. (2007). Are day hospitals effective for acutely ill psychiatric patients? A European multicenter randomized controlled trial. *Journal of Clinical Psychiatry, 68*, 278–287.

Kane, J. M., Quitkin, F., Rifkin, A., Wegner, J., Rosenberg, G., & Borenstein, M. (1983). Attitudinal changes of involuntarily committed patients following treatment. *Archives of General Psychiatry, 40*, 374–377.

Karasch, M. (2003). Where involuntary commitment, civil liberties, and the right to mental health care collide: An overview of California's mental illness system. *Hastings Law Journal, 54*(2), 493–523.

Keilitz, I., Conn, D., & Giampetro, A. (1985). Least restrictive treatment of involuntary patients: Translating concepts into practice. *St. Louis University Law Journal, 29*, 691–745.

Kelly, T. M., Donovan, J. E., Chung, T., Bukstein, O. G., & Cornelius, J. R. (2009). Brief screens for detecting alcohol use disorder among 18–20 year old young adults in emergency departments: Comparing AUDIT-C, CRAFFT, RAPS4-QF, FAST, RUFT-Cut, and DSM-IV 2-Item Scale. *Addictive Behaviors, 34*(8), 668–674.

Keown, P., Mercer, G., & Scott, J. (2008). Retrospective analysis of hospital episode statistics, involuntary admissions under the Mental Health Act 1983, and number of psychiatric beds in England 1996–2006. *British Medical Journal, 337*, a1837.

Kisely, S., Campbell, L. A., & Preston, N. J. (2011). Compulsory community and involuntary outpatient treatment for people with severe mental disorders. Cochrane Database of Systematic Reviews 2011, Issue 2. Art. No. CD004408. DOI: 10.1002/14651858. CD004408. pub3.

Kjellin, L., Andersson. K., Candefjord, I. L., Palmstierna, T., & Wallsten, T. (1997). Ethical benefits and costs of coercion in short-term inpatient psychiatric care. *Psychiatric Services, 48*, 1567–1570.

Knapp, S., & VandeCreek, L. (1987). A review of tort liability in involuntary civil commitment. *Hospital & Community Psychiatry, 38*, 648–665.

Knight, F. H. (1921). *Risk, uncertainty, and profit.* Boston: Houghton Mifflin Co.

Knutsen, E., & DuRand, C. (1991). Previously unrecognized physical illnesses in psychiatric patients. *Hospital & Community Psychiatry, 42*, 182–186.

Kogstad, R. E. (2009). Protecting mental health clients' dignity—the importance of legal control. *International Journal of Law and Psychiatry, 32*, 383–391.

Kumaska, Y., Stokes, J., & Gupta, R. K. (1972). Criteria for involuntary hospitalization. *Archives of General Psychiatry, 26*, 399–404.

Lally, S. J. (2003). What tests are acceptable for use in forensic evaluations?—a survey of experts. *Professional Psychology, 34*, 491–498.

Lamb, H. R., & Mills, M. J. (1986). Needed changes in law and procedure for the chronically mentally ill. *Hospital & Community Psychiatry, 37*, 475–480.

Längle, G., Renner, G., Günthner, A., Stuhlinger, M., Eschweiler, G., U'Ren, R., & Foerster, K. (2003). Psychiatric commitment: Patients' perspectives. *Medicine and Law, 22*, 39–53.

Lidz, C. W., Hoge, S. K., Gardner, W., Bennett, N. S., Monahan, J., Mulvey, E. P., & Roth, L. H. (1995). Perceived coercion in mental hospital admission. Pressures and process. *Archives of General Psychiatry, 52*, 1034–1039.

Lidz, C. W., Mulvey, E. P., & Appelbaum, P. S. (1989). Commitment: The consistency of clinicians and the use of legal standards. *American Journal of Psychiatry, 146*, 176–181.

Lieberman, P. B., & Baker, F. M. (1985). The reliability of psychiatric diagnosis in the emergency room. *Hospital & Community Psychiatry, 36*, 291–293.

Litwack, T. R., Zapf, P. A., Groscup, J. L., & Hart, S. D. (2006). Violence risk assessment: Research, legal, and clinical considerations. In I. B. Weiner & A. K. Hess (Eds.), *The handbook of forensic psychology* (3rd ed.) (pp. 487–533). New York: Wiley.

Lorant, V., Depuydt, C., Gillain, B., Guillet, A., & Dubois, V. (2007). Involuntary commitment in psychiatric care: What drives the decision? *Social Psychiatry and Psychiatric Epidemiology, 42*, 360–365.

Lutterman, T., Berhane, A., Phelan, B., Shaw, R., & Rana, V. (2009). *Funding and characteristics of state mental health agencies, 2007.* (HHS Pub. No. SMA09–4424). Rockville, MD: Center for Mental Health Services, Substance Abuse and Mental Health Services Administration.

Manderscheid, R. W., Atay J. E., Male, A., & Maedke, J. (2002). *Highlights of organized mental health services in 2000 and major national and state trends* (DHS Publication No. SMA04–3938). Rockville, MD: U.S. Department of Health and Human Services. Retrieved from http://mentalhealth.samhsa.gov/publications/all-pubs/SMA04-3938/.

Manschreck, T. C., & Khan, N. L. (2006). Recent advances in the treatment of delusional disorder. *Canadian Journal of Psychiatry, 51*, 114–119.

Marshall, M., Crowther, R., Almaraz-Serrano, A., Creed, F., Sledge, W., Kluiter, H., Roberts, C., Hill, & E., Wiersma, D. (2003). Day hospital versus admission for acute psychiatric disorders. *Cochrane Database Systematic Reviews, 1*, CD004026.

Marshall, M., Crowther, R., Almaraz-Serrano, A., Creed, F., Sledge, W., Kluiter, H., Roberts, C., Hill, E., Wiersma, D., Bond, G. R., Huxley, P., & Tyrer, P. (2001). Systematic reviews of the effectiveness of day care for people with severe mental disorders: (1) Acute day hospital versus admission; (2) vocational rehabilitation; (3) day hospital versus outpatient care. *Health Technology Assessment*, 5, 1–75.

Massachusetts Department of Mental Health. (2009). *Department of Mental Health, Forensic Mental Health Services, report on DMH-operated pre-arrest jail diversion programs 7/1/06 to 10/1/09.* Retrieved from http://www.mass.gov/?pageID=eohhs2modulechunk&L=4&L0=Home&L1=Government&L2=Departments+and+Divisions&L3=Department+of+Mental+Health&sid=Eeohhs2&b=terminalcontent&f=dmh_g_forensic_services&csid=Eeohhs2.

McCusker, P. J. (2006). Use of the COVR in violence risk assessment. *Psychiatric Services*, 57, 142–143.

McDermott, B. E., Gerbasi, J. B., Quanbeck, C., & Scott, C. L. (2005). Capacity of forensic patients to consent to research: The use of the MacCAT-CR. *Journal of the American Academy of Psychiatry and the Law*, 33, 299–307.

McDermott, B. E., Quanbeck, C. D., Busse, D., Yastro, K., & Scott, C. L. (2008). The accuracy of risk assessment instruments in the prediction of impulsive versus predatory aggression. *Behavioral Sciences and the Law*, 26, 759–777.

McGaha, A., Stiles, P. G., & Petrila, J. (2002). Emergency involuntary psychiatric examinations in Florida. *Psychiatric Services*, 53, 1171–1172.

McNiel, D. E., Gregory, A. L., Lam, J. N., Binder, R. L., & Sullivan, G. R. (2003). Utility of decision support tools for assessing acute risk of violence. *Journal of Consulting and Clinical Psychology*, 71, 945–953.

Melton, G. B., Petrila, J., Poythress, N. G., & Slobogin, C. (with Lyons, P. M., Jr., & Otto, R.K.). (2007). *Psychological evaluations for the courts: A handbook for mental health professionals and lawyers* (3rd ed.). New York: The Guilford Press.

Meyer, J. M., & Simpson, G. M. (1997). From chlorpromazine to olanzapine: A brief history of antipsychotics. *Psychiatric Services*, 48, 137–139.

Miller, P. R., Dasher, R., Collins, R., Griffiths, P., & Brown, F. (2001). Inpatient diagnostic assessments: 1. Accuracy of structured vs. unstructured interviews. *Psychiatry Research*, 105, 255–264.

Miller, R. D. (1992). Involuntary civil commitment. In R. I. Simon (Ed.), *Review of clinical psychiatry and the law* (Vol. 2) (pp. 95–172). Washington, DC: American Psychiatric Press.

Miller, R. D., & Fiddleman, P. B. (1983). Emergency involuntary commitment: A look at the decision-making process. *Hospital & Community Psychiatry*, 34, 249–254.

Miller, R. D., Ionescu-Pioggia, R. M., & Fiddleman, P. B. (1983). The effect of witnesses, attorneys, and judges on civil commitment in North Carolina: A prospective study. *Journal of Forensic Sciences*, 28, 829–838.

Miller, R. D., & Fiddleman, P. B. (1984). Outpatient commitment: Treatment in the least restrictive environment? *Hospital & Community Psychiatry*, 35, 147–151.

Monahan, J. (1992). Mental disorder and violent behavior: Perceptions and evidence. *American Psychologist, 47*, 511–521.

Monahan, J., Hoge, S. K., Lidz, C., Roth, L. H., Bennett, N., Gardner, W., & Mulvey, E. (1995). Coercion and commitment. Understanding involuntary mental hospital admissions. *International Journal of Law and Psychiatry, 18*, 249–263.

Monahan, J., & Silver, E. (2003). Judicial decision thresholds for violence risk management. *International Journal of Forensic Mental Health, 2*, 1–6.

Monahan, J., & Steadman, H. J. (1994). Toward a rejuvenation of risk assessment research. In J. Monahan & H. J. Steadman (Eds.), *Violence and mental disorder: Developments in risk assessment* (pp. 1–18). Chicago, IL: University of Chicago Press.

Monahan, J., Steadman, H. J., Appelbaum, P. S., Robbins, P. C., Mulvey, E. P., Silver, E., Roth, L. H., & Grisso, T. (2000). Developing a clinically useful actuarial tool for assessing violence risk. *British Journal of Psychiatry, 176*, 312–319.

Monahan, J., Steadman, H., Appelbaum, P., Grisso, T., Mulvey, E., Roth, L., Robbins, P., Banks, S., & Silver, E. (2005a). *The classification of violence risk.* Lutz, FL: Psychological Assessment Resources.

Monahan, J., Steadman, H. J., Robbins, P. C., Appelbaum, P., Banks, S., Grisso, T., Heilbrun, K., Mulvey, E. P., Roth, L., & Silver, E. (2005b). An actuarial model of violence risk assessment for persons with mental disorders. *Psychiatric Services, 56*, 810–815.

Monahan, J., Steadman, H., Silver, E., Appelbaum, P., Robbins, P., Mulvey, E., Roth, L., Grisso, T., & Banks, S. (2001). *Rethinking risk assessment: The MacArthur study of mental disorder and violence.* New York: Oxford University Press.

Morgan, C., Mallett, R., Hutchinson, G., et al. (2005). Pathways to care and ethnicity. 1: Sample characteristics and compulsory admission. Report from the AESOP study. *British Journal of Psychiatry, 186*, 281–289.

Mossman, D. (2006). Critique of pure risk assessment or, Kant meets Tarasoff. *University of Cincinnati Law Review, 75*, 523–609.

Mossman, D. (2008). Analyzing the performance of risk assessment instruments: A response to Vrieze and Grove (2007). *Law and Human Behavior, 32*, 279–291.

Mossman, D., & Hart, K. J. (1993). How bad is civil commitment? A study of attitudes toward violence and involuntary hospitalization. *Bulletin of the American Academy of Psychiatry and the Law, 21*, 181–194.

Mossman, D., Noffsinger, S. G., Ash, P., Frierson, R. L., Gerbasi, J., Hackett, M., Lewis, C. F., Pinals, D. A., Scott, C. L., Sieg, K. G., Wall, B. W., & Zonana, H. V. (2007). AAPL practice guideline for the forensic psychiatric evaluation of competence to stand trial.

Journal of the American Academy of Psychiatry and the Law, 35, S3–S72.

Mossman, D., Schwartz, A. H., & Lucas E. (in press). Risky business versus overt acts: What relevance do "actuarial," probabilistic risk assessments have for judicial decisions on involuntary psychiatric hospitalization? *Houston Journal of Health Law and Policy* (forthcoming).

Mulder, C. L., Koopmans, G. T., & Lyons, J. S. (2005). Determinants of indicated versus actual level of care in psychiatric emergency services. *Psychiatric Services, 56,* 452–457.

Mulvey, E. P., & Lidz, C. W. (1984). Clinical considerations in the prediction of dangerousness in mental patients. *Clinical Psychology Review, 4,* 379–401.

Munetz, M. R., & Geller, J. L. (1993). The least restrictive alternative in the postinstitutional era. *Hospital & Community Psychiatry, 44,* 967–973.

Munetz, M. R., Grande, T., Kleist, J., & Peterson, G. A. (1996). The Effectiveness of outpatient civil commitment. *Psychiatric Services, 47,* 1251–1253.

New York State Office of Mental Health. (2005). *Kendra's Law: Final Report on the Status of Assisted Outpatient Treatment.* Retrieved from http://www.omh.state.ny.us/omhweb/Kendra_web/finalreport/.

New York State Office of Mental Health. (2006). *An Explanation of Kendra's Law.* Retrieved from http://www.omh.state.ny.us/omhweb/Kendra_web/Ksummary.htm.

Nicholson, R. (1986). Correlates of commitment status in psychiatric patients. *Psychological Bulletin, 100,* 241–250.

Niendam, T. A., Jalbrzikowski, M., & Bearden, C. E. (2009). Exploring predictors of outcome in the psychosis prodrome: Implications for early identification and intervention. *Neuropsychology Review, 19,* 280–293.

O'Donoghue, B., Lyne, J., Hill, M., Larkin, C., Feeney, L., & O'Callaghan, E. (2010). Involuntary admission from the patients' perspective. *Social Psychiatry and Psychiatric Epidemiology, 45,* 631–638.

Opjordsmoen, S., Friis, S., Melle, I., Haahr, U., Johannessen, J. O., Larsen, T. K., Røssberg, J. I., Rund, B. R., Simonsen, E., Vaglum, P., & McGlashan, T. H. (2010). A 2-year follow-up of involuntary admission's influence upon adherence and outcome in first-episode psychosis. *Acta Psychiatrica Scandinavica, 121,* 371–376.

Osborn, D. P., Levy, G., Nazareth, I., Peterson, I., Islam, A., & King, M. B. (2007). Relative risk of cardiovascular and cancer mortality in persons with serious mental illness from the United Kingdom's General Practice Research Database. *Archives of General Psychiatry, 64,* 242–249.

Otto, R. K., & Douglas, K. S. (2010). *Handbook of violence risk assessment*. New York: Routledge; Taylor & Francis Group, LLC.

Packard v. Packard (2010). *Packard v. Packard—Significance, Reverend Packard's Case Against His Wife, Mrs. Packard Defends Her Sanity*. Retrieved from the Law Library-American Law and Legal Information website:http://law.jrank.org/pages/13236/Packard-v-Packard.html#ixzz0t6LI0111.

Palmstierna, T., Lassenius, R., & Wistedt, B. (1989). Evaluation of the Brief Psychopathological Rating Scale in relation to aggressive behavior by acute involuntarily admitted patients. *Acta Psychiatrica Scandinavica, 79*, 313–316.

Palmstierna, T., & Wistedt, B. (1990). Risk factors for aggressive behaviour are of limited value in predicting the violent behaviour of acute involuntarily admitted patients. *Acta Psychiatrica Scandinavica, 81*, 152–155.

Parry, C. D., & Turkheimer, E. (1992). Length of hospitalization and outcome of commitment and recommitment hearings. *Hospital & Community Psychiatry, 43*, 65–68.

Parry, C. D., Turkheimer, E., & Hundley, P. L. (1992). A comparison of commitment and recommitment hearings: Legal and policy implications. *International Journal of Law and Psychiatry, 15*, 25–41.

Patel, J., Pinals, D. A., & Breier, A. (2008). Schizophrenia and other psychoses. In A. Tasman, J. Kay, & J. A. Lieberman (Eds.), *Psychiatry* (3rd ed.). Chichester, UK: John Wiley & Sons, Ltd., pp. 1201–1282.

Patterson, D. A., & Lee, M. (1995). Field trial of the Global Assessment of Functioning Scale–modified. *American Journal of Psychiatry, 152*, 1386–1388.

Perlin, M. L. (1998). *Mental disability law—Civil and criminal* (2nd ed.). Charlottesville, VA: LEXIS Law Publishing.

Pierce, G. I., Durham, M. L., & Fisher, W. H. (1985). The impact of broadened civil commitment standards on admissions to state mental hospitals. *American Journal of Psychiatry, 142*, 104–107.

Pies, R. (2007). How "objective" are psychiatric diagnoses? (Guess again.). *Psychiatry, 4*, 18–22.

Pinals, D. A., Glancy, G. D., & Lee, L-W., G. (2011). Civil and sex offender commitment. In A. Buchanan & M. A. Norko (Eds.), *The psychiatric report: Principles and practice in writing for the courts*. Cambridge, Cambridge University Press.

Pinals, D. A., Packer, I., Fisher, B., & Roy, K. (2004). Relationship between race and ethnicity and forensic clinical triage dispositions. *Psychiatric Services, 55*, 873–878.

Pinals, D. A., Tillbrook, C. E., & Mumley, D. L. (2006). Practical application of the MacArthur competence assessment tool-criminal adjudication (MacCAT-CA) in a public sector forensic setting. *Journal of the American Academy of Psychiatry and the Law, 34*, 179–188.

Pinals, D. A., Tillbrook, C. E., & Mumley, D. (2009). Violence risk assessment. In F. M. Saleh, A. J. Grudzinskas, J. M. Bradford, & D. Brodsky (Eds.), *Sex offenders: Identification, risk assessment, treatment & legal issues*. New York: Oxford University Press, pp. 49–69.

Power, A. K. (2009). Focus on transformation: A public health model of mental health for the 21st Century. *Psychiatric Services, 60,* 580–584.

Poythress, N. G. (1978). Psychiatric expertise in civil commitment: Training attorneys to cope with expert testimony. *Law and Human Behavior, 2,* 1–23.

Poythress, N. G., Cascardi, M., & Ritterband, L. (1996). Capacity to consent to voluntary hospitalization: Searching for a satisfactory Zinermon screen. *Bulletin of the American Academy of Psychiatry and the Law, 24,* 439–452.

Priebe, S., Katsakou, C., Glöckner, M., Dembinskas, A., Fiorillo, A., Karasterigiou, A., Kiejna, A., Kjellin, L., Nawka, P., Onchev, G., Raboch, J., Schuetzwohl, M., Solomon, Z., Torres-González, F., Wang, D., & Kallert, T. (2010). Patients' views of involuntary hospital admission after 1 and 3 months: Prospective study in 11 European countries. *British Journal of Psychiatry, 196,* 179–185.

Prinsen, E. J., & van Delden, J. J. (2009). Can we justify eliminating coercive measures in psychiatry? *Journal of Medical Ethics, 35,* 69–73.

Quinsey, V. L., Harris, G. T., Rice, M. E., & Cormier, C. A. (2006). *Violent offenders: Appraising and managing risk* (2nd ed.). Washington, DC: American Psychological Association.

Rain, S. D., Williams, V. F., Robbins, P. C., Monahan, J., Steadman, H. J., & Vesselinov, R. (2003). Perceived coercion at hospital admission and adherence to mental health treatment after discharge. *Psychiatric Services, 54,* 103–105.

Ramirez Basco, M., Bostic, J. Q., Davies, D., Rush, J., Witte, B., Hendrickse, W., & Barnett, V. (2000). Methods to improve diagnostic accuracy in a community mental health setting. *American Journal of Psychiatry, 157,* 1599–1605.

Ramirez Basco, M., Jacquot, C., Thomas, C., & Knack, J. M. (2008). Underdiagnosing and overdiagnosing psychiatric comorbidities. *Psychiatric Times, 25*(12). Retrieved from http://www.psychiatrictimes.com/display/article/10168/1342694#.

Rawls, J. (1971). A theory of justice. Cambridge, MA: Harvard University Press.

Ray, I. (1864). American legislation on insanity. *American Journal of Insanity, 21,* 21–62.

Redding, R. E., Floyd, M. Y., & Hawk, G. L. (2001). What judges and lawyers think about the testimony of mental health experts: A survey of the courts and bar. *Behavioral Sciences and the Law, 19,* 583–594.

Redelmeier, D. A., Tu, J. V., Schull, M. J., Ferris, L. E., & Hux, J. E. (2001). Problems for clinical judgment, 2: Obtaining a reliable past medical history. *Canadian Medical Association Journal, 164*, 809–813.

Reisner, R., Slobogin, C., & Rai, A. (2004). *Law and the mental health system* (4th ed.). St. Paul, MN: Thomson West.

Resnick, P. (2008, October 20). *Violence risk assessment.* Presented at the Forensic Psychiatry Review Course of the American Academy of Psychiatry and the Law, Seattle, Washington.

Ridgely, M. S., Borum, J., & Petrila, J. (2001). *The effectiveness of involuntary treatment: Empirical evidence and the experience of eight states.* Santa Monica, CA: RAND Health, RAND Institute for Civil Justice.

Roessler, W., & Reicher-Roessler, A. (1992). Fortschritte der neurologie. *Psychiatrie, 60*, 375–382.

Rogers, R. (2003). Standardizing DSM-IV diagnoses: The clinical applications of DSM-IV diagnoses and structured interviews. *Journal of Personality Assessment, 81*, 220–225.

Rogers, R., & Shuman, D. W. (2000). *Conducting insanity evaluations* (2nd ed.). New York: Guilford.

Rosenstein, M. J., Steadman, H. J., MacAskill, R. L., & Manderscheid, R. W. (1986). Legal status of admission to three inpatient psychiatric settings, United States, 1980. *Mental Health Statistical Note 178.* Rockville, MD: U.S. Department of Health and Human Services, Substance Abuse and Mental Health Administration.

Roth, L. H. (1979). A commitment law for patients, doctors, and lawyers. *American Journal of Psychiatry, 136*, 1121–1127.

Roth, L. H. (1980). Mental health commitment: The state of the debate 1980. *Hospital and Community Psychiatry, 31*, 385–396.

Roth, L. H. (1989). Four studies of mental health commitment. *American Journal of Psychiatry, 146*(2), 135–137.

Roy-Byrne, P., Dagadakis, C., Unutzer, J., & Ries, R. (1996). Evidence for limited validity of the Revised Global Assessment of Functioning Scale. *Psychiatric Services, 47*, 864–866.

Rubenstein, L. S. (1985). APA's Model Law: Hurting the people it seeks to help. *Hospital & Community Psychiatry, 36*, 968–972.

Ruggeri, M., Koeter, M., Schene, A., Bonetto, C., Vàzquez-Barquero, J. L., Becker, T., Knapp, M., Knudsen, H. C., Tansella, M., Thornicroft, G., & the EPSILON Study Group. (2005). Factor solution of the BPRS-expanded version in schizophrenic outpatients living in five European countries. *Schizophrenia Research, 75*(1), 107–117.

Ruskin, P. E., Reed, S., Kumar, R., Kling, M. A., Siegel, E., Rosen, M., & Hauser, P. (1998). Reliability and acceptability of psychiatric diagnosis via telecommunication and audiovisual technology. *Psychiatric Services, 49*, 1086–1088.

Saldaña, D. (2001). *Cultural competency: A practical guide for mental health service providers.* Austin, TX: Hogg Foundation for Mental Health, University of Texas at Austin.

Sattar, S. P., Pinals, D. A., Din, A. U., & Appelbaum, P. S. (2006). To commit or not to commit: The psychiatry resident as a variable in involuntary commitment decisions. *Academic Psychiatry, 30,* 191–195.

Schopp, R. F., & Quattrocchi, M. R. (1995). Predicting the present: Expert testimony and civil commitment. *Behavioral Sciences and the Law, 13,* 159–181.

Schwartz, J. E., Fennig, S., Tanenberg-Karant, M., Carlson, G., Craig, T., Galambos, N., Lavelle, J., & Bromet, E. J. (2000). Congruence of diagnoses 2 years after a first-admission diagnosis of psychosis. *Archives of General Psychiatry, 57,* 593–600.

Segal, S. P., Watson, M.A., & Nelson, L. S. (1986). Indexing civil commitment in psychiatric emergency rooms. *The Annals of the American Academy of Political and Social Science, 484,* 56–69.

Segal, S. P. (1989). Commitment standards and patient mix in England/Wales, Italy, and the United States. *American Journal of Psychiatry, 146,* 187–193.

Segal, S. P., Laurie, T. A., & Segal, M. J. (2001). Factors in the use of coercive retention in civil commitment evaluations in psychiatric emergency services. *Psychiatric Services, 52,* 514–520.

Shannon, P. J. (1976). Coercion and compulsory hospitalization: Some patients' attitudes. *Medical Journal of Australia, 20*(21), 798–800.

Shear, M. K., Greeno, C., Kang, J., Ludewig, D., Frank, E., Swartz, H. A., & Hanekamp, M. (2000). Diagnosis of nonpsychotic patients in community clinics. *American Journal of Psychiatry, 157,* 581–587.

Simon, H. A. (1982). *Models of bounded rationality* (Vol. 1): *Economic analysis and public policy.* Cambridge, MA: MIT Press.

Simpson, S. G., McMahon, F. J., McInnis, M. G., MacKinnon, D. F., Edwin, D., Folstein, S. E., & DePaulo, J. R. (2002). Diagnostic reliability of bipolar II disorder. *Archives of General Psychiatry, 59,* 736–740.

Sjöstrand, M., & Helgesson, G. (2008). Coercive treatment and autonomy in psychiatry. *Bioethics, 22*(2), 113–120.

Slobogin, C. (2006). *Proving the unprovable: The role of law, science, and speculation in adjudicating culpability and dangerousness.* New York: Oxford University Press.

Slovenko, R. (2006). Commentary: Deceptions to the rule on ultimate issue testimony. *Journal of the American Academic of Psychiatry and the Law, 34,* 22–25.

Snowden, R. J., Gray, N. S., Taylor, J., & Fitzgerald, S. (2009). Assessing risk of future violence among forensic psychiatric inpatients with the Classification of Violence Risk (COVR). *Psychiatric Services, 60,* 1522–1526.

Söderberg, P., Tungström, S., & Armelius, B. A. (2005). Reliability of global assessment of functioning ratings made by clinical psychiatric staff. *Psychiatric Services, 56*, 434–438.

Spiegel, D. R., Dhadwal, N., & Gill, F. (2008). "I'm sober, doctor, really": Best biomarkers for underreported alcohol use. *Current Psychiatry, 7*(9), 15–27.

Spitzer, R. L., Forman, J. B., & Nee, J. (1979). DSM-III field trials: I. Initial interrater diagnostic reliability. *American Journal of Psychiatry, 136*, 815–817.

Spitzer, R., Gibbon, M., Williams, J., & Endicott, J. (1994). Global Assessment of Functioning (GAF) Scale. In L. Sederer & B. Dickey (Eds.), *Outcomes assessment in clinical practice* (pp. 76–78). Baltimore, MD: Williams & Wilkins.

Steadman, H. J., Gounis, K., Dennis, D., Hopper, K., Roche, B., Swartz, M., & Robbins, P. C. (2001). Assessing the New York City involuntary outpatient commitment pilot program. *Psychiatric Services, 52*, 330–336.

Steadman, H. J., Silver, E., Monahan, J., Appelbaum, P. S., Robbins, P. C., Mulvey, E. P., Grisso, T., Roth, L. H., & Banks, S. (2000). A classification tree approach to the development of actuarial violence risk assessment tools. *Law and Human Behavior, 24*, 83–100.

Stefan, S. (1987). Preventive commitment: The concept and its pitfalls. *Mental and Physical Disability Law Reporter, 11*, 288–302.

Stefan, S. (2006). *Emergency department treatment of the psychiatric patient: Policy issues and legal requirements.* New York: Oxford University Press.

Steinert, T., & Schmid, P. (2004). Effect of voluntariness of participation in treatment on short-term outcome of inpatients with schizophrenia. *Psychiatric Services, 55*, 786–791.

Stone, A. A. (1975). *Mental health and law: A system in transition* [DHEW Publication No. ADM-76-176]. Rockville, MD: NIMH Center for Studies of Crime and Delinquency.

Stone, A. A. (1985). A response to comments on APA's model commitment law. *Hospital and Community Psychiatry, 36*, 984–989.

Strasburger, L. H., Gutheil, T. G., & Brodsky, A. (1997). On wearing two hats: Role conflict in serving as both psychotherapist and expert witness. *American Journal of Psychiatry, 154*(4), 448–456.

Stromberg, C. D., & Stone, A. A. (1983). A model state law on civil commitment of the mentally ill. *Harvard Journal on Legislation, 20*, 275–396.

Swanson, J., Swartz, M., Van Dorn, R. A., Monahan, J., McGuire, T. G., Steadman, H. J., & Robbins, P. C. (2009). Racial disparities in involuntary outpatient commitment: Are they real? *Health Affairs (Millwood), 28*, 816–826.

Swartz, M. S., Swanson, J., Hiday, V. A., Wagner, H. R., Burns, B. J., & Borum, R. (2001). A randomized controlled trial of outpatient commitment in North Carolina. *Psychiatric Services, 52,* 325–329.

Swartz, M. S., Swanson, J. W., Steadman, H. J., Robbins, P. C., & Monahan, J. (2009). *New York State assisted outpatient treatment program evaluation.* Durham, NC: Duke University School of Medicine. Retrieved from http://www.omh.state.ny.us/omhweb/resources/publications/aot_program_evaluation/.

Swartz, M. S., Swanson, J. W., Wagner, H. R., Burns, B. J., Hiday, V. A., & Borum, R. (1999). Can involuntary outpatient commitment reduce hospital recidivism?: Findings from a randomized trial with severely mentally ill individuals. *American Journal of Psychiatry, 156,* 1968–1975.

Swartz, M. D., Wilder, C. M., Swanson, J. W., Van Dorn, R. A., Robbins, P. C., Steadman, H. J., Moser, L. L., Gilbert, A. R., & Monahan, J. (2010). Assessing outcomes for consumers in New York's assisted outpatient treatment program. *Psychiatric Services, 61,* 976–981.

Szasz, T. (1960). The myth of mental illness. *American Psychologist, 15,* 113–118.

Szasz, T. (1974). *The myth of mental illness: Foundations of a theory of personal conduct* (revised edition). New York: Harper & Row.

Talbott, J. A. (1979). Deinstitutionalization: Avoiding the disasters of the past. *Hospital & Community Psychiatry, 30,* 621–624.

Teplin, L. A., & Pruett, N. S. (1992). Police as streetcorner psychiatrist: Managing the mentally ill. *International Journal of Law and Psychiatry, 15,* 139–156.

Thatcher, B. T., & Mossman, D. (2009). Testifying for civil commitment: Helping unwilling patients get treatment they need. *Current Psychiatry, 8,* 51–55.

Thomas, A., Donnell, A. J., & Young, T. R. (2004). Factor structure and differential validity of the expanded Brief Psychiatric Rating Scale. *Assessment, 11,* 177–187.

Toews, J., el-Guebaly, N., & Leckie, A. (1981). Patients' reactions to their commitment. *Canadian Journal of Psychiatry, 36,* 251–254.

Tonge, B. J., Hughes, G. C., Pullen, J. M., Beaufoy, J., & Gold, S. (2008). Comprehensive description of adolescents admitted to a public psychiatric inpatient unit and their families. *Australia and New Zealand Journal of Psychiatry, 42,* 627–635.

Torrey, E. F. (1972). *The mind game: Witchdoctors and psychiatrists.* New York: Bantam.

Torrey, E. F., & Kaplan, R. J. K. (1995). A national survey of the use of outpatient commitment. *Psychiatric Services, 46,* 778–784.

Troisi, A., Kustermann, S., Di Genio, M., & Siracusano, A. (2003). Hostility during admission interview as a short-term predictor of aggression in acute psychiatric male inpatients. *Journal of Clinical Psychiatry, 64,* 1460–1464.

Tseng, W.-S., Matthews, D., & Elwyn, T. S. (2004). *Cultural competence in forensic mental health: A guide for psychiatrists, psychologists, and attorneys.* New York: Brunner-Routledge.

Tyler, T. R., & Blader, S. L. (2003). The group engagement model: Procedural justice, social identity and cooperative behavior. *Personality and Social Psychology Review, 7,* 349–361.

U.S. Department of Health and Human Services Office of Minority Health. (2000). *National standards on culturally and linguistically appropriate services (CLAS) in health care* (Federal Register 65, 80865–80879). Washington, DC: U.S. Department of Health and Human Services.

U.S. Public Health Service. (1952). *A draft act governing hospitalization of the mentally ill* (Revised). Washington, DC: U.S. Government Printing Office.

Van Dorn, R. A., Swanson, J. W., Swartz, M. S., Wilder, C. M., Moser, L. L., Gilbert, A. R., Cislo, A. M., & Robbins, P. C. (2010). Continuing medication and hospitalization outcomes after assisted outpatient treatment in New York. *Psychiatric Services, 61,* 982–987.

Visvanathan, K., Santor, D., Ali, S. Z., Hong, I. S., Davidson, N. E., & Helzlsouer, K. J. (2006). The importance of cytologic intrarater and interrater reproducibility: The case of ductal lavage. *Cancer Epidemiology, Biomarkers and Prevention, 15,* 2553–2556.

Vittinghoff, E., Douglas, J., Judson, F., McKirnan, D., MacQueen, K., & Buchbinder, S. P. (1999). Per-contact risk of human immunodeficiency virus transmission between male sexual partners. *American Journal of Epidemiology, 150,* 306–311.

Vobecky, J., Leduc, C. P., Devroede, G., & Madarnas, P. (2006). The reliability of routine pathologic diagnosis of colorectal adenocarcinoma. *Cancer, 64,* 1261–1265.

Wallsten, T., Kjellin, L., & Lindström, L. (2006). Short-term outcome of inpatient psychiatric care—impact of coercion and treatment characteristics. *Social Psychiatry and Psychiatric Epidemiology, 41,* 975–980.

Warner, M. D., & Peabody, C. A. (1995). Reliability of diagnoses made by psychiatric residents in a general emergency department. *Psychiatric Services, 46,* 1284–1286.

Warren, K. R., & Foudin, L. L. (2001). Alcohol-related birth defects: The past, present, and future. *Alcohol Research & Health, 25,* 153–158.

Wawer, M. J., Gray, R. H., Sewankambo, N. K., Serwadda, D., Li, X., Laeyendecker, O., Kiwanuka, N., Kigozi, G., Kiddugavu, M., Lutalo, T., Nalugoda, F., Wabwire-Mangen, F., Meehan, M. P., & Quinn, T. C. (2005). Rates of HIV-1 transmission per coital act, by stage of HIV-1 infection, in Rakai, Uganda. *Journal of Infectious Disease, 191,* 1403–1409.

Way, B. B., Allen, M. H., Mumpower, J. L., Stewart, T. R., & Banks, S. M. (1998). Interrater agreement among psychiatrists in psychiatric emergency assessments. *American Journal of Psychiatry*, *155*, 1423–1428.

Webster's II New Riverside University Dictionary. (1988). Boston, MA: Houghton Mifflin Company.

Weidow, J., Cederlund, C. G., Ranstam, J., & Kärrholm. J. (2006). Ahlbäck grading of osteoarthritis of the knee: Poor reproducibility and validity based on visual inspection of the joint. *Acta Orthopaedica*, *77*, 262–266.

Whitty, P., Clarke, M., McTigue, O., Browne, S., Kamali, M., Larkin, C., & O'Callaghan, E. (2005). Diagnostic stability four years after a first episode of psychosis. *Psychiatric Services*, *56*, 1084–1088.

Witt, P. H., & Conroy, M. A. (2008). *Evaluation of sexually violent predators*. New York: Oxford University Press.

World Publishing Company. (1951). *Webster's new twentieth century dictionary of the English language, unabridged*. New York: World Publishing Company.

Yesavage, J. A., Werner, P. D., Becker, J. M., & Mills, M. J. (1982). Short-term civil commitment and the violent patient. *American Journal of Psychiatry*, *139*, 1145–1149.

Zanni, G. R., & Stavis, P. F. (2007). The effectiveness and ethical justification of psychiatric outpatient commitment. *American Journal of Bioethics*, *7*, 31–41.

Zealberg, J. J., Santos, A. B., & Puckett, J. A. (1996). *Comprehensive emergency mental health car*e. Washington, DC: Beard Books.

Zimmerman, M. (2008). Is diagnosis of comorbidities obsolete? *Psychiatric Times*, *25*(12). Retrieved from http://www.psychiatrictimes.com/display/article/10168/1343018.

Zimmerman, M., & Mattia, J. I. (1999). Psychiatric diagnosis in clinical practice: Is comorbidity being missed? *Comprehensive Psychiatry*, *40*(3), 182–191.

Zimmerman, M., & Mattia, J. I. (2000). Principal and additional DSM-IV disorders for which outpatients seek treatment. *Psychiatric Services*, *51*, 1299–1304.

Tests and Specialized Tools

AUDIT: Alcohol Use Disorders Identification Test (Saunders et al., 1993)

BPRS: Brief Psychiatric Rating Scale (Original 16 items: Overall & Gorham, 1962; Revised 18-items: Overall & Gorham, 1988)

BPRS-A: Brief Psychiatric Rating Scale–Anchored Version (Woerner et al., 1988)

BPRS-E: Brief Psychiatric Rating Scale–Expanded Version (Lukoff et al., 1986)

BVC: Brøset Violence Checklist (Almvik & Woods, 1999; Almvik et al., 2000)

CAGE Questionnaire (Ewing, 1984)

COVR™: Classification of Violence Risk™ (Monahan et al., 2005)

GAF: Global Assessment of Functioning (American Psychiatric Association, 1987)

HCR-20 (Webster et al., 1997)

MacCAT-CA: MacArthur Competence Assessment Tool–Criminal Adjudication (Poythress et al., 1999)

MacCAT-CR: MacArthur Competence Assessment Tool for Clinical Research (Appelbaum & Grisso, 2001)

M.I.N.I.: Mini International Neuropsychiatric Interview (Sheehan et al., 1998)

MMSE: Mini-Mental State Examination (Folstein et al., 1975)

PANSS: Positive and Negative Symptom Scale for Schizophrenia (Kay et al., 1987)

RAPS4: Rapid Alcohol Problems Screen (Cherpitel, 1995, 2000)

SADS: Schedule for Affective Disorders and Schizophrenia (Endicott & Spitzer, 1978)

SCID: Structured Clinical Interview of *DSM–IV* Disorders (First et al., 1996)

TRIAD: Three Ratings of Involuntary Admissibility (Segal et al., 1986, 1988a, 1988b, 1988c)

References for Tests and Specialized Tools

Almvik, R., & Woods, P. (1999). Predicting inpatient violence using the Brøset Violence Checklist (BVC). *International Journal of Psychiatric Nursing Research, 4,* 498–505.

Almvik, R., Woods, P., & Rasmussen, K. (2000). The Brøset Violence Checklist: Sensitivity, specificity, and interrater reliability. *Journal of Interpersonal Violence, 15,* 1284–1296.

American Psychiatric Association. (1987). *Diagnostic and statistical manual of mental disorders* (3rd ed.). Washington, DC: American Psychiatric Association.

Appelbaum, P. S., & Grisso, T. (2001). *The MacArthur Competence Assessment Tool for Clinical Research (MacCAT-CR)*. Sarasota, FL: Professional Resource Press.

Cherpitel, C. J. (1995). Screening for alcohol problems in the emergency room: A rapid alcohol problems screen. *Drug Alcohol Dependence, 40,* 133–137.

Cherpitel, C. J. (2000). A brief screening instrument for problem drinking in the emergency room: The RAPS4. *Journal of Studies on Alcohol and Drugs, 61,* 447–449.

Endicott, J., & Spitzer, R. L. (1978). A diagnostic interview: The schedule for affective disorders and schizophrenia. *Archives of General Psychiatry, 35,* 837–844.

Ewing, J. A. (1984). Detecting alcoholism: The CAGE questionaire. *Journal of the American Medical Association, 252,* 1905–1907.

First, M. B., Spitzer, R. L., Gibbon, M., & Williams, J. B. W. (1996). *Structured clinical interview for DSM-IV axis I disorders, clinician version (SCID-CV)*. Washington, DC: American Psychiatric Press, Inc.

Folstein, M. F., Folstein, S. E., & McHugh, P. R. (1975). "Mini-mental state." A practical method for grading the cognitive state of patients for the clinician. *Journal of Psychiatric Research, 12,* 189–198.

Kay, S. R., Fiszbein, A., & Opler, L.A. (1987). The positive and negative syndrome scale (PANSS) for schizophrenia. *Schizophrenia Bulletin, 13,* 261–276.

Lukoff, D., Nuechterlein, K. H., & Ventura, J. (1986). Brief Psychiatric Rating Scale (Expanded–1986). *Schizophrenia Bulletin, 12,* 594–602.

Monahan, J., Steadman, H. J., Appelbaum, P. S., Grisso, T., Mulvey, E. P., Roth, L. H., Robbins, P. C., Banks, S., & Silver, E. (2005). *Classification of Violence Risk (COVR)*. Lutz, FL: Psychological Assessment Resources.

Overall, J. E., & Gorham, D. R. (1962). The brief psychiatric rating scale. *Psychological Reports, 10,* 799–812.

Overall, J. E., & Gorham, D. R. (1988). The Brief Psychiatric Rating Scale (BPRS): Recent developments in ascertainment and scaling. *Psychopharmacology Bulletin, 24,* 97–99.

Poythress, N., Nicholson, R., Otto, R. K., Edens, J. F., Bonnie, R. J., Monahan, J., & Hoge, S. K. (1999). *The MacArthur Competence Assessment Tool—Criminal Adjudication: Professional manual*. Odessa, FL: Psychological Assessment Resources.

Saunders, J. B., Aasland, O. G., Babor, T. F., de la Fuente, J. R., & Grant, M. (1993). Development of the Alcohol Use Disorders Identification Test (AUDIT): WHO Collaborative Project on Early Detection of Persons with Harmful Alcohol Consumption—II. *Addiction, 88*(6), 791–804.

Segal, S. P., Watson, M., Goldfinger, S., & Averbuck, D. (1988a). Civil commitment in the psychiatric emergency room: I. The assessment of dangerousness by emergency room clinicians. *Archives of General Psychiatry, 45,* 748–752.

Segal, S. P., Watson, M., Goldfinger, S., & Averbuck, D. (1988b). Civil commitment in the psychiatric emergency room: II. Mental disorder indicators and three dangerousness criteria. *Archives of General Psychiatry*, *45*, 753–758.

Segal, S. P., Watson, M., Goldfinger, S., & Averbuck, D. (1988c). Civil commitment in the psychiatric emergency room: III. Disposition as a function of mental disorder and dangerousness indicators. *Archives of General Psychiatry*, *45*, 759–763.

Segal, S. P., Watson, M. A., & Nelson, L. S. (1986). Indexing civil commitment in psychiatric emergency rooms. *The Annals of the American Academy of Political and Social Science*, *484*, 56–69.

Sheehan, D. V., Lecrubier, Y., Harnett-Sheehan, K., Amorim, P., Janavs, J., Weiller, E., Hergueta, T., Baker, R., & Dunbar, G. (1998). The Mini International Neuropsychiatric Interview (M.I.N.I.): The development and validation of a structured diagnostic psychiatric interview. *Journal of Clinical Psychiatry*, *59*(Suppl. 20), 22–33.

Webster, C. D., Douglas, K. S., Eaves, D., & Hart, S. D. (1997). *HCR-20: Assessing Risk for Violence (Version 2)*. Burnaby, BC, Canada: Mental Health, Law, and Policy Institute, Simon Fraser University.

Woerner, M. G., Mannuzza, S., & Kane, J. M. (1988). Anchoring the BPRS: An aid to improved reliability. *Psychopharmacology Bulletin*, *24*, 112–117.

Case Law and Statutes

104 Code Massachusetts Regs. § 27.05[1].

Addington v. Texas, 441 U.S. 418 (1979).

Alabama Code §§ 22–52-10.49a and 22–52-1.1(1).

Alaska Statutes §§ 47.30.915(9) and 47.30.915(10) and 47.30.915(10)(B).

Arizona Statutes §§ 36–501(20)(a), 36–501 (22), 36–501(26), and 36–501(26)(b).

Arkansas Code 20–47-207.

Buck v. Bell, 274 U.S. 200 (1927).

Civil Rights Act of 1964 (Pub. L. 88–352, 78 Stat. 241), 1964.

Colorado Revised Statutes 25–1-302(1), 25–1-311.

Commonwealth v. Lamb, 365 Mass. 265 (1974).

Community Mental Health Centers Construction Act, Public Law 88–164 (1963).

Covington v. Harris, 419 F. 2d 617 (D.C. Cir. 1969).

Daubert v. Merrell Dow Pharmaceuticals, 509 U.S. 579 (1993).

Donaldson v. O'Connor, 493 F. 2d 507 (5th Cir. 1974).

Ecker v. Worcester State Hospital, 2010 Mass. Super. LEXIS 222 (June 30, 2010).

Estates of Morgan v. Fairfield Family Counseling Center, 77 Ohio St. 3d 284 (1997).

The Fair Housing Act of 1968 (FHA) (42U.S.C.A. §§ 3601–3631).

Federal Rules of Evidence, Rule 703.

Federal Rules of Evidence, Rule 801, Article VIII, 28 U.S.C. App.

Florida Statutes §§ 394.467(2b) and 397.675.

Frye v. United States, 293 F. 1013 (D.C. Cir. 1923).

Heller v. Doe, 509 U.S. 312 (1993).

Idaho Code § 66–317(m).

In re Civil Commitment of Renz, 2008 Minn. App. Unpub. LEXIS 1287, 2008 WL 4706962 (Minn. Ct. App. 2008).

In re E.S., 2005 Iowa App. LEXIS 819 (Iowa Ct. App. Aug. 17, 2005).

In Re Gault, 387 U.S. 1, (1967).

In re J.P., 574 N.W. 2d 340, 344 (Iowa 1998).

In re Kottke, 433 N.W. 2d 881 (Minn. 1988).

In re McGaughey, 536 N.W. 2d 621, 623 (Minn. 1995).

In re McKinney, 8 Ohio App. 3d 278, 456 N.E. 2d 1348 (Ohio Ct. App., Franklin County 1983).

In re Melton, 597 A. 2d 892, 908 (D.C. 1991).

In re Miller, 63 Ohio St. 3d 99, 585 N.E. 2d 396, 404 (1992).

In re Ratz, 2003 Ohio 1569, 2003 Ohio App. LEXIS 1497 (Ohio Ct. App., Montgomery County Mar. 28, 2003).

In re the Mental Health of DLT, 2003 MT 46, No. 02–555.

Indiana Code §§ 12–26-7-2 and 12–7-2–130.

Interest of Pollard, 3 NCA 854 (Neb. App. 1993).

Iowa Code §§ 229.1(15) and 229.12(3).

Jablonski v. U.S., 712 F. 2d 391 (1983).

Jackson v. Indiana, 406 U.S. 715 (1972).

Kansas Statutes Annotated 59–2946(f)(1) and 59–2946(f)(3).

Kansas v. Henricks, 521 U.S. 346 (1997).

Kumho Tire Co. v. Carmichael, 526 U.S. 137 (1999).

Lake v. Cameron, 364 F. 2d 657 (D.C. Cir. 1966).

Lanterman–Petris–Short (LPS) Act, Cal. Welf & Inst. Code § 5000 *et seq.*

Lessard v. Schmidt 349 F.Supp. 1078 (1972).

Lipari v. Sears, 497 F.Supp. 185 (D. Neb. 1980).

Maine Revised Statute Title 34-B § 3801(5).

Massachusetts General Laws, chapter 123, §§ 1, 7, and 8.

Matter of Josiah Oakes, 8 Law Rep. 123 (Mass. 1845).

Matter of Laura L., 54 Mass. App. Ct. 853 (2002).

McCabe v. City of Lynn, 875 F. Supp. 53, 63 (D. Mass. 1995).

Michigan Compiled Laws Annotated § 330.1400(g).

Minn. Stat. §§ 253B. 02(17) and 253B. 02, Subd. 13. (a).

Miranda v. Arizona, 384 U.S. 436 (1966).

Mitterbach v. Cuyahoga Cty. Probate Court, 2007-Ohio-6489.

Naidu v. Laird, 539 A. 2d 1064 (Del. 1988).

National Voting Rights Act of 1965, 42 U.S.C. § 1973 *et seq.*

Nevada Revised Statutes § 433.164.

New Jersey Statutes Ann. § 30:4–27.2(r).

New York Mental Hygiene Law §§ 1.03(20), 9.01, 9.27, and 9.43.

O'Connor v. Donaldson, 422 U.S. 563 (1975).

Occupational Health and Safety Management Systems, OHSAS 18001, Clause 3.21.

Ohio Rev. Code §§ 5122.01(A), 5122.01(B), 5122.01(B)(4), 5122.10, 5122.11, and 5122.15(E).

Oklahoma Stat. Ann. § 43A-1–103.

Olmstead v. L.C., 98–536, 527 U.S. 581 (1999).

Parham v. J.R., 442 U.S. 584 (1979).

Pennsylvania Laws, Act of April 8, 1869, Pub. L. No. 78.

Pennsylvania Statutes Annotated (2003) 50 Sec. 7301(a).

People v. Doan, 141 Mich. App. 209, 215 (Mich. Ct. App. 1985).

People v. Lang, 113 Ill. 2d 407, N.E. 2d 1105 (1986).

Rehabilitation Act of 1973, Retrieved from http://www.dotcr.ost. dot.gov/documents/ycr/REHABACT.HTM.

Rennie v. Klein, 720 F. 2d 266 (3d Cir. 1983).

Rev. Code Wash §§ 71.05.020(23)(a)(iii), 71.05.020(17)(b), 71.05.040, 71.05.360, 71.05.360(9), 71.05.390(17), 71.05.390(19), and 71.09.030.

Rivers v. Katz (and Grassi v. Acrish), 495 N.E. 2d 337, 1986.

Roe v. Wade, 410 U.S. 113 (1973).

Rogers v. Commissioner of Mental Health, 458 N.E. 2d 308 (1982).

South Carolina Code of Laws §§ 44–17-580(A)(1) and 44–52-10.

South Dakota Codified Laws § 27A-1–1(18).

State ex rel. L.C.F., 96 S.W. 3d 651 (Tex. App. El Paso 2003).

Tarasoff v. Regents of the Univ. of Cal., 118 Cal. Rptr. 129 (Cal. 1974).

Tarasoff v. Regents of the Univ. of Cal., 551 P. 2d 334 (Cal. 1976).

Texas Evid. R. 509(e)(6).

Texas Health and Safety Code §§ 573.012(e) and 574.031(A).

The Fair Housing Act of 1968 (FHA) (42U.S.C.A. §§ 3601–3631).

Utah Code Annotated § 62A-15–102.

Vermont Stat. Ann. 18 § 7101 (14).

Virginia Code §§ 32.1–127.1:03(D)(12–13) and 37.2–817C(a)(2).

Vitek v. Jones, 445 U.S. 480 (1980).

Wisconsin Statute s. 51.001 stats. 13(b), 51.20(1)(a)2. d, 51.20(1) (a)2. e, 51.22(5), 51.15(1)(a), and 51.01(8).

Wyatt v. Aderholt, 503 F. 2d 1305 (5th Cir. 1974).

Wyatt v. Stickney, 325 F. Supp 781(M.D. Ala. 1971).

Youngberg v. Romeo, 457 U.S. 307 (1982).

Zinermon v. Burch, 494 U.S. 113 (1990).

Key Terms

Affidavit: Latin for "he has declared upon oath"—a sworn written statement that the declarant signs before a magistrate or notary, who affirms the veracity of the declarant's signature.

Civil commitment: the legal mechanism through which the government deprives persons of their liberty and places them in a hospital for the treatment of mental illness.

Collateral data: information obtained from sources other than the patient-respondent, such as legal documents, medical records, and the reports of acquaintances and relatives.

Conclusory statement: a statement that speaks only to the conclusion and not to the details or facts that support the conclusion. In the civil commitment context, an example would be to testify that the respondent is "psychotic" rather than saying that the respondent hears voices and expresses beliefs that someone is poisoning the respondent's food.

Deinstitutionalization: a term designating the movement of severely mentally ill people out of large state psychiatric hospitals (largely accomplished between 1965 and 1985) and the subsequent closure of many of those hospitals.

Forensic Assessment Instruments (FAIs): instruments developed using structured techniques and scoring mechanisms to help address forensic questions. They generally provide for systematic assessments of specific forensic issues, and they often provide a basis for comparing individual evaluees to a normative or relevant population.

Grave disability: condition of persons who have neither expressed wishes to harm themselves nor made direct attempts to do so, but have so neglected their basic needs that they have placed themselves in physical peril.

***Habeas corpus* petition**: a legal request made to seek a remedy for an individual's confinement or detention. From the Latin for "you [shall] have the body."

Hearsay exceptions: exceptions to the usual requirement in court that witnesses testify only about what they have personally done or experienced with their senses. Hearsay exceptions in civil commitment hearings allow experts (i.e., mental health professionals) to testify about relevant matters beyond what they have personally witnessed (e.g., what a staff member or relative of the respondent reported about the respondent's conduct).

Lanterman-Petris-Short Act (LPS Act): passed in California in 1969, this was one of the first state statutory reforms that increased procedural protections to subjects of civil commitment proceedings.

Least restrictive alternative (LRA): a phrase that has come to represent the need to determine whether forms of care less confining than involuntary institutionalization would meet an individual's needs for treatment and care.

Outpatient civil commitment: a court order for a person to get mental health care while living in the community.

Parens patriae **doctrine**: one of the traditional justifications for civil commitment, this legal principal recognizes that because some persons need institutional care for their health and well-being, the state must act to protect these persons much as parents protect their children. From the Latin for "father of the people."

Perceived coercion: the degree to which an individual feels forced or coerced into treatment.

Police power rationale: refers to the state's obligation to prevent persons from endangering others or themselves as a justification for the deprivation of liberty involved in civil commitment.

Respondent: in a civil legal action, the party who is must answer a petition for a court order that would require the party to take some action, halt some activity, or obey a court order. In the civil commitment context, the respondent is the individual alleged to be mentally ill and in need of hospitalization.

Sexually Violent Predator (SVP) laws: typically allow courts to order long-term postconviction confinement of persons who have committed sexually oriented crimes if a court finds that those persons have "mental abnormalities" that make them "likely" to engage in additional acts of sexual violence.

"Thank you" theory: posited by Alan Stone, M.D., it argues that civil commitment might be justified by showing that persons who need involuntary hospitalization but cannot currently recognize or think rationally about their needs will, once they have recovered, *in fact* recognize that they needed treatment and will be grateful for having had treatment forced on them.

Ultimate opinion: an opinion, offered in the form of an opinion or inference in a written statement in a forensic report or in testimony, that embraces the legal issue at stake in a matter about which an expert witness is providing an opinion; often regarded as objectionable because such an opinion appears to invade the moral province of the trier of fact (the judge or jury).

Index

Note: Page numbers followed by "*f*" and "*t*" denote figures and tables, respectively.

About the Authors

Debra A. Pinals, M.D. is the Assistant Commissioner of Forensic Mental Health Services for the Massachusetts Department of Mental Health and an Associate Professor of Psychiatry and Director of Forensic Education at the University of Massachusetts Medical School. Dr. Pinals has worked as a treating psychiatrist in hospitals, correctional facilities, court clinics, outpatient, and emergency mental health settings and regularly conducts forensic psychiatric evaluations. She is Vice President of the American Academy of Psychiatry and the Law (AAPL) and is a Distinguished Fellow of the American Psychiatric Association (APA). She has received the Red AAPL Outstanding Service and the AAPL Best Teacher in a Forensic Psychiatry Fellowship Awards, the Outstanding Psychiatrist Public Sector Award from the Massachusetts Psychiatric Society, as well as awards for teaching and resident-faculty academic collaboration at the University of Massachusetts Medical School. Her areas of interest include the assessment and treatment of violence and suicide risk, informed consent, criminal and civil competence, civil commitment, the interface of mental illness and the criminal justice system, mental health and law enforcement, public policy, and cross cultural issues in forensic psychiatry. Dr. Pinals has made significant contributions to the field of forensic psychiatry as the author of numerous scholarly publications. She is the editor of *Stalking: Psychiatric Perspectives and Practical Approaches* (2007).

Douglas Mossman, M.D. is Administrative Director of Glenn M. Weaver Institute of Law and Psychiatry at the College of Law, University of Cincinnati and Program Director for Forensic Psychiatry Training at the UC College of Medicine. In 2008, Dr. Mossman received the Manfred S. Guttmacher Award from the American Psychiatric Association (APA) for his outstanding contributions to the literature in forensic psychiatry. He is a Distinguished Fellow of the APA, a former councilor of the American Academy of Psychiatry and Law, and past-president of the Midwest Chapter of the American Academy of Psychiatry and the Law. Dr. Mossman has given more than 200 lectures and pre-sentations to medical, legal, and nonprofessional audiences at local, regional, national, and international meetings, and he serves as a reviewer for more than 20 professional journals. His 100-plus publications cover a wide range of topics, including legal and ethical issues, medical decision-making, statistics, and psychiatric treatment.